THE CIVIL WAR DIARY

of

Berea M. Willsey

THE INTIMATE DAILY OBSERVATIONS OF
A MASSACHUSETTS VOLUNTEER IN THE
UNION ARMY, 1862–1864

Edited by
Jessica H. DeMay

HERITAGE BOOKS
2022

HERITAGE BOOKS
AN IMPRINT OF HERITAGE BOOKS, INC.

Books, CDs, and more—Worldwide

For our listing of thousands of titles see our website at
www.HeritageBooks.com

Published 2022 by
HERITAGE BOOKS, INC.
Publishing Division
5810 Ruatan Street
Berwyn Heights, Md. 20740

Copyright © 1995 Jessica H. DeMay

Heritage Books by the author:

The Civil War Diary of Berea M. Willsey: The Intimate Daily Observations of a Massachusetts Volunteer in the Union Army, 1862–1864
CD: *Civil War, Volume 2*
CD: *The Civil War Diary of Berea M. Willsey*

All rights reserved. No part of this book may be reproduced or transmitted in any form or by any means, electronic or mechanical, including photocopying, recording or by any information storage and retrieval system without written permission from the author, except for the inclusion of brief quotations in a review.

International Standard Book Number
Paperbound: 978-0-7884-0168-8

CONTENTS

Editor's Note	v
Biography of Berea M. Willsey	viii
History Of The Regiment	ix
Poem	xi
Genealogy Chart	xii
The Diary–1862	1
The Diary–1863	71
The Diary–1864	121
Appendix	161
Letters & Obituaries	175
Index	183

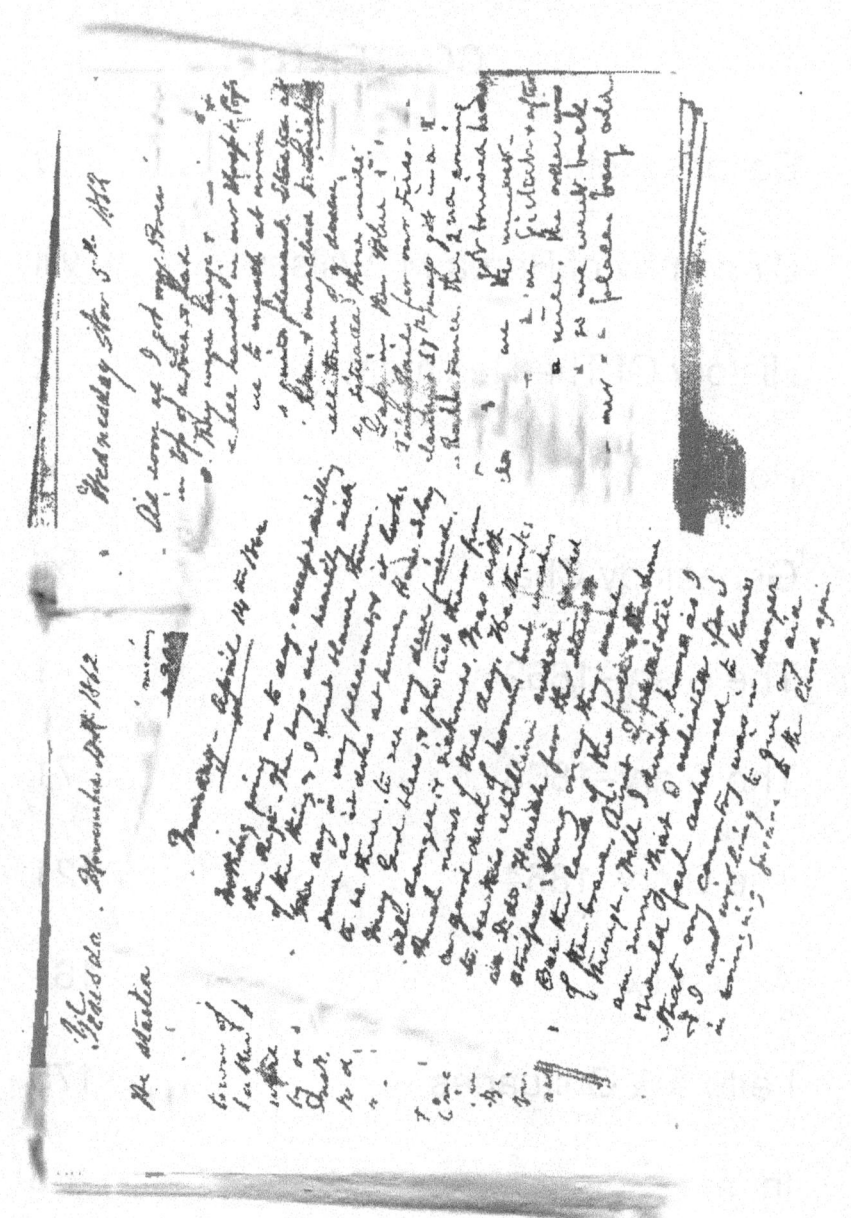

REPRODUCTION OF DIARY ENTRY

EDITOR'S NOTE

"Please take care of these for me, you are my only relative who can do it for me." Those were the words of Lucille Dennis Higgins when she gave me these three worn diaries. She had kept these books secure in her attic since the death of her mother in 1951. Her mother, Caroline "Carrie" Willsey Dennis, had cherished the Civil War diaries of her father, Berea M. Willsey, a member of Co. C, 10th Massachusetts Volunteers. She had them in her possession when she married George G. Dennis, an Agent for the Northwestern Railroad and moved to Deadwood, South Dakota, in the late 1890's. After her husband's death in 1906 she returned to Nebraska and ultimately made her home with her son, Waldo Willsey "Jack" Dennis. After their mother's death Lucille kept the diaries, hoping to preserve this small, but vanishing, glimpse of history of the Civil War and her grandfather.

The fact that these tattered and fading notebooks have survived is overwhelming. Berea carried the 1862 diary as he boarded the steamer *Seashore* and started the trip down the Potomac River and Chesapeake Bay with McClellan's Army of the Potomac. He marched through the mud and swamps, fought and nursed the sick all through the Peninsular Campaign. He wrote during the Battle of Fair Oaks, crossing and recrossing the Chickahominy River. He survived the Battle of Malvern Hill, carrying the hospital knapsack weighing 69 pounds. It was here that his younger brother, Buel "Buck" Willsey, was killed at the age of nineteen. His body was never found. He undoubtedly lies in an unmarked grave in the Glendale National Cemetery near Richmond, Virginia.

He withdraws with the troops back to Yorktown and sails up Chesapeake Bay and the Potomac River back to Washington. He ultimately fights at Antietam, Fredericksburg, Chancellorsville and Brandy Station.

He fights at Gettysburg - arriving on the second day of the battle in July, 1863. In the spring of 1864 he engages in the Battle of the Wilderness, Spotsylvania Court House, North Anna River and Cold Harbor.

On June 7th, 1864, two weeks before his three year enlistment is to be concluded, he has a near brush with death as a shell explodes at his feet as he is eating his evening meal! He vows with his friend Coop to stay close together until their time is up to help each other make it to their final day of enlistment.

At first it was with personal interest that I laboriously started transcribing the diaries for my children and grandchildren. Many times I had to use a magnifying glass to decipher the words. But as my work progressed I became fascinated with this uneducated man who so meticulously kept track of weather, troop movements, medical care, cooking and his comrades' names and company numbers. His observations about military strategy, or lack thereof, his evaluation of Commanding Officers, the "Preaching" of visiting Clergy and the use of "spirits" by the troops.

He became depressed over the poor rations and uniforms, supply system, the terrible living conditions, suffering from the bitter cold and the flies in the heat. But he never faltered in his commitment to the Union. He writes of seeing General McClellan, whom he loved, and President Lincoln who reviewed the troops on two different occasions. Undoubtedly, he survived because of his work as a Company Nurse in Battlefield hospitals which kept him, at times, away from the front line. He of course took his turn at "firming in line" of battle and going on picket.

When I transcribed the last page I knew I had to pursue getting this document published. I felt like he was an old friend. I visited his home of origin, North Adams, Massachusetts, and found a letter of his that was published in the *Transcript* in October of 1863. I also went to Blair, Nebraska, where he and his wife "Lucy" are buried. He had homesteaded there in 1869 and made his home and raised his family.

It is with great pride that I finished my work, hoping it will be a new insight to the common soldier of the Civil War and a help to historians and those interested in this period.

It also will be of great interest and help to genealogists tracing the history of their ancestors during the Civil War. I might even discover more descendants of Berea M. Willsey with this publication.

This work could not have been completed without the help of my husband, Richard F. DeMay, who put it all on the computer and his patience with my four year research project. I also want to thank my daughter Ann Higgins Cox who found one portion of the 1863 diary in the Willsey family Bible and gave it to me so it could be included; my daughter, Molly Higgins O'Holleran for her consistent encouragement and proof reading; my son John R. Higgins, Jr. for his legal advice; and last, but not least, my daughter Lucy Higgins Sinkular for her assistance in researching the 10th Regiment. I also want to thank the North Adams Public Library, North Adams, Massachusetts; The Blair, Nebraska Public Library; The Edith Abbott Public Library, Grand Island, Nebraska; The Denver Public Library; The Fort Collins Public Library; The Massachusetts State Historical Society; the National Archives of Washington, D.C.; the Washington County Genealogical Society; and the Scottsbluff Historical Society; and all of those who helped me in getting the family tree completed. I have transcribed the diaries as they are written, the spelling is his. I have only changed the punctuation where it was necessary to convey the meaning.

Jessica H. DeMay

Private Berea M. Willsey
Co. C., 10th Massachusetts Volunteer Infantry

Served in the Union Army from June 21, 1861 to July 1, 1864. He fought, and sometimes served as a nurse, in the Army of the Potomac in the Peninsular Campaign, Battle of Fair Oaks, Battle of Malvern Hill, Battles of Antietam, Fredericksburg, Chancellorsville and Brandy Station. He fought at Gettysburg, Battle of the Wilderness, Spotsylvania, North Anna River and Cold harbor.

Born: Troy, New York, June 26, 1839.
Married Lucy A. Gooodrich on 10-18-1864 at Stamford, VT
Died: Lincoln, Nebraska January 24, 1918.
Homesteaded in Blair, Washington County, Nebraska in 1869.
Buried with his wife, Lucy, in Blair, Nebraska.

HISTORY OF THE REGIMENT

After my initial transcribing of Berea M. Willsey's diaries, I had so many questions. Not being an expert on the Civil War, or even a serious student, I wanted to find out about the "Tenth Massachusetts." When were they formed, and where did they serve?

I found two viable sources of information on the Regiment. "The Tenth Regiment Massachusetts Volunteer Infantry 1861-1864" by Alfred S. Roe and "The 10th Regiment" Salient Points in its History, a paper prepared by its commander, Col. Joseph B. Parsons. This paper was delivered to the Loyal Legion on April 3, 1901 and at the 34th annual reunion of the 10th Regt Assoc. at Orange, Mass., June 21, 1901. I quote in part from the latter:

"The Tenth Massachusetts regiment was the first contribution from the western part of the state to the War of the Rebellion. It was a militia regiment and it offered its services to the Governor early in April, 1861. The different companies of the regiment were engaged in drill, fitting themselves and waiting for the orders from the Governor to move to the front. These were not issued until early June, when the regiment was ordered to Camp Springfield. Col. Briggs, who was already at the front with the eighth regiment, was summoned home to reorganize and assume command.

"The regiment was mustered into the service on the 21st day of June, 1861, for three years, and probably not more than 20 percent of the members who served on the militia continued with the regiment. It was increased to a thousand, composed of the best young men from the western part of the state; it was ordered to Washington and went into camp at Brightwood. There it was engaged in drilling and building fortifications for nearly eight months, when it was ordered to the Peninsular under the command of Gen. McClellan, and thereafter participated in all the battles of the Army of the Potomac".

In checking Berea M. Willsey's Civil War service from the office of the National Archives I found from his Co. Muster-out Roll that he joined for duty and enrolled on June 14, 1861 for 3 years. He was mustered out on July 1, 1864. He was a Pvt. for his whole enlistment and from October 1861 to March 1862 he was a Hospital Nurse and from May 1862 to November1863 he was on extra or daily duty as a Hospital Dept. Nurse.

Colonel Parson's commentary was so informative I have taken the liberty of inserting his narrative throughout the diary to better illustrate the movements of the Army of the Potomac, as described by Berea. Colonel Parson's narrative will be in italics.

THE TENTH AND HER COLORS
ON THE RETURN OF THE REGIMENT

Hurrah for the flags, battle-stained and worn,
Which the bold, brave Tenth so nobly hath borne
Through wearisome marches and many a fight;
Three cheers for the flags that now greet our sight.
But three times three for that patriot band
Who went forth with the flags and their lives in their hand;
Throughout our land, from its length to its breadth,
We'll gratefully honor the "Glorious Tenth."
Then three cheers for the flags, and nine for the men,
Let the shout re-echo again and again,
Let the cannon boom and the drum sound afar -
For the Tenth and her colors, Hurrah! Hurrah!!

                        - By a Chicopee lady

From the Book THE TENTH REGIMENT,
MASSACHUSETTS VOLUNTEER INFANTRY,
1861–1864, By Alfred S. Roe,
A veteran of the Civil War.

DESCENDANTS OF BEREA M. WILLSEY

1st Gen.	2nd Gen.	3rd Gen.	4th Gen.	5th Gen.	6th Gen.

Berea M. Willsey (b. 6-26-1839 in Troy, NY, d. 1-24-1918 at College View, NE.)
  m. Lucy Goodrich (b. 4-10-1841, d. 3-5-1920)
    Hattie Louise Willsey (b. 9-11-1866 in North Adams, Mass., d. 2-25-1923)
      m. J. Frank Kinney (b. in Iowa)
        Russell Jay Kinney (b. 12-2-1892, d. 3-17-1930)
          m. Hazel Rothwell (d. before 1930)
            Harriet Jane Kinney (b 2-10-1917)
            Eloise May Kinney (b. 10-12-1918)
            Rothwell Jay Kinney (b. 9-8-1920)
            Ruth Elaine Kinney (b. 4-21-1922)
    Caroline "Carrie" M. Willsey (b. 7-11-1868 in North Adams, Mass., d. 1-6-1951)
      m. George Dennis (b. 8-23-1863, d. 5-29-1906)
        Waldo Willsey Dennis (b. 7-16-1891, d. 9-20-1976)
        Lucile Dennis (b. 9-26-1894, d. 6-17-1968)
          m. Ray M. Higgins (b. 4-24-1889, d. 3- -1965)
            Ray M. Higgins, Jr. (b. 6-10-1920, d. 10-13-1931)
            John Richard Higgins (b. 4-4-1922, d. 7-2-1977)
              m. Jessica Stocking (b. 6-16-1929)
                John R. Higgins Jr. (b 4-18-1953)
                  m. Karen Martinson (b. 11-22-1951)
                    Christine D. Higgins (b. 9-9-1982)
                    John V. Higgins (b. 10-5-1985)
                    Suzanne J. Higgins (b. 9-28-1989)
              Molly Higgins (b. 5-20-1954)
                m. Timothy O'Holleran (b. 3-26-1953)
                  Colleen O'Holleran (b. 6-29-1980)
                  John O'Holleran (b. 8-18-1981)
                  Meghan O'Holleran (b. 3-13-1984)
                  Brigid O'Holleran (b. 6-30-1986)
                  Daniel O'Holleran (b. 10-29-1989)
              Ann E. Higgins (b. 8-17-1955)
                m. Michael Cox (b 11-1-1955)
                  Abbie M. Cox (b. 8-17-1981)
                  Sara Cox (b. 2-28-1983)
                  Maggie Cox (b 5-26-1986)
              George M. Higgins (b. 5-27-1956, d. 5-27-1956)
              Lucy J. Higgins (b. 2-1-1969)
                m. Scott Sinkular (b. 2-5-1970)
            Jessica Stocking Higgins
              m. Richard F. DeMay (b. 6-21-1925) on 11-6-1983
    Lois Estelle Willsey (b. 2-27-1873 in Blair, Nebr., d. 5-31-1954)
      m. Ed. R. Duffie (b. - - , d. 1-1913)
      m. Joseph B. Schrock
        Joseph Benson Schrock (b. 6-18-1920)
          m. Helen Elizabeth
            John Benson Schrock (b. 2-26-1944)

BEREA M. WILLSEY
COMPANY C, TENTH MASSACHUSETTS VOLUNTEERS
ARMY OF THE POTOMAC
CIVIL WAR DIARY
March 10, 1862–December 31, 1862

Monday - March 10th 1862 - Left our camp at Brightwood at 7'30 A.M. joined the Regts. (7th Mass. 2nd R.I. & 56th NY) at Gen Couchs Headquarters, one mile from the old camp. We passed through Tennalytown, DC at 9 1/2 O'Cl'K A.M. Crossed Chain Bridge at 11 Ocl'k. Cooked our dinner one mile from Ft. Marcy in Va. Marched about ten mile from the Potomac River to aplace called Prospect Hill. arrived at the said place 5 P.M. went in camp, cooked our supplies & lay out in open field all night. After a poor nights rest we were awakened at reveille. Loose word came to remain here, until further orders.

Tuesday - March 11th 1862 - Staid at Prospect Hill all day visited the Regts of other Divisions in the forenoon. After dinner took a tramp to see the far famed McClellan Lancers. They were a fine body of men and done their drilling in good shape. They belonged to Banks Army, but I understand they are now transferred to the Army of the Potomac. It is a splendid day & I often am thinking of the loved ones at home. Dress Parade at retreat. Had supper of fresh beef & crackers, went to bed on a lot of Pine boughs with three blankets over me.

Wednesday - March 12th 1862 - Nothing new agoing on in camp. We hear the report that the enemy have evacuated Manasses & that we are a going back to Brightwood. Do not like the idea at all. The people that live here seem to be ignorant side of people. Mostly Seces. The darkies are as smart as stick traps. One of them has been in our camp all day singing & dancing like the nig's I used to read about. Dress Parade at retreat. Glad for supper. Oysters put up can's. As it was so cold I concluded to pitch a tent & crawl in for the night.

Thursday - March 13th 1862 - Reville at five Ocl'k A.M. Rations of hard bread, Pork, coffee & sugar, given out for three days.

Hear we are to march in the morning back to Chain Bridge & go in camp for a week, until boats can be got ready to take us away. Richmond is a going to be taken by some other route. I don't believe the report about the boats & that we shall go in a week. Went in the afternoon to see the Batteries of our Division throw shell. It was a treat & no mistake. My brother Buel went with me. He is very lame today with a sore toe. I have tried to have him have the nail pulled out. Wrote home to Father & also to Lucy of the same place. Went to bed at 8 1/2 P.M.

Friday - March 14th 1862 - Started this morning at Nine Ocl'k for Chain Bridge, was three hours in the road, but for some reason did not go in Camp until dark. Our Regt. most of the afternoon halted under the guns of Ft. Marcy. They fired their guns some six rounds apiece. The Ft. is mounted with guns of 10 lbs to the heavy pieces of 52 lbs. It commenced to rain just as we got in the woods for the night. It was bitter cold. Soon the mud was from 4 to 10 inches deep & the water was running in streams. I was wet to the skin. I tried to sleep, but didnt make out. I found the Hospital boys all together in our baggage wagons. They were a blue as whetstones & as wet as I was. Charlie Wells our Hospital Steward was a man after my own heart that night fer he have me a good drink of hot whiskey.

Saturday - March 15th 1862 - After a night, never to be forgotten I got my breakfast, & such a breakfast I little dreamed of ever eating, before I could get the victuals off my plate it was filled with water. My overcoat weighed just about fifty pounds. I was wet & so was every body & everything else. It rained all day as hard as ever & the boys were getting in an awful condition covered with mud from head to foot. About 8 Ocl'k P.M. General Couch told our Col. if he wished he could take his Regt. back to Brightwood. The boys heard of it & such a hubbub I never see before. They all started in a few minutes, but I was left behind to look after our Hospital stoves. The Regt. went off in a jolly good humor.

Sunday - March 16th 1862 - After a good nights rest in the Col's tent with C. Wells, & John Warner on top of two boxes I got up much refreshed. Wells & Warner started after breakfast for Brightwood leaving me to come with the goods. Soon a wagon came & after getting myself covered with mud, I got all our stuff inside, mounted the seat with the driver & started. The sun was shinning as bright as ever, but the mud was awful, crossed the bridge, wel down through Georgetown & into the City of Washington. The passed up 7th st on the way to the old camp, arrived there at noo all safe & sound with no bones broken. After a good warm dinner went to see Buel & found him well. His adventures on his way bac were doleful enough. Some of the time he went up to his hips in th mud holes. Went to bed in good season.

  Monday - March 17th 1862 - Got up at five Ocl'k, eat breal fast, fixed up our tents a little, nothing going on. Reports of ever description flying around camp about what we are agoing to do what the Rebels are doing. I can't believe anything. The stories ar so absurd. Had a good dinner of <u>Beef Heart stuffed</u>. For supper ha fried & stewed oysters. In the evening had a game of backgammon Dominoes. The day was very pleasant. Recd letters from Father one from Lucy.

  Tuesday - March 18th 1862 - Eat my breakfast at sunrise then got some water ready for washing. Washed one shirt, pr drav ers & socks. After dinner went to see the battery belonging to ou Brigade practice in throwing shell & solid shot. It was fine sport fc me after the gunners got the range of their pieces. They would sen every shot right to the mark. I believe if they ever see the enemy the will do good execution. Buel was with me. I had a good time wit him. I think he is not as wild & reckless as he used to be! Dres parade at sundown. The band played some excellent pieces. Wer to bed at nine.

  Wednesday - March 19th 1862 - After eating breakfast went with the Regt down to Columbia College where the Divisio were drilling under the command of Gen. Hayes. There also was review. Gov Andrew from Mass reviewed us. Some 10,000 soldiers were there. It was a splendid sight. Got back to camp at 4 OCl'k P.M. Wrote home a letter to Father & also one to Hatfield, had a good supper of roast beef at 8 OCl'k. went to bed at ten.

  Tuesday - March 20th 1862 - Nothing new today. The Regt had a Battallion drill in the afternoon. The mud has not dried up yet. Recd a letter from Lucy, also wrote to her & one to H. R. Graves of Hatfield. All well at home not withstanding my fears to the contrary. I am feeling well, tough & hearty as ever. Feel to praise God for his goodness in giving me good health. Retired at nine P.M.

Friday - March 21st 1862 - After eating breakfast I went up to Mrs Blairs to get some milk. Had a nice time in going over the grounds & seeing the way the big <u>bugs</u> live in the State of Maryland - where the darkies have the management of the land. Went back to camp & made a nice pudding. It was excellent & I think if I ever go home I shall learn some of the folks how to do things. Had a game of dominoes in the evening with Charlie Wells - John Warner & G. C. Clark. Went to bed at 10 -

Saturday - March 22nd 1862 - Heard today that the transports were nearly ready for receiving us. Can't believe yet that we shall leave this place. Mr Blair is using all his influence to keep us here. If something ain't done I fear he will accomplish the undertaking. I long to be on the march & to see the rebels. If they don't get a taste of the bullets from the 10th then I am no judge. We are all eager & ready for the fight. Went in the afternoon & bought a turkey fer tomorrow dinner. Orders were read at dress parade that every one must have his clothing brushed up nice, also each mans equipments fer the regular Sunday morning Inspection. Crawled in bed at nine -

Sunday - March 23rd 1862 - After surgeons call had Breakfast cleaned up our quarters & then brushed up my clothes for Inspection. Dr Chamberlain complimented us in our good look - the way we fixed our quarters. We of course felt "<u>greatly flattered</u>". In the afternoon had a discourse from our Chaplain, Mr Barton. Went back to quarters & then the dinner bell rang fer Mr Turkey. Maybe I didn't eat & may be I did. It just made a meal for five of us. Went to my tent & read my bible & triesd to fix my thoughts on heavenly things. I often think of home & of the many blessed priviledges I once enjoyed while there. I trust the Lord will bring me back safe to my home & friends. But I feel to say - his will be done.

Monday - March 24th 1862 - Today we recd orders to march tomorrow & so I have been busy at work packing up our goods sending off our sick ones, & selling what things I could not carry - such as the crockery I recd from home, old coats & pants. I was very tired but not so much so that I cant do anything more. Wrote a letter to father informing him or our movements. We don't know where we are agoing after leaving Washington - But hope it will be somewheres near the enemy. Went to bed in good spirits thinking of our leaving to morrow.

Tuesday - March 25th 1862 - Crawled out of bed at three Oclk A.M. packed my knapsack, got my haversack full of rations & then ate breakfast. Soon the teams came & while loading them the Regt went away. I worked hard fer 2 1/2 hours pulling down tents & trying to get the teams off. About ten A.M. they were all loaded & I mounted the load while the driver straddled his wheel mule & off we went. I found the Regt on the grounds of Columbia College. We staid there all day. The boats were not ready fer us. Gov Sprague from R. Island was there. The Regts of our Brigade were ordered back to camp & to start the next morning at 3 OClk A M. I staid with the teams on the grounds of the College with Dr Clark. We slept on a wagon & a jolly night we had. The mules kept up their noise & at times it seemed as if bedlam had broke loose. Curious.

Wednesday March 26th 1862 - Just as the sun was rising I got out of the wagon & the first thing I beheld was our Regt marching by, but as I was on duty - at the wagon I had to let them go - After the mules were fed the train started - we passed down 7th St as far as Pensylvania Avenue, then down to the Arsenal. We remained around the arsenal until night, then we went on board the vessels ready for us. I went with the left wing of our Regt on board the Seashore. The right wing with the baggage of our Regt went on board the Mystic & John A. Warner. All the boats were North River Steamers that had been chartered by the Government. We started down the river & stopt at Alexandria until morning. The other boats staid at the wharf where they loaded. I got in the cabin & made my quarters there with the officers. I had my bed on a lot of water casks & so passed the night.

Thursday - March 27th 1862 - I got up about three this morning as my bones began to ache. I went on the upper deck & all the boys were sleeping as soundly as they would in their Mothers bed. They were scattered all around in every shape - under benches, on the coils of rope & in the boats that hung by the side of the vessel. It was a great sight to see them & when I got on the wheel house & looked around me, the sight was greater still. Vessels of every description were as thick as they could be. The the City of Alexandria just opposite was visible. I could see the Marshall House with its large observatory (the place where Col Ellsworth was killed) & the places of other importance. The other boats soon came down & then we steamed away with two brigs in tow down the Potomac. Just exactly eight months ago we were on the sameplace (that we are now) as we were sailing from Boston to Washington.

  Friday - March 28th 1862 - Today the sun shines warmly & it is pleasant on deck. Yesterday we passed Mt Vernon & the Band played a Dirge. National Times YE. Today we see boats going up & down the river. Old & dilapidated houses on either shore. Little nigs are running & I can almost see the whites of their eyes as they turn around. We got in the bay a little after 9 this morning. A large Steamer passed us just now, we think it is the Vanderbilt. Well here we are at Fortress Monroe & yonder is the little Monitor. Surely we look like a cheese box on a raft & there is a large vessel they are putting cotton bales around her machinery. We sail past the Fortress & my eyes cant see half enough. The Rip Rap in the distance, the big guns at the Fortress & The Frigates all around us is enough to make one wild with delight. We got to Hampton & then disembarked about 3, Oclk. The whole place was burnt by the rebels & now there is not a house standing. encamped out side from the warf.

  Saturday - March 29th 1862 - After eating my breakfast of salt beef & hard bread, I went down to Hampton to view the ruins. The houses were all built of brick & walls of most of them were standing, while on my ramble through town. I came across a small hut & seeing a crowd of boys around thought I would see what was to pay. I found they were looking at an old negro & his wife. Their heads looked just like the wool to a sheep. They were near 100 yrs old. They talked of Gen Washington & the noble deeds he done. They have always lived here & were here the time the place was burned by the rebels. I visited the old church & grave yard, saw a grave & age of the person was 137 years. The stone was placed in the year 1688. I should judge by that, that the church was over 200 yrs old. Went back to camp, got rations for three days & then got ready for inspection. It looks rainy-

  Sunday - March 30th 1862 - After a good nights rest I had a good breakfast of oysters, fish & small pies as large as a tea saucer. Had inspection at nine, & then were ordered to march. We went near five miles & encamped in an old swamp hole. It commenced raining just as we started & as I had nothing with me I got wet through. My own knapsack was on the wagon. I have to carry the hospital knapsack & a big load it is, chucked full of medicines, splints, bandages etc. I went with Clark & Warner in the woods near by thinking I would get out of some of the rain. I borrowed a rubber blanket to keep my self dry. We made a fire, but I had nothing to cook - but one solitary hard tack to eat. Things began to look dubious & I was discouraged Awful hungry & wet to the skin. I hung my rubber on a bush & crawled under it with nothing over me. Clark & Warner were with me In the dead of night I found the water over three inches deep & I just awoke the boys & told them I was about drowned.

Monday - March 31st 1862 - I was out from under my blanket about one Oclk A.M. It was raining as hard as it could pour down & my back was as sopping wet with water, & mud as it could be. My patriotism was at a low ebb & I would have sold my Commission fo less than three cents. I thought of home & the splendid bed there was for me & then Mothers cupboard came before my eyes with bread & butter enough for a good meal. I never dreamed of being in such a predicament. At day light we went down to the Regt - found the hospital tent put up & the Steward as mad as a March hare. I didn't care though, but told him I wanted some thing to eat. I got my knapsack, changed my clothes & after a good hot whiskey punch to keep from getting sick I eat my breakfast, while eating Buel came down & from him I learned that he had fared a great deal better than I did. Worked all day fixing up the hospital, getting wood etc.

Tuesday - April 1st 1862 - My sleeping during the past evening was of a little different style & I thought it a great deal better than the night before. I went up to see Buel & to find out if he knew what day of the month it was. After thinking a spell he looked up & laughed. I told him I would not hurt him that day, but wait until we go home. He is 19 yrs old today. I went down to my quarters & got D Jewett our assistant surgeon, & then started fer Buels bunk. I told Buel to haul off his sock fer I was bound he should have his toe nail out. So after a good deal of coaxing it was done & Dr took it out slick & clean. I took it & put it in a paper, saying there was a young lady wanted that to put with his other one. However he wanted it himself & so I let it go fer a birthday present. There was Company & Battallion drill but he was excused. We had five sick ones in the hospital & I took care of them during the night.

Wednesday - April 2nd 1862 - About one Oclk I commenced writing a letter to Lucy to send in Buel's letter to his ladye love. After a great deal of patience with my sick ones I got it wrote & sealed. I then kept myself busy the rest of the night in thinking of home & the dear one I left behind. I often think of old times & am busy in building castles for the future. But the dead only know whether they will come true or not. We had a heavy thunder storm in the afternoon with some hail. A spy was brought into Headquarters. A woman dressed in mans clothings. Went to the Sutlers to get some cheese & cakes, paid for one dozen cookies 20 cents, cheese 25 cents per pound. Everything is very high in the eating line especially with these Sutlers. They are almost robbers in my way of thinking. Went back to quarters & at dress parade visited the 23rd Penn Regt. They can drill equal to the old 10th.

Thursday - April 3rd 1862 - This morning we had inspection & an extra twenty round of cartridges were given out to the soldiers. We recd today our new tents called dee Aubrey. They are about 4 1/2 feet square in two pieces. Each man carries a piece & two pieces make a tent. Soon the soldier will be nothing but a pack mule. We cut two poles, or crutches about 4 feet high, then have a ridge pole. A pin for each corner & then the tent is up. They are a handy thing, but I believe they will leak as bad as a sieve. However we are nothing but soldiers, so what is the use. Orders to march tomorrow at daylight, came at 4 P.M. We have sent our sick to Hampton & now we expect stirring times. We hear that the right wing of our army have gone through big & little Battle driving a lot of rebel cavalry before them. Hope it is true but doubt it.

Friday - April 4th 1862 - Revielle beat at 3, Oclk, we eat our breakfast & started at 4 fer Yorktown (20 report said) I had the Hospital Knapsack & as it was a rather a curious looking concern, everyone asked me if I would play them a tune. I told them yes, but I wanted a monkey to make the performance pay, & if they would just let themselves we would go halves. Others called it a band box, or bureau & some a chest of drawers. It was all the same to me, however as I was in my countrys service. The roads were very very bad & we did not get but 10 miles. We bivoucked fer the night near a piece of woods. A rebel camp had been there but a short time before.

The boys shot a lot of hogs, & one of them had a hide on three inches thick. It certainly was a great curiosity to me. I should judge that he must have been pretty old. Looks rainy.

Saturday - April 5th 1862 - (The Siege of Yorktown) - Started at 3 A.M. Oclk on our march, got but a short distance when our advance reported the enemy in front. We were wide awake I'll bet. Our battery went up & fired a few shots. The enemy left in a hurry, it was the outpost of the enemy. The place was Youngs Mills & it was enclosed or barricaded very strongly. They had a breastwork for & guns. It commenced raining at this time & I was destitute of a rubber. When our Regt got to Youngs Mills we halted & Buel gave me a blanket. It didnt do me much as I was so wet. We then started & took our way to the left. We went over ploughed fields & such walking I never see, no stopping to rest, we went six miles & when we halted we did not have 300 men with us out of 1000. After they came up we pressed on again & soon we heard firing. Our Regt fanned in line at the double quick loaded their guns - sent out skirmishes but no ending there. The firing was 1 1/2 miles ahead.

Sunday - April 6th 1862 - It rained all night very hard, but as I was pretty tired I didn't get up. I could feel the water running next my flesh, but as there was no prospect of my condition I lay still & tried to sleep. It was a poor show, but I stuck to my text. At daylight I found we were at Warwick C. House. The firing was from Smiths Division. Our cavelry have crossed the country in front & they say there is a long line of breastworks, Fort & everything else in front. Have not had anything to eat in 24 hours. The teams are stuck in the mud 1 mile below Youngs Mills. Sent some of our boys down to back up rations. Nearly two thirds of our Regt have gone. Went in camp in the woods where we first formed in line of Battle. It has rained all day & I guess will all night. What shall I do. Have had only three crackers to eat today.

Monday - April 7th 1862 - I couldn't sleep much as it was so cold & as I had no blankets with me. I had to make the best of it. I got up pretty early made a fire & then went to sleep sitting up until reveille. I had no breakfast, went to see Buel about 8 Ocl'k & he gave me some salt jerk & hard crackers. If ever anything tasted good, that did. Our teams got up about noon & we unloaded our stuff in a jiffy. Our provisionsbox was opened the first thing & our cook went to his work like a good fellow. Soon we had victuals enough & we laid in some I reckon. Pitched our tents & Hospital tent, but no sooner done than it commenced raining again. However I was bound to have a good nights rest so I took our Hospital boxes & lay on them. I was awakened several times by the noise outside from the boys. It rained as hard as it could pour, all night long.

  Tuesday - April 8th 1862 - I awoke this morning very much refreshed - eat a good breakfast & then took a good plate down to Buel, as I knew he had nothing but hardtack to eat. He received it with a great deal of pleasure. He bunks with Lieuts Wells & Trevor. They think a good deal of him. He has made quite a respectable looking house for them out of pine logs & boughs. Nothing going on in front. Our whole army, I guess, have run against a stump. Now we will see what our General is made of. The report is circulated that we are agoing right into them, hammer & tongs. I hope so at any rate. Worked around fixing up our Hospital & our tents. Had a good fire in the evening & we also had a good sing. Clark, Wells & myself making the woods ring with National Songs. We are as patriotic as ever.

  Wednesday - April 9th 1862 - It has commenced raining again this morning & our rations are giving out. The roads are in an awful condition. Six mules can't draw a wagon with 400 pounds of stuff in. If this is a sample of the weather we are to have, I hope the rebels will just lay down their arms. It has done nothing but rain since we landed in Virginia & everything is gloomy. The boys, Officers & the weather. Well, I dont know as we can always expect sunshine, but this mud is awful. The boys have their shoes filled with the sacred soil every step they have taken. If I didn't have a good pair of boots I don't know what I should do. Made out my supper & then started fer the Brigade Commissary as the teams have got along. Thursdays rations are to be given of Beans, Rice, Coffee, Sugar, Bread & Pork. While going up I got stuck in a mud hole going in to my hips - Had to be hauled out.

  Thursday - April 10th 1862 - Got up this morning bright & early, eat my breakfast & then took a stroll up to the C. House to see some rebel prisoners that had been brought in the night before. They were a miserable looking set of fellows. Dirty, ragged & saucey. No two were dressed alike. One had on an old straw hat & a citizens coat. Their pants were of a butternut color. They were from Georgia.

From there I went to see the balloon but as there had been so many there in the morning, I could not get in. Our Paymaster came up in the night & now he is paying off our Brigade. Our Regt was paid of about three Ocl'k. I recd $40.75 - $14.75 of it being for extra duty at the Hospital. Now that I have got it, I hardly know what to do with it Buel recd $26.00. W. H. Coop was also paid & now we feel bully -

Friday - April 11th 1862 - Turned out of my bunk at revielle cooked my breakfast & then got some fer a couple of sick ones Made them a meal out of corn starch & Tea. Pretty dry fodder, should think, but it is all fer the Union. Went up to C. House again today & from there went over to the 23rd Penn Suttlers to get something to eat, as we were nearly out. Found about 2000 men around each of their wagons & so I gave up the job as a bad one. I ther went back to C. House, found Tip Coop, had a long talk with him about home & our friends we left. The mud is awful deep & it is very hard going. Went back to camp took supper. Then let my patriotism ooze out a little by singing the Star Spangled Banner & other tunes Wound up with old Hundred & then went to bed.

Saturday - April 12th 1862 - Had a good nights rest & feel as gay & festive as they make them. Wrote a letter to Father & sent him thirty five dollars. Buel sent ten with mine. We believes in living as he goes along, & I believe in letting Uncle Sam pay fer my living, that is all the difference between us. I enclosed a letter to Lucy also & sent them by E. B. Whittlesey to Fortress Monroe there to have them go by Express. I have sent home, since I enlisted, one hundred & thirty five dollars & to others a small bit. I have used but about twenty dollars for myself in eight months. If I live I expect to realise the benefit of doing so. The day was passed in much the usual way as the day preceeding it. Had supper of Pork & Hardtacks. Went to roost at nine P. M.

Sunday - April 13th 1862 - I awoke this morning just as the sun was rising. It has been a splendid day. The mud is drying up fas & the roads are getting in good condition. We were called out this forenoon to hear preaching by our Chaplain. The Regt were fermed in a hollow square & we all doffed our hats. It has been the first discourse we have heard since coming on the peninsula. I saw J. J White fermerly of S Adams. He is a Capt in the 33d N. York & is as fat as a porpoise. He says he lives on nothing but Governement rations. I guess though he has the best there is. No duties & no parade. I feel in good spirits & praise God for all his mercies to me. Oh, how good he is to me. I read my bible every day. Three chapters every weekday & Sundays I read five, by doing this I will read it though in one year.

Monday - April 14th 1862 - Nothing going on today, except drilling the Regt. The boys are heartily sick of the thing & I dont blame them. The day is very pleasant & it looks some as it does at home. How I long to be there, to see my dear friend. May God bless & protect them from all danger & sickness. Was with Buel most of the day. He thinks a great deal of home but wishes to see this rebellion ended as bad as I do. Hurrah for the Stars & Stripes, long may they wave oer the land of the free & the home of the brave. Aint I patriotic though. Well I dont know as I am sorry that I enlisted fer I would feel ashamed to know that my country was in danger & I not willing to give my aid in bringing peace to the land again.

Tuesday - April 15th 1862 - The same duties today as yesterday. I forget to say in duties of yesterday that a detail from our Regt was made to work on the roads, chopping down trees & laying those across the roads & thus making what is called Corduroy roads. Our Regt built a bridge today & made a road a quarter of a mile in length. The weather is pleasant, the sun shinning warm. The birds sing gaily & everything looks like spring. We cleaned the ground in front of our tents & then went to bed. Hoping that on another spring we would be a home enjoying the feather beds instead of the hard grounds.

Wednesday - April 16th 1862 - We were awakened before day light & told to cook our breakfast & pack up as we would move in an hour. We were to go without knapsacks & so we thought we were in for a fight. After fooling around all day we got the distance of four mile. Then two of the Regts in the Brigade were sent back to get their knapsacks while the other staid on guard. Our Regt went back about 9 oclk & got back to camp at 11. Staid until three in the morning. I staid in an ambulance & took care of Adjutant Porter, of the General Staff, so saved a tramp of 8 mile. I was tired & hungry & did not get much sleep, felt pretty sick - had a severe headache.

Thursday - April 17th 1862 - This morning we started again,

after a mile we halted & lingered around until near night. I felt pret[ty]
well in the morning, but at noon I felt worse, thought I should have [a]
fever. Doctor Chamberlain told me to be careful & not eat muc[h]
gave me a hot whiskey punch & two Quinine Pills, went to bed in th[e]
brush & leaves until the Regt went off. We went a mile farther,
thought I could never get there, had on my back the Hospital kna[p]
sack & a blanket. I got up to the Regt & then went right to bed fer t[he]
night. My head felt as big as a pumkin. The Regt were called out [in]
line at midnight by an alarm from the pickets. I heard that there ha[d]
been quite a fight with the rebels. One Vt. Regt getting pretty well c[ut]
up.

   Friday - April 18th 1862 - The Regt were called again at tw[o]
Oclk & formed in a line of Battle, as the report came the rebels we[re]
coming. I felt pretty bad, but was bound not to be sick while the[re]
was a fight. I staid up until morning & then tried to eat something, b[ut]
it was no go. The surgeon ordered me into the tent & told me to sta[y]
there. He gave me one dose of pills also a good scolding for bein[g]
up in the night. I was very sick all day, but I did not mean to let the[m]
know it. I heard that the Regt were chopping down trees to block u[p]
the road, in case the rebels should make a dash on us. Skirmishin[g]
going on all day at the front.

   Saturday - April 19th 1862 - We were routed out of our bed[s]
at one Oclk A.M. by the pickets firing & I thought I would get up to[o]
but dare not as I felt no better. The Regt moved off from their cam[p]
several rods & fermed in line of Battle & so they staid all night. Th[e]
picket got into quite a lively dance. At daylight I took a dose of Cast[or]
Oil on my own hooks, felt much better at night. Some of the boy[s]
went to the front, to see the rebel batteries & our Sharpshooter[s].
They brought back a glowing account of them & I made up my min[d I]
would take a peep at this the first opportunity. Had a good supper [of]
Beef Broth & Boston crackers & then went to bed.

   Sunday - April 20th 1862 - We were called out again th[is]
morning about two Oclk & marched up towards the point to see wh[at]
was the trouble. I did not get (up) but stuck to my bed like a good fe[l]
low. It was raining like shot. At daylight I got up & had a goo[d]
Breakfast. The Regt came back the same time. After dinner I took [a]
walk with Buel to see the batteries of the Rebels. We got up there [&]
found that a flag of truce had been sent in. We had a splendid vie[w]

of their Batteries, saw their flag & our sharpshooters. The 3rd Vt. Regt were there bringing in their dead & wounded, some of their wounded had lain out three days in the mud & rain without anything to eat in all that time. I felt sorry for the poor fellows. Went back to camp pretty well tired out.

Monday - April 21st 1862 - We were not called out during the night. I suppose on account of its being so rainy. It rained all day & the mud was awful deep. We recd orders to march back to our old camp, the next morning. I thought it was retreat, but was told that we only came there to support Gen. Davidson & that he would still hold his old position. I felt better & was glad to know that we were agoing to move, as the place we were in was nothing but a swamp hole. I went in the evening over to the Sutlers with the rest of the Hospital Boys & had a good stew of oysters. Felt tip top, went to bed in good spirits & slept well all night.

Tuesday - April 22nd 1862 - Recd orders to march at 9 Oclk A.M. & after working hard all day we got to our old camp at Warwick C. House where mud was knee deep & such going I never see before. Our teams got stuck every rod or two & we had to lift them out. I was tired, dirty & hungry as could be. This on ward to Richmond is a hard road to travel especially such weather as this. I hope it will be better before long. It was quite cold walking. After getting to camp I saw a Sutlers cart, went there & by a streak of good luck got half a dozen loaves of bread. Was offered after I got them - fifty cents a loaf, but it was no temptation. After the best supper I ever eat I went to bed & slept well until morning.

Wednesday - April 23rd 1862 - Put up the Hospital tent, & got two sick ones inside. I took care of them & slept with them. The other duties of today were the same as usual.

Thursday - April 24th & Friday April 25th 1862 - The same duties both days, one of my boys died this morning of the 25th. He was sick but three days. He belonged to Co. C & his name was Frederick Goodrich. He was buried under an old cherry tree, it was a solemn time, & a sad sight to behold. We wrapped him up in his blanket & laid him in the ground. No one of his friends at home near him. Heard that a Col. & Maj. of the 93rd N Y Regt had been taken prisoners.

Saturday - April 26th 1862 - I was awakened in the morning by the wind & rain pattering on my shelter tent & on crawling out, the first salutation I met with, was a pair of wet feet, I thought it was a pretty good beginning for the day, but was not disheartened, as I have had the good, or bad luck, to have my feet wet most of the time since coming on the peninsula. Nothing going on in camp, but the same old duties of Mounting Guard, & C. I was in the Hospital all day taking care of the sick. Two of the boys are not expected to live. But if careful nursing will cure them they shall have it.

Sunday - April 27th 1862 - After watching the sick all night I was relieved from my duties & after eating Breakfast I went to bed. I had a pretty good snooze, but was awakened at two Oclk by a terrible hubbub outside. On getting up to see what was to pay, I found, that the boys were feeling pretty jolly, in meeting some of their old friends. Lieut Hager of Co. D had arrived in camp with a lot of recruits from old Mass, for our Regt. I scanned each face with care, not knowing but I might find somone that I knew. But it was no go & so I went back to bed again & slept until Dark. Then fer another night watch.

Monday - April 28th & Tuesday April 29th 1862 - Monday was passed as other days, with nothing new to occupy our minds. Tuesday morning we were mustered in for two months pay & after that the boys started a game of Ball. We had a good time of it. I often thought of the splendid games I used to have at home & for once wished myself there. At sundown we recd orders to hold ourselves in readiness to march at a moments notice. Heavy firing had been heard all day long, in the vicinity of Yorktown, now for a fight, we all think.

Wednesday - April 30th 1862 - Firing commenced this morning at day light & in the same vicinity of yesterday. We waited anxiously fer orders to march but none came, & we passed the day playing Ball, Jumping, Pulling Sticks & other games. In the evening took my turn watching with the sick. One of the boys is pretty near done with this world in my opinion.

Thursday, Friday & Saturday - May 1st, 2nd & 3rd 1862 - Went to bed at daylight & slept all day, went to work again at dark watching the sick. Staid up all night & Thursday ferenoon. One of the

15

boys died at nine Oclk A.M. of congestion of the lungs. His name was Falvey of Co. I from Holyoke, Mass. He was buried in his blanket by the side of Goodrich under the old cherry tree. Friday was very warm & pleasant. It seemed like summer to me. Nothing new in camp.

Sunday - May 4th 1862 - Had orders to march at noon. After packing my worldly goods in my knapsack & getting everything in order, I was told that I would have to stay behind to take care of the sick in the Brigade. I felt blue enough after that order. I was pleased to learn that the Steward Charles Wells, & one of the Nurses, would stay with me, besides our apt Surgeon Jewett. The Regt did not leave until 4 P.M. & then I had to put up a tent & get the sick all together, found I had 24 sick ones to look after. My tent was more than full, yet I managed to get them in. A fellow from Co. I was detailed to stay in the tent & look after them during the night. It commenced (raining) at dusk. I got a rubber & laid myself down on a board under a tree & went to sleep.

Monday - May 5th 1862 - (Battle of Williamsburg) - I got up this morning with a wet coat, but as the clouds were clearing away & the sun just rising I put on a bright face & began to think what I should get for Breakfast to feed my sick ones. The sick from the other Regts didnt have the first bit of anything in their Haversacks & what to do fer them I couldnt tell. I went to the Surgeon & told him how I was situated. He gave me an order to get Bread, Meat & C from the Brigade Commisary, & at 11 oclk the boys had their Breakfast. Then orders came fer me to sent them all to the General Hospital, especially those from the 7th Mass & 2nd R. Island. I got their tent all up & everyone of them comfortable with bread enough & to spare, before dark. Their tent was by the side of Warwick CH.

Tuesday - May 6th 1862 - I was up at midnight looking after my boys, one of them is very sick. I dont know how in the world we can move him; if the Regt should not come back. He is as crazy as a bear & I have got my hands full to take care of him. Our other nurse S. P. Williams is sick a bed, & no one to help me but the Steward. Our Quartermaster came to camp at noon, & says our men had a big fight at Williamsburgh yesterday & that we drove them before us. He knows but little about the old 10th whether they were in it or not. All our baggage had to go tomorrow from here & all the sick have to go back to Yorktown, 100 ambulances will be here at daylight to take them away. Oh! how I long to see the Regt & to know if any are dead. I never will stay behind again. Thats SO

Wednesday - May 7th 1862 - After a very poor nights sleep, I got up, eat breakfast & then got the sickones all ready for their jaunt. Soon my eyes beheld a long train of baggage wagons coming to the C. House. I was told Utro (?) that these were our ambulances. Oh didn't I pity the poor fellows that would ride in them. We had only one wagon to carry the sick ones of our Regt, our number was eight - that could not walk, we stowed them away in the bottom of the wagon & I never felt so bad in my life, as I did to see the poor fellows cry & beg us to take them out & let them die. Oh, it was a sad sight. I rode in one of the wagons a mile & such a ride I never had. My head would go one side & then the other. I finally concluded that I would get out & walk especially while we were on a corduroy road. The teams all stopt after going two mile, & while there, we buried 12 men that had dies while coming over the roads.

Thursday - May 8th 1862 - As I had got the sick off my hands, we were told to go to Yorktown & there await further orders. I started on the road with several of our men (convalescents) fer the town. I lost my way several times & it was not until near sundown that I found myself at the place. I followed the line of earthworks that were built by our men all the way, & if it was not a grand sight, then I am no judge. While passing through Yorktown I saw all the entrenchments of the enemy Their Rifle Pits, Forts & the big guns that they had left. I cant think for the life of me, why! They left so good a position as this, I wandered all over the place & almost forgot where I was. Then it got so dark that I could not see very well. I began to think about a place to sleep & on walking around a little, I beheld friend Bidwell with his cart of dry goods. Now says I, I am all right for the night & so I was, Had a good, nights rest.

Friday - May 9th 1862 - I got up this morning feeling well & after eating breakfast, I took a stroll around town, to see the place by daylight. I went on the Hill where the Rebels had their Hospital & where our own sick were being conveyed. I had a good view of the river, of Gunboats, Sloops & Steamers. Troops were going on board transports fer West Point, to cut enemy off from their retreat to Richmond. I went back to Bidwells & hired out to him fer one day. I sold Books, Writing paper, pens, ink, shirts, Hats & everything else in the line of trash, at 2 Oclk P.M. I went to peddling papers & if I didnt have my hands full then I wouldnt say so. I drove a smashing business. After my days work was done Bidwell gave me eight dollars & told me, he guessed I had earnt it. I then went over to the tents on the hill & got our 10th boys all fixed up, as they had just come in they were tired & hungry & I went to work with a will. Staid up all night.

Saturday - May 10th 1862 - While eating my breakfast this morning, the Surgeons came around & appointed Stewards & Nurses for the Hospital & as I had not been reckoned in the lot, I thought I would go to the Regt, if I could find them. I heard they were some 24 miles away & travelling still. I told the Steward [C. Wells] & our nurse Sam Williams what I thought of doing & they said they would go too. We then spoke to Dr. Jewett [our apt. Surgeon] He said if we could get away on the sly, we might go. So off we started. On the road we overtook a fellow that had deserted the rebels the morning of the fight at Williamsburg. He told us everything about how they lived, what they thought of us, & stories, any quantity. He was from New Jersey, but was on board an oyster sloop on the York River at the time of the rebellion. He showed us all the Ferts at Williamsburg & the battle field where we had the hardest fight. We stopt & took dinner at Fort Magruder by the side of a good spring of water, one that this fellow had made. We had marched in all 12 mile & my feet were pretty sore but I was bound to catch the Regt. So after taking a good rest we started again. Passed through Williamsburg & such a sight I never beheld before. Prisoners were stuck in all the large buildings in the place. Wounded soldiers were being carried hither & thither & my heart did ache for the poor fellows. St. James & Marys Colleges were the nicest looking buildings in the town. I longed to stay & visit the different places of notoriety, but the old 10th were ahead & I must away. We marched ten mile farther & then camped for the night as the boys got played out & I wasnt much better. I had carried the Hospital knapsack all the way [weight 45 lbs] I slept the best that I have for a long time.

Sunday - May 11th 1862 - We all got up bright & early & started on the march without anything to eat. Our rations failed us yesterday, after marching one mile we came across a lot of the 10th boys, Guarding the rations for our Brigade. We filled our empty stomachs after learning that the Regt were only five mile ahead. We then made tracks & just at noon, I found the Regt - a happier fellow than I could't be found. I went to see Buel the first thing, found him well & in good spirits. He gave me a letter from L___ & then he told me what he thought of fighting. It took him a good while to tell his story & I listened with rapt attention. He was with me all day. I went to bed pretty early. The place where we encamped is called Ropers Church.

Monday - May 12th 1862 - I laid in my bunk until 8 Oclk this morning, then after eating found Buel, and we took our Portfolios, and went into the woods to write to our friends at Home. We had a nice time together in talking over old times before we were soldier boys. I often think to myself if we shall ever see home again, or see the dear friends that are endeared to our hearts. May God grant us his blessing, and spare our lives to see the end of this unholy rebellion. We went back to camp at dinner time, & then went to see some of the other Regts, Recd orders to march at 7 Oclk tomorrow morning. In the evening our Band out serenading & good music they played. Went to bed in good season -

Tuesday - May 13th 1862 - We started this morning at 7 Oclk on our march & in eight hours, we got just one mile over the road. The delay was caused by the troops, & wagons ahead. At three Oclk we got under weigh & put sticks as tights as we could jump. Passed through New Kent C House at sundown. We bivoucked on a high hill after firming in Line of Battle with orders to sleep near the stacks. I cooked some coffee, & after eating a Hardtack & a piece of raw salt Pork, I turned in fer the night. My dreams were delicious & delightful-

Wednesday - May 14th 1862 - Orders came early this morning to pack up & start. Dr Chamberlain wished me to go back to New Kent C. House with a lot of sick ones, so off I started in as hard rain storm as ever there was. Got to New Kent, found the Dr, & he piloted the way to a house he had got for a Hospital. The house was full of dirt, old tools, bedsteads & Feather beds. After a heap of hard work, I got it cleaned out. Beds arranged with sheets & pillow cases, I had three beds in one room & seven patients to occupy them. Had a Tip Top time all day. At night hauled into the room another featherbed & laid myself down fer the night - bound that I would have a night rest fer once, on a feather bed, while in the army & so I did.

Thursday - May 15th 1862 - After rolling & tossing about for a good while on my feather bed, I concluded I would finish the night by sleeping on floor, & I must say give me a hard board, sooner than your feathers, to sleep on. I got up at daylight, fixed up my boys all nice & then commenced looking for relics. Found in the garret, things too numerous to mention. While engaged in the pursuit of happiness, I was aroused by a voice from the stairway yelling "Hallo Wools! where ye at?" I looked & saw Charley Wells, then says I, "bout yere! Whats to pay? Nothing, only I've come after you to go back to the Regt." "Good" says I, & off I started with my old Pill Box on my back, leaving my Bro Nurse (Williams) to take care of the sick ones. Found the Regt on picket, about two mile from where I left them with orders to march in three hours, orders countermanded, & so we staid overnight.

Friday - May 16th 1862 - Recd orders to march at seven A.M. Got all ready to go, then the order countermanded again. Recd orders at noon that we should go at three Oclk P.M., & some did. Marched five mile, unslung knapsacks, & then went one mile farther, to reconnoiter & post pickets. Keyes Corps. is in the advance of the army & Couch's Division, the advance of the Corps. We found no enemy, posted the pickets & then turned in fer the night.

Saturday - May 17th 1862 - We got up pretty early & started back fer our knapsacks, leaving a portion of the Regt to look after things a little. After getting our knapsacks we went back to where we were on picket; took the remainder of the Regt & then went on. Traveled some four mile & then camped down in one of the most pleasant places I have seen since coming on the Peninsula. The people have fled for parts unknown to us & left us masters of all we survey. Our Regt were posted on a road in a Pine woods. Our Videttes report the enemy in front. All are wide awake. Our pickets are supported with heavy reserves, so I camp down feeling mightly secure. Two of our men are very sick.

Sunday - May 18th 1862 - I did not rest very well, as I had to give medicine every two hours all night long. At daybreak the Dr went to the town to find a house fer a Hospital. He soon came back having found one & sent four of us down with Hospital Pill Box, & C to clean out the Shantie, & fix up a little. After getting the thing done I was ordered back to camp, left the Medicine Chest, with Dr. G. C. Clark &

marched back to camp again. After eating a good hearty dinner o Broiled Beef Steak & Hardtack, I pitched my tent in the woods, I ther lay myself down to think, read & pray. How different the Sundays are spent in the army, to what they are at home. Here we have nc preaching, no meetings of any kind, & everything & everybody is ful of wickedness.

Monday - May 19th 1862 - Nothing going on in the old 10th today different from other days while in Camp. The 7th Mass are ou in picket & they have seen the enemy, fired at them & the rebels firec in return, wounding one of the 7th boys pretty seriously - . I went tc see him, but as there was such a crowd around the tent, I concludec to pospone my visit. In the evening, Signal rockets were sent up, by our Signal Corps & as it was the first time I had seen the performance, I was very much pleased. It put me in mind of the 4th of Julys I used to spend at home.

Tuesday & Wednesday - May 20th & 21st 1862 - (Skirmish at Bottom Bridge) - Nothing going on Tuesday. It commenced raining in the morning & rained all day long. I staid under shelter most of the time. Wednesday we recd orders to pack up & march, after a great deal of trouble we got started & marched about three mile, to a place called Bottom Bridge, on the Chickahominy River. There was no bridge there for the Rebels had burned it down. We encamped on a nice piece of grass land & our Hospital was in an old corn crib. There had been two Graneries, House & Barn burnt by secesh. The graneries were filled, I should judge by the depth of the ashes. Had a good hard oak floor for a bed & I slept tip top.

Thursday - May 22nd 1862 - After a good nights rest I got up & as there was some corn scattered about, I though I would have a Breakfast of Hasty Pudding. So after pounding a sufficient quantity into coarse meal, I went at the task of cooking it. By dint (?) of a good deal of patience & perseverence I managed to make a pudding fit for a king. Buel came along soon after & I tried to make him eat some, but it was no go, as he complained of being sick. I gave him a dose of Whiskey & Quinine & sent him off to Bed. Most of the Regt went off in Picket across the River, Lieut. Wheeler of Co. D had finished building a bridge over the Chickahominy & now I expect we shall all go on one tramp again tomorrow. We have had one of the hardest rain storms of the season, but as my lodgings are under cover of a good roof, I didnt mind it much.

Friday - May 23rd 1862 - We recd orders to march this morning, but after waiting quite awhile, we thought it would be no go. However at 4 P.M. we started & crossed the noted Chickahominy & now I expect we shall meet with resistance. After going one mile, we turned to the left, on the Charles City road, & marched two mile farther. Encamped in an old swamp hole, but our Surgeon took us boys into a niggers shanty close by, telling us to clean it up & use it fer a hospital. We went to work, & soon there was a decided improvement in the looks of the building, got all our sick inside, made them a supper & then went to bed out of doors, under a <u>Hedge fence.</u>

Saturday - May 24th 1862 - I was awakened this morning by some of the niggers driving the cows to pasture. I got up, just in time to see the boys go after them, double quick with cups in their hands, to get a taste of milk, but they were doomed to be disappointed, fer they had been stripped clean & dry. Staid in camp all day, while the Regt went on Picket. Our Lieut. Co. (J. M. Decker) come to our shantie, sick with chills & touch of Rheumatis. I made him up a good bed on a lot of husked corn in the garret. Went to bed in good season, and heard we would march in morning.

Sunday - May 25th 1862 - It has been a splendid day. The sun shining warmly all day long & the birds have been singing, as if there never was such a wicked thing as men hunting after each other to kill. We started from our camp at 11 A.m. on our road to Richmond. Went back the two miles we come Friday & took the direct road for the secesh Capitol. Marched two mile farther & encamped in a large wheat field, near a nice mansion. Our Quarters fer the Hospital were in a corn crib. Buel was quite sick & could hardly march with us. I got his knapsack, Gun & Equipments carried fer him, & then got him in the Hospital, where I could take care of him. I fear he will have a Fever. Got him a good rousing punch, covered him up with blankets & let him sleep. I laid myself down by his side to watch his every care.

Monday - May 26th 1862 - [Memoranda from rear of diary: "Out on a Reconnissance, under heavy Artillery fire for half an hour or more. Drove the enemy, but lost no men."]
We were ordered this morning to march without knapsacks to reconnoiter & see if we could find the enemy. We had gone but a short distance before we found them in force, after a brisk cannon-

ade of hours duration, we drove them from their position & put pickets on the ground we drove them from. Then went back to Camp of the morning. We lost none in our Regt, although several were killed & wounded belonging to the Battery. It rained all the while we were gone, & the mud was awful deep. I was wet through. I found Buel not better than when I left him in the morning. The Dr. gave him Lead & opii alternate with Quinine & Capsicarn. After getting him a supper of Farina Gruel I went to bed.

Tuesday - May 27th 1862 - My brother kept me awake most of the night, he being so restless & feverish. I gave him a good scrubbing in the morning & put a clean change of clothing on him. The Dr. thought he was in better condition than he was the night before. Gave him for medicine one dose of (illegible), then Quinine & Opii. Think he is improving tonight. Our regt have been to work building Breastworks, Rifle Pits & C. in expectation of a Battle. The enemy are reported to be in force one mile & a half, in advance of us. Probably they think we will run, but I guess they will find themselves mistaken. Gen. Couchs Headquarters are in the mansion belonging to Mr. Allen. The women folks have all gone to Richmond.

Wednesday - May 28th 1862 - Buel is much better this morning having obtained a good nights rest, & I think with care will get along. Our Regt, our Division were ordered on another Reconnoitering excursion & I took the old Pill Box & started with the rest. After going 1/2 a mile up the main road we passed what is called the Seven Pines. Then took the road to the right & passed Fairoaks Station. Distance from Camp 2 1/2 mile & distant to Richmond only five mile. Found the enemy in force & after they fired several shots at us, we left, first establishing a picket line. Caseys Division were just in rear of us & we left them going into Camp at that place. I got back to Camp just at dusk. Went to bed after eating supper of Hard Bread & Coffee.

Thursday - May 29th 1862 - Recd orders to march at daylight & after a tramp of two miles we came to a halt 1/4 of a mile in the rear of Caseys Division. We established our Hospital in a nigger shantie, about 20 rods in front of our Regt. Buel was reported to quarters after we got here, as he is getting a great deal better. Recd letters from Home & from a dear friend. Fixed up my tent outside as I did not like the idea of sleeping in a house all the while, especially when the lice were as thick as toads in a thunder shower. I then went down to the brook & took a grand good wash, & then turned in for the night.

Friday - May 30th 1862 - I got up this morning feeling as happy as a lark. Wrote letters to Father & Lucy, one to my cousin in Pittsfield & another one in Hatfield. It took me nearly all day to do it. There has been considerable firing to the right of our lines, but what is the cause of it, is not known in Camp. Went to sleep at 8 P M, but was aroused by a false alarm of the pickets at 11 P.M. Did not go to bed again until midnight.

> Colonel Parsons continued to review the service of the regiment,"*At the battle of Fair Oaks, with seven companies in line, the other three on picket, it sustained a loss of 126 men, including four officers killed and a number of officers severely wounded; among the number was Col. Briggs, shot through both legs, and the writer of this article, Capt. Parsons, who was severely wounded in the head and thigh and left for on the field for dead.*"

Saturday - May 31st 1862 - (Battle of Fair Oaks or Seven Pines. "Of the Mass. 10th 122 killed & wounded.") - Nothing was stirring in Camp this forenoon but just as we had all got our dinners eaten, firing commenced in our front. Whole volleys of musketry, & the booming of the artillery, fairly made the ground shake. Orders were given at once to Fall in, not knowing what might happen. Everyone left their tents up, knapsacks all undone & most of the boys left their coats. Soon orders came from Brigade H Quarters to fall in, as the enemy were driving Gen. Casey. Now fer a fight & will give the rebels a taste of the 10th boys. I was told to take a stretcher & follow the Regt. We went about 10 miles in front of the building we had used for a Hospital & lay down in the Rifle Pits. The shells from the enemy would come over us & go schreeching by like mad. Our batteries were stationed just in the rear of our Regt & the shells from them, wounded several of our Regt. I had work then to get the poor fellows off from the field. I had to creep on my hands & knees, as our cannon were firing as fast as they could. Case Division came straggling along back & they could not be made <u>fall in</u> line. It was one continual string of them for an hour & such a rabble I never see.

Cowards was hissed in their ears, but it done no good. Soon there was a lull in the storm & our Regt were ordered out of the Pits to the point. While going up the road our General observed the Rebels planting their guns in exact range, to sweep the road of everything. We were ordered to go in slashing & while wheeling into line, a whole volley of Musketry was fired on us from the left, giving us a terrible raking fire. Many of the poor fellows droped & the order was given to fall back to the old camp. How we got out of the place is more than I could tell. The first I knew of anything, was when I had two men holding them up & hurrying them to the rear. One shot through the leg & the other shot in the mouth. I passed our old Hospital, found it deserted, & then went farther back. I soon found the Dr. & he told me to take them to Savages Station one mile in the rear from where I then was. I got there with my load & then had to stay to assist in dressing the wounds. Had my hands full & worked as hard as I could. At dark, I heard the Rebels had possession of our Camp. So all my relics have gone to smash with my knapsack, all my under clothing Haversack with three days rations & even the coat from my back. Nothing have I got, but my breeches, shirt & cap. I never was so hard up before & never felt quite so blue. Our loss was not known at midnight. I hear Buel is safe.

  Sunday - June 1st 1862 - I worked all night as hard as I could work dressing the wounds of the boys & getting them coffee & crackers. Col. N. L. Briggs & Gen Devens were brought in the house wounded & from them I hear good news from the 10th, at daylight heavy firing commenced again & soon it was a continual roar. I had no fears however, as lots of reinforcements had come up the past evening. We drove the Rebels from the field & there the pursuit was stopt. Hookers Division encamping on the old camp, left by us. I assisted in getting the boys of on the cars to the White House landing, there to go to the Hospitals in the North. I hear our loss is 130 in killed, wounded & missing.

  Monday - June 2nd 1862 - After sleeping two hours I was up & at it again. I found one of the boys with my blouse on his back. I was pleased to find my Bible all safe & sound. Heard Lew Amidon was killed, started fer the Battlefield to find him, when I heard he had been found & taken to the Hospital wounded, went back & took care of him.

Tuesday - June 3rd 1862 - <u>Lew</u> Amidon was sent off in the cars bright & early, while I was asleep. Was sorry it so happened, but as I had had no sleep of any amount for three days. I could not keep awake any longer. Went back to the Regt found them in Rifle Pits 1/2 a mile back from our first position. Capt. Smart was buried today, as was Capt. Day, & Lieut Leland. The boys feel awfully the way Capt. Smart was murdered, & swear <u>revenge</u>, another show is all they ask, & all they want.

Wednesday - June 4th 1862 - It rained all the last night, but cleared off this morning, moved our camp, some 1/4 of a mile up the road & occupied another line of Rifle Pits. The Regt are in a sorry plight, having no blankets, & good many without coats. We almost freeze everynight. Our Quartermaster has gone to Fortress Monroe to get us a new supply. We all feel downhearted as we miss the familiar faces of our commanders.

Thursday - June 5th 1862 - I had a nice mud hole for my bed & after enjoying it until near daylight, I got up & run around to get warm. Oh this soldiering, how I wish myself back at home in mothers nice warm bed. There has been very heavy firing off to the right of us, & it is reported than Gen. Franklin has crossed the Chickahominy & gained a position. Nothing stirring in camp, all dull & down hearted.

Friday - June 6th 1862 - Lots of troops have been passing by us to the front. Our boys do nothing but eat, sleep, & talk of the fight, & of the bravery of some missing comrades. Our Major (Wm. Marsh) is under arrest for running away from the Regt. & it is hinted that our adjutant will go the same way. They are both errant cowards & not fit to be called men. I hope they will be put through.

Saturday - June 7th 1862 - Nothing unusual transpired today in our camp. It commenced raining in the afternoon & such a shower ain't to be seen everyday. Heavy firing on our right & we hear that Franklin Corps are giving the Rebels a taste of <u>Yankee Doodle</u>. I made a bunk today of boards & pine boughs & after getting it finished I went to bed.

Sunday - June 8th 1862 - We heard in the morning that the Paymaster was on the road to see us. At noon he was with us & he soon began to deal out the Greenbacks. I recd. $41.25 for my share.

Buel got his 26 dollars & after paying his debts had money left. I wrote to father & enclosed $35 dollars, sent it in a package that the No. Adams boys were getting up, to go by express. Went to bed feeling better in spirits, than I had for a long time.

Monday - June 9th 1862 - The day has been very pleasant, & the boys having been playing Bluff & Monte all day long. Report says that Gen. Porter took 10 cannon from the Rebels & lots of prisoners. Also that on the rail road in our front we took a train of cars, Engines & all. The Rebs came from Richmond to take some supplies that they had piled up while on their way to annihilate us - But instead we took them, cars & all. Bully for Joe Hooker.

Tuesday - June 10th 1862 - Nothing transpired today of any importance. Most of the boys are busy in playing fer money. I have seen a number of bets, made in the amount of 100 dollars. Went to bed in good season.

Wednesday - June 11th 1862 - I arose this morning feeling pretty well. Our clothing & tents have arrived & are to be given out tomorrow or as soon as the Quartermaster can get ready. Gen. Palmer of Caseys Division has taken command of our Brigade, while Gen. Devens is absent. He is said to be a brave officer & distinguished himself at Fairoaks. Nothing going on in camp of importance.

Thursday - June 12th 1862 - Our clothing was given out today. I got me a blanket, knapsack, & haversack also a Dee Aubrey tent. I wanted me a coat, but thought I would wait a spell. A gentleman from Northhampton came after the bodies of Sargeant Braman & Private, Perry Coleman, to take them home to their friends. He says everyone speaks well of the old 10th. Went to bed at Tattoo.

Friday - June 13 1862 - It has been a very pleasant day & as warm as any day that I can remember. Mr Clapp has gone home with the bodies of Braman & Coleman & we all feel glad to know that they will be buried where their friends can have the priviledge of going to their last resting place. Nothing unusual has transpired in the camp duties. Laid me down to rest at Tattoo.

Saturday - June 14 1862 - I went with Buel to Savages station this forenoon, to buy him some shirts. He was taken sick while there, & it was with a great deal of trouble, that I got him back to Camp. However after getting there, I gave him a dose of Ginger & Opii which brought him out all right. Heard that Stewarts Cavelry had made a <u>raid</u> near the White House, also a dash on a train of cars, killing two of our men, that were coming back to the Regt.

    Sunday - June 15th 1862 - It has been very warm today & all of us boys have done nothing, but loll & sweat. I should hate to live in such a climate, always where the days are so hot & the nights so cold. However it has been raining some this afternoon, & I guess we will have a wet night. The boys are pretty well prepared for it, so I say let <u>her come</u>.

    Monday - June 16th 1862 - After eating breakfast the Hospital boys were ordered to pitch a tent. A new tent having been sent us. We worked hard all day in cleaning the ground, putting up the tent, making beds & C. Our Steward was taken sick with Congestion, chills & fever. I went to bed at Tattoo, feeling pretty tired.

    Tuesday - June 17th 1862 - I got up at Revielle feeling very unwell. My throat was sore & I couldn't speak a loud word. After getting the tent all up in shape, I went back to bed. In the evening took some Quinine & Capsienan. I heard that our gunboats had taken Fort Darling on the James River, but as there were no land forces, to cooperate with them, the Gunboat had to relinquish the prize.

    Wednesday - June 18th 1862 - We rec'd orders to march at a moments notice. Everything was packed up & got ready for moving, but here we are yet. My throat is no better & I have a severe headache in the bargain. After taking a big dose of Hot stuff I went to bed, hoping I would feel better in the morning.

    Thursday - June 19th 1862 - I laid in my bunk all day, sick as I wished to be. I heard our quartermaster was put under arrest for going to Washington without leave. Six of sick men were sent to the White House Hospital, as we were expecting to move. No news of any importance worth writing.

    Friday - June 20th 1862 - Rec'd letters from home, before I got out of my bed. After eating a little I took my Portfolio & went with

Buel to write dear ones at home. Feel almost well - Gen. Palmer calls our Regt. wild & unruly set of fellows, not fit to live with Hottentots. I believe he will live to see the day when he will think different.

Saturday - June 21st 1862 - Everything is quiet in Camp. All the Regts have to turn out at three Oclk every morning & stand an hour with muskets in hand. Ready for any emergency. The boys don't like it much as they say it is just the time they want to sleep. Our Army took a Fort from the Rebels & we are presssing hard on to Richmond - Retired at Tattoo.

Sunday - June 22nd 1862 - I got up at daybreak, cooked some breakfast & then went in the Hospital to look after the sick. Found everything in good shape. Staid with them until midnight, was then relieved from duty. The usual going on except occasional firing from the pickets.

Monday - June 23rd 1862 - Nothing going on in Camp but the usual routine of duty. Firing from the pickets is kept up. What it amounts too, I have not learned. For some reason or other, I feel downhearted. I have no doubt, but we shall have a hard battle. Everything seems to indicate as much.

Tuesday - June 24th 1862 - The same duties as yesterday & I feel the same in spirits. Reports are flying from mouth to mouth, of victories & defeats from the Army of the West, & no one can tell what to believe. I hope if a Battle we are to have, that it will come soon. Went to bed at midnight as I had to watch with the sick.

Wednesday - June 25th 1862 - (The Seven Day Campaign - a skirmish near Fair Oaks.) - At eight A.M. firing commenced in our front & it was kept up until one P.M. We hear Gen Hooker & Heintzleman have given Battle to the enemy & drove them some distance. Orders came fer our Brigade to relieve the Brigade in front. While going up we passed several Regts that had been in the fight. The first Mass. lost nearly 75 in killed & wounded. As we went by they gave three rousing cheers & told us to give them fits. We got in position & found that the enemy had been driven over a mile, our Regt. well in front. 7th Mass. in the rear of us & the other Regt in the rear of them. A Gun came alright, & the 2nd R. Island, Regt like a pack of fools commenced to cheer. They had hardly got done before the shells came flying in where we were. Killing & wounding a number in our Brigade, one of our Hospital Corps was hit in the head slightly with a bullet. The Hospital boys were all ordered out of the woods, where our Regt were by Gen. Couch & Hooker. At eight Oclk in the evening our Regt. commenced digging Rifle Pitts as fast as they dug it filled with water. I went to the rear with another fellow, & took a stretcher along. We lay down fer the night on a lot of sticks with nothing over us. About midnight, a terrible fire of musketry was commenced & soon the 7th Mass. came running back scart to death. Brave fellows. I staid to hear them talk a spell & then laid down again, but it was so cold I could not sleep. I then went to the building back of where I then was to find our surgeon. I found him there fast asleep, with my blankets over him. I awoke him taking my blankets & started for the stretcher.

Thursday - June 26th 1862 - (The Seven Day Campaign) - I awoke at sunrise, heard our Brigade were relieved after leaving our pickets. Soon they came back & went in some Rifle Pitts or Breastworks. I followed them with my knapsack of medicines & began to deal out the stuff to the sick ones. I found Buel well. After waiting a spell, our Brigade marched back to their old camp. Very heavy firing was agoing on, to our right & report said that McClellan had gained a crossing over the Chickahominy. The firing didnot cease until after nine Oclock P.M. I believe that I am 23 years old today, yet my duties have prevented me giving much thought about it.

Friday - June 27th 1862 - (The Seven Day Campaign) - Firing commenced at daylight, in the same direction as yesterday. Report says Stonewall Jackson is in our rear. Our Brigade are ordered to move. Load in wagons everything we can & pile the rest up & set Fire to it. I staid behind with the sick & at Dark went with them to the Hospital at Antioch Church. The Brigade have gone up to the right to help Porter. I went to bed at 11 P.M. in an ambulance.

Saturday - June 28th 1862 - (The Seven Day Campaign) - Was aroused at two Oclk A.M. by our Surgeon with the report that our army were falling back & that all the sick were to be sent to the White House. We got them all away in ambulances to Dispatch Station at four Oclk. We left six poor fellows to die alone, in the church, two of them died in the night. Heard our Brigade had passed by on the Charles City Road. Started after with my knapsack. I had my haversack filled with <u>Boston</u> <u>crackers</u> & <u>lemons</u>. Found the Regt. after travelling as fast as I could for three hours by the side of the road fast asleep. Buel was well, he told me all the particulars of the night march. We went about a mile farther, firmed a line of Battle, sent out skirmishes & at night posted pickets. I went to sleep in a jiffy tired as I could be.

Sunday - June 29th 1862 - (The Seven Day Campaign) - I got up at daylight, nothing happened until about 10 A.M. Then a party of Cavalry came charging down the road & such a skiedaddling I never see, whole Regt. in the rear goin like sixty, as they heard the report of the musket. I had no fears, though, as I knew the old 10th were in the advance & wouldn't run without a hard tussle. After some time the Regts. were brought back by their Officers, but not until the muss was over. We killed & wounded some 29 of the rebels not losing a man on our side. I went out with the Surgeon to dress their wounds, our videttes were a mile in our front. At dark we were ordered to move. We marched all night through a swamp called the 9 mile Swamp. The march was one I never shall forget. We went at a snails pace & most of us would sleep while walking, not a loud noise was made & no one would have known we were there; if they had been within 10 rods of us -

Monday - June 30th 1862 - (The Seven Day Campaign) - At daylight we got out of the swamp & found ourselves in a large wheat field near the James River. Wagons by the hundreds were there, & so were soldiers by the thousand. We halted in the middle of the field & then stacked arms & went to sleep. The sun was burning hot & we were almost roasted, yet it made no difference. A lot of the boys went down to the river to bathe, Buel went with them. He seems to be in excellent spirits. The place we are in is called Berkleys. About three O clock P. M. firing commenced but a short distance from us. Our Division were ordered to go & soon they started. I didn't go with them as the surgeons, were unwilling. Soon however we all started after them, found them at Malvern Hill just at dusk in the line of Battle. The Hospital corps took up their quarters in the side on a high hill, near a large house & went to sleep on a pile of chips.

"In the battle of Malvern Hill, Tuesday, July 1st, the Tenth regiment suffered severely, and among the killed was Major Miller, then in command of the regiment. The regiment fired over 100 rounds of ammunition per man, and lost in killed and wounded 82."

Tuesday - July 1 1862 - (The Seven Day Campaign, Battle of Malvern Hill, Mass. 10th loss of 88 men.) - At 8 Oclk A.M. Gen McClellen came riding by with his staff. Gen. Couch took him along our lines as we were in front. Nothing but skirmishing was going on until about three P. M. I went up to the Regt. in the afternoon with a stretcher & staid there until I was ordered away by Gen's. <u>Couch</u> & <u>Palmer</u>. While there I saw two Brigades of the Rebels killed by our shell & shot. Such firing I never heard. Our Regt. had not got into business, but soon after I left they had their hands full. The fight lasted until after dark & when our Regt. had fired their ammunition all away they charged bayinets & stood their ground. After being relieved Gen. Palmer came riding along & raised himself in saddle with hat off, exclaiming: These are the Sharp Shooters, & other words, thereby showing, he had altered his mind in regard to us. I was at the Hospital in large brickhouse. Maj Miller & Lieut Wheeler were brought in wounded, from <u>Lieut</u> W- I was told that the boys fought like tigers. At 10 1/2 oclk P.M. I was told that my Brother had been wounded & taken from the field to a farm near the Battleground. I told the Dr. I wanted to go & find him, but he discouraged me saying it was so dark I could not find him. I however went out trying to get someone to show me the house or barn, but could not. The Surgeon said I could have his horse in the morning & go after him as it was some two mile to the place. I went to bed 11 1/2 but could not sleep.

Wednesday - July 2nd 1862 - I laid awake nearly all the night. At 3 1/2 A. M. I got up & found that the Regt. had gone, & so had the whole army. Some of the nurses of the 10th were left behind to take care of the wounded. I was told all the wounded had been brought in from the field, & part of them taken to Harrison Landing. What to do, I didn't know. I must soon make up my mind as the enemy were advancing to take possession of what remained. I started after a good deal of <u>reluctance</u> fer the Regt. It was raining as hard as it could pour & I went up to my knees in mud at every step. I was wet through to the skin & as cold as I could be. Our Hospital Steward

& John Warner were with me. I met a fellow on the road from the 10th & he told me that Buel had been wounded, but not very badly. I found the Regt. at Harrisons Landing & even the whole Army of the Potomac - such an immense lot of men I never saw before. Cannon & everything else in abundance all on one level piece of ground. Everybody was covered with mud from head to foot & wet as they could be. I could get no news from Buel, although I saw the boys who brought him from the field. I am just discouraged. Oh, that I could find him. I went to the Hospital Wagon, got out my knapsack, changed my clothes, put up my tent, as the Regt. had encamped. I laid myself down to think & so the day passed.

Thursday - July 3rd 1862 - Awoke at daylight feeling much refreshed about 8 oclk A. M. we were aroused by the noise of cannon, & we were greeted with a lot of solid shot, striking in the ground in our midst. None were hurt however, but how it happened is more than I know, as our whole army, were encamped close together. Gen. McCall started out to see what was to pay. He soon brought in a lot of prisoners & 6 piece of cannons that he had taken from the enemy. We recd orders to march at 3 P.M. went about 2 mile, sent out skirmishes established a picket line & turned in. Oh, where is Buel! If he is a prisoner & wounded I know he will be taken care of, as our nurses look to him. I got a bundle of straw & laid down for the night.

Friday - July 4th 1862 - I was awakened at 2 1/2 oclk by the Pickets firing. My blanket were done up in a twinkling & I was ready fer a muss, but as we heard nothing more, I again laid down & slept until broad daylight. Our skirmishes have advanced over a mile & we are to remain here for the pursuit. The sun shines very warm & we have no trees to crawl under. We are in a wheat field, after wasting all day, until five P.M., we were ordered to pack up & march in the woods some half a mile. We soon got there & I pitched my tent with Wm. Lane, cooked some supper & at 9 P.M. went to bed.

Saturday - July 5th 1862 - The Regt. have been hard at work building a Redoubt or Breastwork. Michael Timothy had 2 Ribs broken by a tree falling on him down to the Hospital at the landing. The Redoubt we are building, is 800 ft. long & 4 ft. high. Nothing of importance going on.

Sunday - July 6th 1862 - The day has been a splendid one & we rec'd orders to march at 8 A.M., but did not get started until after dinner, then only went 1/2 a mile & encamped in a swamp Hole, where the Ivy (poison) was as thick as hops, cleaned off a spot of ground & then pitched my tent. Went some two mile after water, didn't get back for three hours, as I lost my way & could not find the Regt. Went to bed after supper.

Monday - July 7th 1862 - We pitched a tent for the sick this morning & in trying to suit to many of the Bosses, I learned I didn't suit any of them & finally concluded I would pitch it, to suit myself. After it was done I found I had hit the nail on the head. I hardly know what we shall do fer water to drink. Co. C. have dug down 25 feet & yet there is no sign of water.

Tuesday - July 8th 1862 - Went after water this morning to a spring some 2 mile off. The sun pours down its melting rays & it is as much as I can do to stand it. I am afraid I shall be nothing but a grease spot unless I can keep out of the sun. Our camp has an awful stench & the flies are as thicker than toads in a hot skillet. President Lincoln visited our army at 4 P.M. It is the first time I have seen him.

Wednesday - July 9th 1862 - I had to go into the Hospital today to take care of the sick ones. I have two sick with the Bilous Cholic, caused by drinking so much of this nasty water. I got a New York Herald & read over the names of the Prisoners in hopes of seeing my Brothers name, but was disappointed. My patients are better at 7 P.M.

Thursday - July 10th 1862 - I was on the same duty as yesterday, but as my patients are better the duty is light. We had a very hard shower in the afternoon & the streets between the different Companies are a perfect mud puddle. No news of any importance from the rest of the Army. We heard that the Rebels had sunk one of our Boats from a point opposite Harrisons Landing, also that a Lieut. & 20 men of the Rebellion came into Camp. Doubt the story.

Friday - July 11th 1862 - It has rained most of the day & it is nothing but mud out of doors, so I stay in my tent, answering letters I rec'd from home yesterday. Rec'd a letter from Lucy, also one came directed to my Brother. I hardly know what to do, but write to his friend. I must, & tell her just what I think. Oh I hope he is alive & well. Retired at 8 1/2 P.M.

Saturday - July 12 1862 - Dr. Jewett has come back to the Regt. He was released from durance vile by the Rebels at Richmond. I read over the list of names he had with him of all the persons that were wounded & that came under his care, but couldn't find my Brother. He told me he thought he was at Richmond but couldn't say for certain. The more I think of it, the more I think he was killed, or mortally wounded. Poor fellow, why couldn't I have seen him.

Sunday - July 13th 1862 - It has been a most splendid day and seemed a good deal like the Sundays at home, everything is quiet. I see three men from Pittsfield, Mass. who came on to find friends in the army. Rec'd a letter from H. P. Goodrich. Wrote to Lucy & one to Calista. The sick are getting along nicely.

Monday - July 14th 1862 - Duties in Camp same as usual - nothing new. The sun shines very warm & we are almost roasted. Do as little as possible, some of the boys have rec'd their discharge from the service on account of disability. Went to bed pretty early.

Tuesday - July 15th 1862 - Our Brigade was Inspected by Gen. Keyes this A. M. Our Regt. were complimented for their neat appearance & C. Had a shower in the afternoon with very sharp lightening & terrific thunder, crawled in my bunk & say I, Let her Rip. After the shower it was very cool. Retired at 9 P. M.

Wednesday - July 16th 1862 - We had another fine shower of Rain about 10 A.M. & got caught out in it while going after water to the Spring some two mile distant. I got as wet as ever I was in my life, but it felt good & after getting back to camp I changed my clothes & after it got through raining, I hung my others out to dry. We had a box of lemons come to the hospital & I made out to get a couple - went to roost at 9 P.M.

Thursday - July 17th 1862 - Nothing worth mentioning happened today in camp, I remained in my bunk writing letters & reading the papers. Our Surgeon (Dr. C. N. Chamberlain) started for home on a leave of absence of 30 days. Have in the Hospital three sick ones, one of them is dangerously ill, & requires a great deal of attention.

Friday - July 18th 1862 - Duties in camp the same as usual. We were visited with a Rain storm in the afternoon & the ground is very muddy. Two soldiers from Co. D. (Pittsfield) came back to the Regt. after an absence of several months. Their absence was caused by sickness. They brought messages to a good many boys from friends in Pittsfield & vicinity. Had some potatoes today for the first time since leaving Brightwood.

Saturday - July 19th 1862 - It has been a very disagreeable day out of doors, damp, with a heavy mist & some rain. Rec'd a letter from my friend in Adams & answered without delay. I often wish that I could see the faces of my friends again, but dare not hope. Retired at 9 1/2 P. M.

Sunday - July 20th 1862 - Another glorious Sunday. How still & pleasant it has been today. I have been thinking of home nearly all day & the many priviledges I once enjoyed. Report came in camp at 4 P.M. that we were to move tomorrow. Well I really hope to, for if ever I was tormented it is in this place. The air is perfectly black with flies & they bite like all possessed. No comfort night or day.

Monday - July 21st 1862 - I went in the Hospital this morning to look after the sick. Ed Stanley of Co. C. is very sick & I have been by his Bedside all day long, bathing his head & trying to keep the flies from bothering him. I should think all the Flies in Christendom had made these woods their place of resert. Wm. Lane done my washing fer me.

Tuesday - July 22nd 1862 - After watching by the bedside of my patient all night I was relieved from my position by A. S. Kellogg. I went to bed at 10 A.M. & slept until three P. M. Then took a stroll around the different camp of the Corps. Our front line all around the Army have thrown up Earth works & we consider ourselves impregnable to Jeffs whole Army.

Wednesday - July 23rd 1862 - I started this morning, after eating Breakfast of Potatoes & boiled onions, to a large Pond near by to have a good swim. I found on my arrival about 3000 soldiers enjoying themselves hugely. Had a nice time & then went back to camp, where I arrived just in time to see one of our boys before going home. E. S. Joy.

Thursday - July 24th 1862 - After eating breakfast I took one of the Doctor's horses & rode out in the country some three mile looking after straw for beds, but could not find any. Had a splendid ride. The day has been very warm & we have all suffered very much. Flies are hungry as can be. Nothing else to do through the day. Red'd a letter from Father & one from Lucy.

Friday - July 25th 1862 - After Revielle I done a few chores around the Hospital & at Surgeons Call I acted the part of Steward, dealt out the Medicines to the sick as fast as prescribed fer by the Dr. I then took another jaunt over to the Pond, to have a good dinner. Duties in camp the same as usual. One year ago today the 10th Regt. left Medford, Mass. for Washington.

Saturday - July 26th 1862 - I wrote a letter to Father & one to Goodey. It has been very warm, no one does any more work than is necessary. Capt. Clapp of Co. D. has returned to camp having been away on a sick leave since our fight at Fair Oaks. A heavy thunder storm this evening; but as I was in the Hospital loooking & watching with the sick. It did not disturb me much. Ed Stanley is much worse fear he will not live.

Sunday - July 27th 1862 - Stanley died this morning at 1 1/2 oClk. His last words were tell my Wife & little one I died thinking of Them. His end was peaceful. It was very fatiguing to take care of him, as our supplies & conveniences are so limited. He was buried this afternoon under a large Oak. Nothing stirring in Camp.

Monday - July 28th 1862 - Orders came this morning to have the Regt. go to drilling. The same as in Camp Brightwood. While on drill several of the boys fainted as it was so warm. It created some excitement. Biny Blaise, orderly Sergeant of Co. B. was admitted in the Hospital today. He is very sick was taken Sunday morning. I shall have to go in the Hospital in the morning, so I shall go to bed pretty early.

Tuesday - July 29th 1862 - After eating Breakfast I went in

the Hospital, found the Orderly no better, but rather worse. Oh, what a time I had all day. The flies were thicker than anything I every saw. I gave him a piece of Ice as large as a Walnut every 15 minutes & the rest of the time my hands were full in keeping off the flies.

Wednesday - July 30th 1862 - Biny Blaise Died this morning at one oclock A.M. I called his offficers Traver & Wells to see him die. Such a picture of despair, I never beheld before. He died hard, was sent Home to his friends. I paid one dollar for that purpose. Went to bed in the morning at sunrise & slept until the flies woke me up - & that wasn't long.

Thursday - July 31st 1862 - Rec'd orders to pack up & be ready to march at a moments notice. Everything was hurly burly for spell, but the order was contramanded at noon. Wellington Kingsley shot his fingers off, to get rid of going. There never was a greater Coward lived than this same Kingsley.

Friday - August 1st 1862 - There was a terrible cannonading commenced this morning at the landing & everybody was up & dressed in short-time. Hear that the Paymaster has arrived. Hope it is true. Nothing of importance has happened today besides this. Went to bed pretty early.

Saturday - August 2nd 1862 - Our Paymaster (Maj. Ladd) came in Camp & commenced to pay off our Regt. I rec'd $41.25 pay due to July 1st. I tried to get my Brothers pay, but could not. Everything & everybody was looking bright & cheerful, as they always do on Pay day. All duties were laid aside fer the time being.

Sunday - August 3rd 1862 - It has been very still & quiet in our Camp today. I suppose the boys are busy playing Bluff. The 36th New York Reg. are being paid off & they are noisy enough, some of them have had a knock down. Corporal John Moon has rec'd his discharge papers & starts fer home tomorrow. I shall send my money by him. Have been in the Hospital all day, with two sick fellows from Co. F.

Monday - August 4th 1862 - Corporal Moon started fer No Adams today, sent 35 dollars by him to Father. I have done but little of anything, as it is so warm, & the flies are so troublesome that it

38

don't pay to stir much. It beats everything I ever heard or have ever seen. Horses & mules are fairly eaten up by these pesky flies. Heavy firing was heard at Malvern Hill.

Tuesday - August 5th 1862 - All quiet in Camp this morning, until 2 P.M. when we recd orders to pack up & be ready to march at 6 P.M. Hookers Division went up to Malvern Hill Sunday evening & now we are agoing to support him. We marched at 7 Oclk from our camp & at 11 1/2 P. M. we got to Berkley landing 5 mile from our camp, but the way we come It was 18 mile, as we followed the River all the way up. I laid down to rest in the same ground where I last saw my Brother - tired enough.

Wednesday - August 6th 1862 - We were awakened early in the morning by the Orderlies of the Companies telling us to make no noise, we cooked our Breakfast of Pork & crackers & then marched around the field. While going around the field I saw a soldier of the 36th N. York that had been bitten by a copper Head snake. Gave him a pint of Brandy & then started on our march.

Thursday - August 7th 1862 - We started at one oclk A.M. from the field for Malvern, marched about two mile & then were ordered to go back to camp. Arrived in Camp at daylight. Heard that the Rebels were coming down in strong force to fight us. I went to bed in the forenoon & slept most all day, found we had a sick man in the Hospital by the name of Toomey from Co. K.

Friday - August 8th 1862 - Nothing going on in Camp, everybody is talking of our late March & wondering what the reason was, that we were not allowed to hold our position. Stories of all kinds are going the rounds & a fellow must be pretty well up to snuff or he will get fooled. Toomey from Co. K died at 6 P.M. Complaint - Conjestion of the Bowels.

Saturday - August 9th 1862 - The boys of Co. K. sent the body of Toomey home. It will cost 90 dollars to have him embalmed & other expenses. It is very warm & a fellow will almost roast trying to get in the shade. Thermometer is near boiling heat. I think I never see such a country. The nights are very cool & the days are as hot as can be & not kill a man - went to bed in good season.

Sunday - August 10th 1862 - Had a fine shower this afternoon which made it very pleasant for us boys. Mr. Millet of Co. D. Lieut. Brewster of Co. C, Haskins of Co. B & several others in the Regt started North today to get recruits for our Regt. Recd orders to March tomorrow at 2 Oclock A.M.

Monday - August 11th 1862 - Everything is hurly burly. I got up at 1 oclk A.M. & prepared myself fer marching but finding that we did not start, I went to sleep again & rested until morning. All the sick were sent to Hospitals at the North - no signs of marching tonight & so I shall turn in.

Tuesday - August 12th 1862 - Was up bright & early. All the knapsacks belonging to the men in the army have been taken to the landing & loaded on Barges, so that we can move quickly when we do start. We are all ready to go at a moments notice. I have kept my knapsack, as the Hospital Corps have got a mule & Gocart to take our truck.

Wednesday - August 13th 1862 - The day has passed & such a day. Nothing to do. Everything gone & all turned topsy turvey. The boys have been making Images or Scarecrows of their cast off garments, sticking them up on our line of Breastworks with inscriptions over their heads. I guess when secesh visits the place after we leave, they will laugh in their shoes at our ingenuity, or else be awful mad. Who cares!

Thursday - August 14th 1862 - Another day has past like the preceding one. Fun has been the order of the day & fun we have had. I sometime wonder how men can be so foolish, yet when I think of our situation, everything is explained. No signs of moving.

Friday - August 15th 1862 - Orders came to be ready to march at 12 M. The Baggage wagons started at that time but our Regt did not go. Mr. Lane went with Hospital Wagon. He has been my bunk mate for 10 weeks. Expect to go in the morning - but where no one knows.

Saturday - August 16th 1862 - We started this morning at 3 A.M. Marched 1/2 a mile & halted until noon, such werks I never see. At 12 we again took up our line of march & we went as if the old devil himself was after us. I thought I would have to fall out, but like a good fellow, I stuck & hung. Halted at night on a large plain near Charles City. Cooked some green corn for supper.

Sunday - August 17th 1862 - At daylight we were on our way, stopped at 7 A.M. near a large corn field. Eat all the corn I could stuff down. Reported we are on the wrong road. Went back a mile & then we are ordered to turn around & go back on the same road we were on. Marched all day. Dust 6 inches deep - very warm. My feet were so sore I could hardly walk. Arrived at Chickahominy river at dusk, crossed over, eat supper. Then went in swimming in the River. Never was so tired in my life. Marched 24 mile today.

Monday - August 18th 1862 - I was up at 4 A.M. cooked my ration of Pork & coffee. Then we started again. Halted after marching a mile about 2 hours. Gen. McClellan & Staff have just gone by - 10 A.M. Pontoons all taken up & here we go again. Passed through Williamsburg at 3 P.M. Things looked about the same, as they did four months ago. Rations delivered to us. Camped for the night three miles from Williamsburg.

Tuesday - August 19th 1862 - Moved our camp only about a mile. Then I started out on a foraging expedition. Got two chickens, peck of potatoes & a lot of apples & pears. Had a tip top supper. Sesesh must pay for this war. Thems my sentiments.

Wednesday - August 20th 1862 - This morning we again started on our march. Arrived at Yorktown at noon. Rations almost out. The River was filled with soldiers in swimming, Steamers & sloops were busy at Wharves, loading. At 2 P. M. we went through Yorktown & marched some three miles, halting in a Peach orchard near the River. It used to be the old camp of the 16th Mass.

Thursday - August 21st 1862 - After eating breakfast went down in swimming, while in the water a monstrous great Crab caught me by the toe & I'll bet I came out of that water just as quick as I knew how, bringing the animal with me. I had some work to get the critter off. My toe bled pretty freely. In the afternoon I started with Mr. Mason, fish hook & line to catch a supper of Crabs. Succeeded beyond my expectation & I had a good meal.

Friday - August 22nd 1862 - Went this A. M. fishing after Clams, succeeded in getting about a bushel. Lived on Clams all day. I enjoyed myself nicely. Believe I should like to live in such a place, if I were rich. Commenced raining at noon, were ordered to pack up. We marched 1 1/2 miles farther down the river, our teams here came to us, having been down to Fortress Monroe. Mr. Lane is not well.

Saturday - August 23rd 1862 - Pitched our tents in regular camp Style. We are in a nice place. Rec'd letters from Lucy & Father - Feel well & happy. Hear that we are going to stay here for some time. Made me a bunk of Pine poles.

Sunday - August 24th 1862 - It has been very raw & cold today, we put up our Hospital Tent & took in three sick ones. Done the nursing for them. Shall be up all night. Wish I could get a Herald or a Tribune & see what is to pay in other parts of these great United States.

Monday - August 25th 1862 - Things are the same as yesterday, no news, & no nothing. I was in my Bunk nearly all day, asleep. Rations are all ate up & so I must go hungry until tomorrow noon. Well, what can't be cured, must be endured & so I suppose I will have to grin & bear it. Thinking all the time that it is fer my bleeding country that I suffer. Well, who wouldn't.

Tuesday, Wednesday, Thursday - August 26th, 27th, 28th 1862 - Nothings happened Tuesday or Wednesday worthy of note everything remained quiet as usual. Thursday we rec'd orders to pack up everything but our tents, ready for another tramp. Hear Gen. Keyes is to stay here at Yorktown. No signs of moving tonight. Hear we are to start at 7 A.M.

"The regiment then retreated to Harrison's Landing and August 29th commenced the march down the Peninsular, landed at Alexandria, participated in the second battle of Bull Run, and thence marched to Antietam, in which battle the regiment as engaged."

Friday - August 29th 1862 - Started for Yorktown at 9 A.M. After numerous delays, we arrived at the Wharf about 4 P.M. We carried on board the transport, Key West, a large propellar & glided down stream a short distance. Took on board a large shell (two pounder) fer Dr. Jewett. Mr. Lane & Cromwell of our Hospital stay with the teams.

Saturday - August 30th 1862 - Our Brigade were all on Board this forenoon in several transport. We left Yorktown at 3 P.M. I worked very hard in getting our hospital supplies in the hold of the ship. We lost a keg of Whiskey (all we had in the world) while at work. Some of the deck hands stole it. We had a splendid sail down, the York River.

Sunday - August 31st 1862 - Our sail up the River was a fine one. We passed Aquia Creek at 5 P. M. were hailed by a war vessel & told our destination, which was Alexandria. Arrived at Alexandria in the evening staid on board all night. Heard that we were a little to late as Gen. Pope had been badly whipped. I can't say how I feel, McClellan is removed from the Army & all on account of Traitors at Home.

Monday - September 1st 1862 - At daylight we steamed up to the wharf & disembarked. We got everything unloaded at 12 M. Rations for two days were delivered to us & then orders came for us to march to Fairfax Co. House. While going through Alexandria we met our new Colonel (Henry L. Eustis) passed the 33rd & 34th Mass. Unslung knapsacks 2 mile from the city & then started again. I had the old medicine chest, so my load was no lighter, as that had to go anyway. It commenced raining soon after we started, & wet us through & through. The troops of Popes Army were coming back in great disorder. Marched until 9 P.M. within one mile of our destination & halted fer the night. I lay down by the side of the road with the rest of the Regt. & soon lost myself in sleep. I had no blankets. Mud was my bed & mud was my pillow & finally I was nothing but mud.

Tuesday - September 2nd 1862 - I was up pretty early as I could not sleep being so cold. I went into a potatoe patch & got some potatoes & corn & then had a Breakfast. Orders came to get back to Alexandria. We started at 8: A.M. & at noon we had our knapsacks - Heard we were going to the landing & so Warner & myself started, we could not get through the City & so went back. Our Regt. was gone & we were in a pickle. Went outside the city to the landing -

found the 31st New York & concluded to keep with them as they would go where the old were. Started at 3 P.M. Marched up the old road on the way to Washington. Got opposite the city at 8 P.M. Our destination is Fort <u>Ethan</u> <u>Allen</u> near Chain Bridge. I got tired out before getting there & lay down to sleep, just one mile from the desired haven, with one blanket to cover me.

Wednesday - September 3rd 1862 - At daylight we got up & started fer the Regt, passed Fort Ethan Allen & then found our Regt. They had got on the wrong road & had not got in camp until after we did. The new Regts. from New York & Mass. flocked around us, looking at us like we were <u>Bears</u>. I don't doubt but we were a sight as we were ragged, shoeless & all covered with dirt. The gave us soft bread & we gave them thanks & told them of our hardships. They were eager listeners. The reporter from the Herald came to visit us while here.

Thursday - September 4th 1862 - Today was passed in visiting the new Regts, cleaning ourselves up & in getting Rations fer another start. Hear McClellan has been reinstated & has command of all the troops in & around Washington. Hurrah for Little Mac - Wrote a letter to Lucy & one to Father.

Friday - September 5th 1862 - Received orders to march at 1 P.M. After getting all ready I recd a visit from Mr Millimun, had a long talk over old difficulties & had everything settled. While crossing Chain Bridge I met W. H. Coop not having seen him before fer 6 weeks. We took the old road to Brightwood & I was in hopes we should go there, but after passing through Tennally Town we struck off on the road towards Harpers Ferry. Halted about 10 mile from Tennally town at a place called Potomac Cross Roads fer the night - our boys are pretty tired.

Saturday - September 6th 1862 - Our Brigade staid here all day - The 10th Mass went on picket. I found a Rubber blanket & I shall contrive to carry it as I have no blankets with me. Feasted on potatoes & green corn. My bunk is under a large Oak. Recd a letter from <u>my</u> Lucy.

Sunday - September 7th 1862 - I got me a pair of shoes this morning, so I am already fer another tramp. My feet are pretty sore.

Orders came to march at 12 A.M. We started in good spirits. Gen Couch leading us. After marching 8 mile, we halted at Seneca Creek for the night with orders to sleep at the stacks, in case of surprise. I slept in a barn on some hay.

Monday - September 8th 1862 - The 7th Mass. were detailed to stay behind & guard the ford at the creek. The rest of the Brigade started for Poolesville, at which place we arrived at 3 P.M. The Rebel Cavalry were driven from here this morning, saw a number of their wounded & several prisoners. We lost one man killed on our side. Encamped on a large field 1 1/2 mile from the town. This is the place where our Gen. Devens had his camp while Colonel of the 15th Mass.

Tuesday - September 9th 1862 - It commenced to rain this morning & it has been very unpleasant all day, our supply fer rations came to us this A.M. I had to go down to the Ambulances to get my old Bureau or Medicine Chest filled with a fresh supply. I was not in the best of humor while going down & my old knapsack went over a couple of fences a little quicker than I did, breaking several bottles & C, then I cooled down, staid in the same camp of the night before.

Wednesday - September 10th 1862 - We left Poolsville this morning & went to Barnesville some 10 mile from the first named place. The 36th New York were detailed to guard the Ford at Poolesville. Marched 2 mile from Barnesville, our Regt were on picket. The Rebels were driven from here today. We are near Sugar Loaf Mountain. We have a signal Station at its summit. Col Parsons was taken sick & A. S. Kellogg of the Hosital Department is to take care of him.

Thursday - September 11th 1862 - The Inhabitants of this place have been striped of everything they had by the Rebels that passed through yesterday. We left this place at 9 A.M. crossed the Ford of the Monocacy Creek. This was the greatest sight I ever beheld, over 1000 men wading a creek with pants up to the knees. We halted in a large Pine woods, posted Batteries on a high hill & fixed everything secure.

Friday - September 12th 1862 - Staid in this place all day. Recd our three days rations & rested ourselves. I found a large black snake under my blanket when I went to bed, routed him in fine style.

Saturday - September 13th 1862 - Nothing was done today. Heard our baggage train was on the road to us. Went foraging - Got some potatoes & cabbage. Had a good supper & then retired.

Sunday - September 14th 1862 - Up at 5 1/2 A. M. Started on our march, passed through Adamstown on the B & O R. Road. Eat our dinner near Point of Rocks. Heard firing in the vicinity of Harpers Ferry. Marched until 9 P.M. & halted in a corn field, fer the night, very heavy firing has been heard all day. We just got laid down when orders came to march, passed through Jefferson & halted at 2 A.M. (on the 15th) near South Mountain, a Big fight took place here today.

Monday - September 15th 1862 - Up at 5 A.M., passsed through Birkettsville, over South Mountain & into Valley behind. Saw heaps of dead Rebels, encamped for the day near a woods. Recd rations fer 2 days. Hear Harpers Ferry is in possession of Rebels & that Col. Miles is killed. I must say I am glad of it - or glad Miles is killed, wish every traitor had the same fate.

Tuesday - September 16th 1862 - Heavy firing all day long. We staid here all day, but expecting orders to march. Went in swimming & then done some washing. Recd orders to march in the morning. Went to sleep in a large heap of stones & rocks - after having some words with Dr. Jewett our apt surgeon.

Wednesday - September 17th 1862 - (Battle of Antiedam) - After eating breakfast we started our march to Harpers Ferry. Passed through (illegible) the people came out & gave us water, apples & wished us God speed. I got some potatoes of one of the old women of the place, on the march we saw a great many places where the Rebels had been. The remains of cattle were strewn all over, all the way to the Ferry. Halted within one & a half miles of Harpers Ferry, formed in line of Battle, as soon as we could. We had no sooner done so, than Gen. Couch recd orders to report to McClellans H. Quarters with his Division as soon as possible. We eat our dinners & then started on the back track, the 10th taking the lead. We marched 2 hours as fast as we could go leaving the Batteries & other Regts far behind, when Couch sent word to our Col to halt & not kill his

46

men. Passed our old camp at dark, but had 8 miles more to g(
before reaching H. Quarters. Saw our Baggage train. Got to destina
tion at 11 1/2 P.M. Cooked supper having been without food 12 hour:
& went to sleep.

Thursday - September 18th 1862 - (Battle of Antiedam) - U₁
at 4 A.M., eat Breakfast & then went to the Battlefield. Our skirmish
es were out, but no very serious fighting. We then started for the
Right of our lines. While going through Keedeesville Gen. McClellan
passed by & if the boys of our Division didn't cheer him then I don't
know. Tears run down his cheeks & every man loved him as none
but soldiers can love their General. We then went to our position on
the right. Unloading knapsacks & left them one mile from our position. Gen. Devens horse had a Ball put through his ear, our Hospital
was stationed in a large barn 1/4 mile in the rear, in a large valley out
of reach of shells. Some 80 recruits fer our Regt came to us while
here. No fighting was done & towards night it was hinted that the
Rebels were leaving. Had some Mutton, Pork & Potatoes fer supper.

Friday - September 19th 1862 - At 9 A.M. our army were on
the March following up Secesh while passing over the Battle Field. I
saw a great many of the Rebel killed, one place in particular, behind
a stone wall, there were over two hundred. It was the saddest sight I
every beheld or ever wish to. The stench was almost unendurable.
Passed through the village of Sharpsburgh at 10 1/2 A.M., most of
the buildings were hit by our shells. Horses lay dead in the streets &
everything looked dreary & disolate. Encamped 2 mile from the River
in a beautiful Pinegrove. In the afternoon all of our Cavalry passed
by us to the rear, having chased the Rebels across the River & taken
a great number of prisoners. Our baggage wagons came to us at 9
A.M. I got my knapsack & changed my shirt, having worn it three
weeks. Dr Chamberlain here returned to us having been at
Washington sick, fer 6 weeks. Mr Lane my bunk mate is not well.

Saturday - September 20th 1862 - (Reconnaissance to
Williamsport) - We were called up at Midnight to go on another
expedition. Cooked some coffee & then we started. Hear we are
going to Williamsport, as some Rebels have recrossed the River. We
passed through <u>Sharpsburg</u> & over the old Battlefield again. Halted
after marching five mile until daylight. Most of the soldiers lay in the
road asleep, some of the officers horses broke away & came dash-

ing down the road & as they passed each Regt their numbers became greater, two of our boys were hurt, one quite seriously, fracturing his skull. We left one of our number to take care of him until the ambulances came up. Arrived at Williamsport, fermed in line & advanced, no firing except by the enemy's cannon. They soon dispersed & left us masters of the field. We stayed here for the night - posted pickets & C.

Sunday - September 21st 1862 - Had a good nights (rest) although it was pretty cold. We were relieved from Picket duty at 9 A.M. by Howes Brigade, while forming in a line to go to the rear, a musket in the hands of one of the 7th Mass boys went off, killing his comrade, who was in the rear, instantly. We went in the woods a short distance & all lay down to rest. We are near St. James College & pleasant place it is. Wrote letters to my friends in Adams.

Monday - September 22nd 1862 - Nothing happened this forenoon to excite us. Reports are flying in every direction about the Battle, but there is no use in talking. Our Baggage wagons again made their appearance this P.M. Mr. Lane is quite sick with Fever & Ague. I gave him a dose of Quinine & Whiskey & then went to bed. Morphine & Quinine. I am well, tough & hearty as can be. Thanks to my heavenly father.

Tuesday - September 23rd 1862 - We remained in Camp until after dinner, then recd orders to pack up & march at 4 P.M. I went in the forenoon down to the ambulances after a supply of medicine. We marched 3 miles & encamped fer the night on a side hill. It commenced raining, but throwing our rubbers over us, we lay & took it all night long.

Wednesday - September 24th 1862 - This forenoon orders came to reduce our baggage. All our Hospital supplies we look over & reduced them one quarter, sending them to Washington D.C. fer storage. Marched in afternoon, about one mile & encamped in a large woods near Downsville, MD Put up our Hospital tent & then pitched our own shelter tents. It has been quite cold & uncomfortable all day

Thursday - September 25th 1862 - Worked all forenoon fixing up the Hospital tent. Hear that we are to stop here sometime. In the afternoon wrote to H. P. Goodrich also to my Cousin Kate Atkinson. Went towards evening to an old Farmers & got a large bundle of straw fer my bed, as I lay very cold last night, almost freezing under two wool blankets.

Friday - September 26th 1862 - Our Regt were supplied with a fresh lot of Rations today. Fresh meat, Port & salt jerky & hard crackers. I got me a Beefs liver & then prepared to have a good supper. We have one sick in the Hospital. The regt. are pretty healthy considering the privations they have been called to pass through the last five weeks.

Saturday - September 27th 1862 - This morning our Regt. were blessed by the arrival of our new Chaplain the Rev. Mr. Bingham of Westfield, Mass. he looks like a good man. Our Sutler came in camp this afternoon with a wagon load of cookies, cheese, tobacco & all the other Yankee notions. The boys are around him as thick as Bees in a Sugar Hogshead.

Sunday - September 28th 1862 - This is the most like Sunday of any day we have had in a long time. In the afternoon we had Preaching, by our new Chaplain, nearly everyone of the Regt were out to hear him. We have not had preaching before since we left Warwick, Va. He is going to hold prayer meetings in his tent 3 nights a week. I went this evening. We had a good meeting.

Monday - September 29th 1862 - Nothing has been talked of this forenoon, but the sermon we had yesterday. I hope good results will follow, Our Sutler again made his appearance this afternoon with a load of eatables. It is next to impossibility to get anywhere near him, the crowd being so great. Mr Lane done some washing fer me this afternoon.

Tuesday - September 30th 1862 - No news of any kind, & nothing to write about. It has been remarkably quiet all day. Wrote a letter to Lucy. Wonder why I don't get a letter from her. It has been 25 days since I heard from her, something that has never happened before. Fear that she is very sick, yet cant believe that she would fail in letting me know. Oh dear, such a day.

Wednesday - October 1st 1862 - I remained in camp all day.

A great deal of exitement was caused in camp by the order from the Colonels Headquarters to arrest all the officers that had sent in Resignations. The cause for their doing so is that our Maj. Dexter F. Parker was appointed to that vacancy by H. S. Briggs. The Maj. don't know enough to form a Company. Hence - the dissatisfaction of the Officers.

Thursday - October 2nd 1862 - Nothing is talked of but the way in which our Capt. & Lieuts are used. Some are glad, others are sorry. I myself think injustice has been done us. One of the members of the Regular Battery died last night or rather froze to death & was buried today. Military honors await him at the grave, as a Salute will be fired.

Friday - October 3rd 1862 - All was quiet in Camp until 11:00 A M, When orders were recd to prepare for a Review as the President would visit us. I mounted the Drs horse & started with the Regt after dinner for the review ground. We went 2 mile & after waiting until 3 1/2 P.M the President made his appearance. Salutes were fired & he passed through the lines. It was a grand sight. The whole of Couchs Division were on hand & the thing passed off pleasantly. The President was accompanied by Gen. Franklin our Corps Commander. We returned to Camp at Sundown. Amen.

Saturday - October 4th 1862 - Our officers are being tried by Court-Martial for Conspiracy today. Farther than that nothing is giving in. It is reported that Gen. Franklin has petitioned to have one Division with the rest of his Corps. It is pretty cold weather.

Sunday - October 5th 1862 - Everything all quiet this forenoon. After eating dinner it was reported that the 37th Mass Vols were coming to join our Brigade & sure enough about 2 P.M. the have in sight. The first person I saw was my Uncle Oliver, S. Vining. I was pleased to see him. His Bro had been left in Washington. He came over at night. I gave him as good a supper as I could get up. There are a great many in the Regt. that I know.

Monday - October 6th 1862 - Spent the day in visiting old friends in the 37th - found several boys from No Adams, among them. It seems almost as good as it would to go home. Expected to hear from home tonight - but was disappointed. Oh dear me

Tuesday - October 7th 1862 - Lieut. Charles Wheeler of Co. D. has been appointed Quartermaster of our Regt. John W. Howland having been promoted to Brigade Q.M. We expect good rations hereafter. Our Surgeon has found a Bee tree as he thinks, & wants us Hospital boys to cut it down. We are agoing at it tomorrow, but I think instead of Bees the Surgeon will find Wasps.

Wednesday - October 8th 1862 - I went in the Hospital this morning to wait upon the sick, but I found them all able to help themselves. So I started in Company with Warner, Mason & Save to cut down the Bee Tree. It was a dry White Oak, three foot through at the Butt, & with a dull axe we made out to get it down after a couple of hours of hard work. Bees, proved to be Wasps & the Surgeons had to stand treat to the Field Offices to hush the matter up.

Thursday - October 9th 1862 - Nothing worthy of note has transpired this forenoon. At 3 P.M. I recd letters from Father & one from Lucy dated the 5th. I was very please to hear from her, as it had been just a month since the last time she wrote. I wrote to Father, & also commenced a letter to Luce. It is very cold.

Friday - October 10th 1862 - After a very uncomfortable nights rest I got up & made some Breakfast. Reports are flying thick & fast that the Rebel Stuart & his Cavalry had crossed the River above us & were on a Raid through Maryland into Pennsylvania. Orders came to pack & be ready to march at a moments notice. It commenced raining at 12 M. & rained all the afternoon like shot. The orders were countermanded at dark.

Saturday - October 11th 1862 - We have settled back in our old style of Camp duty. Although reports are flying every way about the Cavalry Raid. I hear that Gen. Pleasanton has been sent out in pursuit of them with Cavalry & Flying Artillery. Hope he will catch them, but fear it will not be his good fortune.

Sunday - October 12th 1862 - Very cold, wet dreary & if we dont get clothes before many days we shall freeze certain, nearly 1/4 of the Regt are without pants & shoes & scarcely underclothing is to be seen. Surely we are in a most wretched condition. We had preaching this afternoon by our Chaplain. It was a very good discourse. Went to Prayer Meeting in the evening &

then retired at 9 P.M.

Monday - October 13th 1862 - It is reported that Gen. Pleasanton has cornered the Rebel Cavalry & that he has taken 300 prisoners with a prospect of capturing the whole of them. I cant believe a word of it yet, although I may be true. I think Stuart has or will outwit us.

Tuesday - October 14th 1862 - Mr. Lane & myself started this morning with a wagon, after Cedar Boughs fer Beds in the Hospital. We went 1 1/2 mile & got a Wagon load, enough fer the Hospital & fer Dr. Chaplain & Cols tent. On getting to Camp I was told another great yarn about the Cavalry, that 14,000 of the enemy had attempted to cross the river, but were driven back.

Wednesday - October 15th 1862 - Again orders have come to pack up & be ready to march at a moments notice. After getting everything all tore down, the orders were countermanded & so we build up again. Dr Clark & A. S. Kellogg have just returned to us. Clark left us at Alexandria & Kellogg was detailed to stay with Col Parsons - at Barnesville, Md.

Thursday - October 16th 1862 - Dr Clark presented me with a very beautiful knife this A. M. fer past favors. We had a very hard shower this afternoon & the weather is a great deal cooler. I recd a letter from Home. Hear that all are well although my dear friend has been quite unwell - Wrote a letter to Kate Joy of No. Adams.

Friday - October 17th 1862 - This morning our eyes were greeted with the sight of three ladies coming in Camp. Capt Travers wife, mother & sister. I had a good chat with Mrs. Traver about the people in Adams. She made inquires concerning the wound of my Brother Buel. I told her just what I thought about him & wished her to state the same to my folks when she saw them.

Saturday - October 18th 1862 - This morning our Camp was cleaned & policed over. At 3 P.M. orders came to pack up & be ready to march at sundown. Dr Jewett was left in charge of all the sick in the Brigade & we started at dusk. I with the old bureau, one rubber & woolen blanket. We passed through Downsville & halted at Williamsport fer an hour - then started again, at 12 midnight we passed through Clear Springs & halted in a corn field fer the night. I made my bed of corn stalks.

Sunday - October 19th 1862 - We were up at 4 A.M. cooking our Breakfast. The night was awful cold & frosty. We then left Clear Springs, passed Fairview or Indian Spring at 11 A.M. At 3 P.M. we passed Stone Point & at 5 P.M. we arrived at Hancock - having marched 31 mile in 23 hours. It is very cold & I am just as tired as I can be. I have carried 69 pounds every step of the way.

Monday - October 20th 1862 - This morning I could hardly walk being all chaffed & foot sore. Went in swimming this forenoon. Some of the 36th New York are pretty drunk & their Col has had them doused in the Canal. Went to bed at 7 1/2 P.M. in a hollow where the wind could not strike me. It was awful cold.

Tuesday - October 21st 1862 - Was awakened at Midnight with the order, "Fall in boys; quick". We were soon up & dressed & then started on the back track. We met our Division Teams on the road. They told us that the Rebels were trying to cross at Cherry Run Ford, about 2 mile from the Fairview Inn. We passed through Stone Pointe at 3 A.M. & at 5 we were at our destination all drawn up in line of Battle ready for anything. At Daylight we went in Camp & soon our Baggage came to us.

Wednesday - October 22nd 1862 - We are all out of Rations, yet we are not discouraged for we expect some tonight. It is very cold. I have been eating Walnuts all day & feel pretty full. We are encamped in a hollow near the Georgetown & Ohio Canal. Our pickets are across the River, 20 prisoners were brought in today. So much fer so much.

Thursday - October 23rd 1862 - Orders came at Midnight to be ready this morning to march. We started at 7 A.M. & we marched one mile. While we were halted a man from Co. A. died in one of our Ambulance wagons & was buried by the side of the road. He had been sick but a day. At 6 P.M. we were ordered to march back to camp, we left this morning & arrived there at 7 - pitched my tent & went to Bed -

Friday - October 24th 1862 - All quiet this morning. It is very cold & I have had to keep a big fire all day in order to keep from freezing. S. P. Williams (who was taken prisoner at Malvern Hill) has just returned to the Regt. He looks pretty tough, yet I think if he been with us on our march through Maryland, he would be among the people that were -

Saturday - October 25th 1862 - I done nothing today but keep us a good fire. We recd some clothing about 4 P.M. & I was lucky enough to get me a Coat which I very much needed. It looks very nice, but I'll bet wont wear three months, as it is nothing but Shoddy. Well it only cost seven dollars & twenty cents. Cheap for cash.

Sunday - October 26th 1862 - Commenced raining at 8 A.M. & has not stopt yet (5 P.M.) I laid in my bunk all day with three wool blanket over me. We have recd orders to March tomorrow morning at 5 o'clk. Which way we shall go is more than I can tell & in fact I dont care. I shall keep with the Regt if they go to Halifax until my three years are out - then I shall take French leave if I cant get away without -

Monday - October 27th 1862 - We started this morning at 5 A.M. on our march. The wind blows a hurricane & it is very cold. Passed Indian Spring at 6 A.M., Clear Spring at 12 N. We halted in Town & took dinner on the sidewalk. The women looked out of the windows at us & seemed to be pleased at the way we soldiers eat. Passed through Williamsport at 6 P.M. & halted.

Tuesday - October 28th 1862 - We are two mile from Williamsport & three from our old camp nears Downsville. Yesterday we marched 15 mile. Most of the Officers are up to Williamsport having a time. All the Company Books were inspected today by a Regular Officer, Some of the Co. Commanders were reprimanded. Good enough fer them.

Wednesday - October 29th 1862 - Orders came to march this morning at 2 P.M. All was confusion fer a time but soon everything was all right. We started at 2 & arrived in our old Camp at 4 A.M. Put up the Hospital tent & then pitched my own. No one sick.

Thursday - October 30th 1862 - We all turned out this morning & policed the Camp, cleaning up all the old stuff & C. Mr. Lane says we shall certainly have orders to march as he never knew the Camp to be cleaned without the order come, & sure enough it did come. We are to get up at 3 tomorrow morning, get our baggage all in by 4 & march by 5.

Friday - October 31st 1862 - Up at 3 A.M. packed up & we were ready to start at five. We passed through Bakersfield & then Smoketown. Smoketown has 2 houses & a barn, but about 100 Hospital tents, accommodations for 1000 sick. This Hospital was established after the Battle of Antietam. The wounded have excellent care. Everything looked neat & clean. Lady Nurses were in abundance. We went near the old Battlefield of Sept 17th, passed through Rohrersville, & Reedyvillle. We encamped fer the night 1/2 mile from Rohrersville & were then mustered in fer our Pay. We have not been paid since we were at Harrisons Landing & our pockets are pretty well drained.

Saturday - November 1st 1862 - We were on the March at 5 1/2 A.M. fer Berlin, Md. We went through Pleasant Valley, over South Mountain, through Crompton Gap & then through Burkettsville. At Burkettsville we halted the 36th New York Band playing several fine pieces. We arrived at Berlin about noon. Encamped 1/2 mile from the town on a very steep side hill by the side of the River & Canal & the Baltimore & Ohio R. Road.

Sunday - November 2nd 1862 - We have been expecting orders every minute fer orders to march. The boys dread going into Virginia again, but I dont care. Most of the Army have gone over, crossing on Pontoons. Clothing has again been distributed to the boys. Orders to March at 9 tomorrow morning. Went in swimming today.

Monday - November 3rd 1862 - The ferenoon was passed in getting ready fer our tramp in Va. I wrote a letter to Father & one to Luce. We started at 1 P.M. & crossed the Pontoons at Berlin 1 1/2 Oclk The whole Division were strung along for several miles as we had to walk in two ranks while crossing the River. I never walked so fast fer so long a distance in my life. I was completely tuckered out, when I got to the head of the column. We marched through Lovettsville at 3 PM & through Bollington at 4 PM also through

Wheaton at 5 1/2 P.M. Encamped in a Pine Woods 2 mile beyond Wheaton. It is pretty cold & chilly, but I have blankets enough so I shall sleep warm.

Tuesday - November 4th 1862 - We started at six & a half this morning passed through Purseville at 9 A.M. Phelmont at 1 PM & through the town of Union at 3 P.M. At this latter place the Cavalry of the Rebels were driven out, with severe loss by our cavalry, on Sunday - the 2nd Inst (?) Gen Newton has marched us today like sixty. I dont believe he knows how fast we go, or how tiresome it is to walk mile after mile & hour after hour without resting. Encamped 2 miles from Union Village in a Woods, at 4 P.M. I made my bed of leaves under a large grape vine, & after eating my supper retired. It was very cold.

Wednesday - November 5th 1862 - As soon as I got my breakfast down I got in top of a tree & had my fill of grapes. They were large & delicious & enough fer all hands in our Hosp. & Corps. We recd orders to march at noon. The day is quite pleasant. Started at one o clock P.M. & marched to Snickersville, a small town of a dozen houses & one hill, situated three mile from Snickers Gap in the Blue Ridge. While getting Rails fer our Fires the 2nd Rhode Island & the 37th Mass got in a Row about a Rail Fence - the 2nd coming off first best. Several got bruised heads, my Uncle being one of the number. We were ordered on picket & after going about a mile, the order was countermanded so we went back again in our old place. Very cold this evening.

Thursday - November 6th 1862 - We were ordered to march this morning at 6 Oclk for White Plains a town on the Manasses R. Road. After marching 7 mile, our General concluded to let us rest a minute. We halted near a farm house where turkeys & chickens were in abundance. Our boys got their share of everything & the inhabitants were very <u>wrath</u>. Some of the officers found a couple of Rebel soldiers hid in the Garret of the house & then the boys went in for destroying everything. We were all heavily laden when we resumed our march. Arrived at White Plains a short time before dark, pretty tired, cooked our suppers & then went to bed. Our rations are all out & we know not when we shall get any more - our poultry came along in the nick of time. Very cold.

Friday - November 7th 1862 - It has been a very tedious day. Commenced snowing this morning at 9 Oclk & has kept it up all day. We have plenty of wood to burn, but nothing to eat in the shape of Bread. In fact our rations are all gone. Most of the boys are out scouring the country fer food. Sheep are being brought in camp, by the dozen & have been all day long, but of our flock of 500, our Brigade got 400. Every man has a quarter of mutton. Several of our Boys are sick & the Surgeon has gone to town to engage a Room fer them while we remain here. A great many of the boys are barefoot & nearly naked, clothing being a thing that money wont buy in this part of the world. Went to bed at 7 1/2 PM with a rousing fire at my feet.

Saturday - November 8th 1862 - Nothing to eat but mutton - very cold & snowing most of the time. The boys have found another flock of sheep & the way they come in Camp is caution to Secessionists - or any other white man. The Provost Guard put a stop to it this afternoon, but I hardly think it will do much good unless we get Rations. Orders to march at day light in the morning.

Sunday - November 9th 1862 - We started this morning at 7 A.M. on our way to Richmond. Our Regt detailed as Wagon Guard. We followed the R. Road down a couple of miles & then after getting in the road we went like shot out of a shovel for some four miles. One of the Hospital boys was run over by a Horseman & quite severely bruised. It was a serious affair, yet I could not keep from laughing, whenever I thought of it. We halted at New Baltimore, encamped on a very steep hill - where wood was a plenty.

Monday - November 10th 1862 - I pitched my tent this morning as we are to stay here a couple of days - or until we get our rations. Gen. McClellan reviewed us this morning - previous to leaving the Army. It is rumored that the Authorities at Washington are dissatisfied with his proceedings. He passed up the Road & troops were in line on both sides. Such cheering I never heard. The Army worships our little Mac. After giving up Porters Corps he came back again, & another grand push was made. The General was muchly affected. Tears were streaming down his face & the boys all felt fer him. Gen. Burnside, his successor was with him, accompanied by their respective staffs & body guard. Wrote a long letter to Henry P. Goodrich of No. Adams.

Tuesday - November 11th 1862 - I was very much amused this morning before getting out of my bunk, at a quarrel going on between old John, our Hosp. Steward & one of the Nurses (Cromwell). The language threats used then I shall always remember. Nothing going on in the Army, much talk of the removal of McClellan. It is reported today that he is ordered to Trenton, New Jersey. The troops do not like the idea of his removal although the Government may know best.

Wednesday - November 12th 1862 - The chief topic of conversation is the removal of McClellan. A great many refuse to serve under the present Gen. A number of Officers high in rank & name are concerned in the trouble. Fitzjohn Porter & others are said to be deep in the mud. Wrote letters to Father & Lucy. Have not heard from Adams (Beaver) in 6 weeks. Very cold & almost starved. Havent had anything to eat all day.

Thursday - November 13th 1862 - Rumors are flying around thick & fast. The enemy are reported to be making preparations for a Forward movement. Rations were delivered to us for three days - the first we have had in a week. A grand rush was made for the commissary, but nothing gained, as he had sold out to Officers. Had a good meal of Hardtack & Pork.

Friday - November 14th 1862 - Nothing transpired today with the exception of one thing. The Mail arrived & brought nearly everyone of us letters from Home & loved ones. Recd a letter from Father, Olson one from my dear friend Lucy, with her Photograph enclosed. It is a treasure indeed & looks exactly like the Original. Wish I could see the dear creature, but suppose I shall have to wait nearly 2 years longer. It is a very pleasant day & reminds me of Home.

Saturday - November 15th 1862 - Wrote letters to my friends at the North. Orders came this evening to be ready to march at daylight tomorrow morning. It is queer that our Generals always select Sunday as a day to begin a March. Most of the Army are camped around Warrenton & we are but 5 mile from there.

Sunday - November 16th 1862 - We commenced our tramp at 9 A.M. arrived at Catletts Station on the Grange & Alexandria R.R.

about noon. Here is where Pope lost his Baggage Train. After eating dinner we again started & went some 15 mile before halting for the night. On our march today we have passed over a good share of the Battle Field of 10 & 12 weeks ago. Horses & mules are lying around dead in every direction, also pieces of muskets & cannon. We are encamped fer the night near a place called Weaverton in a large woods, our march today has been a long one (25 mile)

Monday - November 17th 1862 - Off on our march at 8 A.M. Travelled all day through the woods, not seeing a road once. We are told the Teams occupy that - thus making us go it over hedges - ditches - fences & fallen trees. We hauled up fer the night after marching this way 15 mile to a place called Staffords Store. We are pretty tired & hungry. Caught a Rabbit about dark, so I shall have a good stew in the morning.

Tuesday - November 18th 1862 - We were on our Pins this morning at 7 A.M. for another tramp through this forsaken land. Our march was about as bad as yesterday. We however got to our destination a little earlier, only marching 12 mile & halting in a large open plain some 3 mile from Stafford, C.H. Troops are passing continually & have been for the past six hours. Some of the boys have been down to Aquia Creek - distant only one mile.

Wednesday - November 19th 1862 - We are allowed a day of rest - that is a day of rest from marching. It is raining very hard & the Roads are awful muddy. We are without rations & when we shall get any more the Lord only knows. I should think Government would contrive some way to feed their soldiers. We have not had half enough to eat - during the past two months. I have got to go to Bed without a morsel to put in my bowels. Oh, dear - I wish I were home with my Ma -

Thursday - November 20th 1862 - A detail was made this morning to go after rations, with the teams. The rain is pouring down like all possessed, the mules could hardly draw the empty wagon. They have to go to Belle Plain some 10 mile. We had to borrow 1/4 days rations from the 3d Brigade, so all we have had to eat is 3 crackers & not any Pork. I have the blues most horridly. Have been at work nearly all day putting up the Hospital tent. Am as wet as a drowned rat - tired - cross - & hungry.

Friday - November 21st 1862 - <u>Hurrah</u>, I feel better, our teams have got back from the landing - after working almost incessantly the last 36 hours. Both man & beast are covered with mud from head to foot. We have just drawn 5 days rations of Hard Bread, Sugar, Coffee, & Pork. Droves of Horses have been passing all day. They are fer Cavalry & artillery - some 1000 must have gone by. It is very muddy yet pleasant over head. Our Hospt. is about finished & I am glad.

Saturday - November 22nd 1862 - Our Regiment were detailed to go on Picket. I took the Pill Box on my back & started accompanied by Dr. Clark - Dr Robinson & Mr. Lane. After marching some 3 mile we got to our destination. I pitched my tent with the Reserve. Had a first rate time in getting Grapes - a nice stream ran close by my tent & the large trees were a splendid shelter. It has been a very beautiful day. The inhabitants here are very poor & ignorant looking, as dirty & idiotic as any persons I ever saw.

Sunday - November 23rd 1862 - It was a bitter cold night. Dr. Clark - Lane & myself - sleeping as close as three mice. We had a splendid fire when we went to Bed, but the Major put it out, saying he did not want any fires on his <u>picket line</u>. We built a huge fire this morning, dried our tents & at 10 1/2 A.M. - were relieved from our duty by the 139th Penn. Vol. arrived in Camp at 2 P.M. put up my bunk. The wind is blowing a perfect gale & we have had to strengthen the Hosp. tent also our own.

Monday - November 24th 1862 - At work all day in fixing a Fence & Gateway of brush around our Hosp. tents. Nothing occured in Camp, about dark we were all aroused from our quietness by a report of cannon, the shell bursting, but a few rods from our Camp. It appears the runners & men of the Battery were on a <u>Drunk</u>, got in a fight, where one of them fired off the piece. The fellow has been taken care of & the officers placed under arrest. The weather is quite good.

Tuesday - November 25th 1862 - The same duties in Camp as usual. Worked part of the day fer Surgeon Chamberlain fixing up a shed for his Horses. Very cold. Commenced raining about dusk quite hard. We have recd an addition to our Hospt Corps - Four men were detailed this morning from Co's A, E, H & I.

Wednesday - November 26th 1862 - It rained very hard all night long & the water came in my Bunk, wetting everything generally. I slept the latter part in water 2 inches deep - was very near frozen in the morning - took a good Hot punch of Whiskey with a small dose of quinine. Cavalry have been passing nearly all the afternoon on the way to Falmouth. Gen Sumner who leads the advance had threatened to open on Fredericksburg with 200 guns tomorrow.

Thursday (Thanksgiving Day) - November 27th 1862 - As soon as I awoke this morning my thoughts wandered to the far off Home - where friends & loved ones were to have a Holiday in Prayers & Thanksgiving, & in eating stuffed Turkeys - Oysters & all other kinds of big dishes. I wished that I could be with them, but my country says NO! So I must rest content fer a year, or so, hoping all the while that my friends will not forget me, when they seat themselves before the table, bending under the weight of the good things of the land. All I have had to eat is Pork & Hard Tack. A number of the boys were placed under arrest refusing to go two mile after wood fer our Colonel & Major. The boys having no shoes or stocking to protect their feet from the frozen ground, briars & twigs, but Colonel & Major have but few friends & they are growing less every day.

Friday - November 28th 1862 - Nothing unusual transpired today. Our grounds - fences & C have been fixed up so that now we have a Model Hospt fer any Regiment in the service. Every officer or Private that passed by - sto & admire our peculiar taste fer ornamenting. We have heard our Commanding Generals speak of it. Surgeon Chamberlain is very much pleased & says his Hospt Boys cant be beat.

Saturday - November 29th 1862 - Our Paymaster has arrived in Camp late this afternoon. He will commence paying the 37th Mass first. Four months pay are due us. We have been sadly in need of money the past two months. Some of the officers faring very poorly in consequence. Every one is elated & I shall go to Bed thinking of the benign & glorious Government! Who wouldn't be a Soldier?

Sunday - November 30th 1862 - The boys this morning are all turned topsy turvey - eager to get their pay. The Paymaster made his appearance about 10 A.M. & commended to pay our Regt. I recd $82.75 for my share. I immediately wrote a letter to Father - enclosing 80 dollars & gave it in the charge of Lieut. D. W. Wells who having resigned his commission, would take the first Boat fer Berkshire Co. I tried to settle all of Buels accounts. Wells owed him 7 dollars & promised to pay Father as soon as he saw him. The boys are all sending their money Home. Some by mail - others by Express & others by messengers - very pleasant. A good many of the Boys are visiting the Sutlers to buy clothing. Many of them are nearly naked & not fit to be seen among folks.

Monday - December 1st 1862 - The team of the whole Division started this morning for Aquia Landing to get clothing, they got back about noon & this afternoon everybody was around their officers tent getting their supply. I got me a pair of Pants & Shoes. The day has been very pleasant.

Tuesday - December 2nd 1862 - Done nothing today, but eat my regular rations of coffee, HardTack & Pork, nothing going on. No reports from the front & some think we shall winter here, but I do not. Very cold this evening & looks like a storm of some kind.

Wednesday - December 3rd 1862 - Surgeon Chamberlain got a Team for us & we all started for the woods. Worked quite hard - got up two loads of wood in the forenoon. At 2 P.M. orders came to be ready to march at daylight tomorrow morning. Bully for that. I don't want to stop here, as there is to much Mud.

Thursday - December 4th 1862 - I was up at 5 this morning after eating my breakfast began to pack. Worked very hard packing & loading up the Teams - at 8 Oclk we started in the mud & rain. We got 2 mile in 3 hours - passed Stafford C. House at 12 N. The place has 3 houses - Jail - & C. House. Passed Brooks Station, on the Aquia & Falmouth R. Road at 3 P.M. marched three mile farther towards Belle Plains & camped fer the night having marched 8 mile since morning. Had a rabbit fer supper - saw two men fighting in Co. B.

Friday - December 5th 1862 - It was a very cold night & this morning I got up pretty early - built a fire & cooked my Breakfast. At 8 OClock we started on our march again - went through woods &

everything else for the distance of 5 miles when we halted & pitched our tents. Commenced raining very hard & every drop frose as it struck the ground. Just got our tents pitched when orders came to pack up - as our Generals had found a better place to camp. It was provoking enough but we must obey orders. So off we started cross lots, some 2 miles farther & their halted fer over an hour before we could find out where we were to camp. Everyone was wet through & nearly frosen. We however got our frosen tents up & a good fire agoing about dark. The rain turned to snow & we suffered a good deal. Had to turn out at 10 P.M. & help get our Baggage up to us as they were stuck in the mud.

Saturday - December 6th 1862 - I got up at daylight almost frose to death. If ever I suffered it was last night - my blankets were wet & cold & so I lived through the night. Went to work clearing up the ground. Put up the Hospt. tent, made beds fer the sick & built a brush fence on the East side of our yard to protect us from the cold winds. Recd three men in Hospt, all sick with chronic diarrhea

Sunday - December 7th 1862 - Worked pretty much all day chopping fire wood to keep warm. Moved my Bunk & fixed up things generally. We are fixed quite comfortably. We have one man in the Hospt. dangerously sick - think he will not live long. Mason & Haywood are watchers tonight.

Monday - December 8th 1862 - This has been the coldest day of the season. I have had to work hard to keep warm. We have had huge fires - but it was no use. One side of us would freese while the other was roasting. Recd. letters tonight from Home & my friend Lucy. A man in the 37th Mass was brought in camp reported to have been murdered. My turn in Hospt this 24 hours commencing this morning. Black is with me.

Tuesday - December 9th 1862 - Had a very busy time all last night in watching & nursing the sick. I had a good fire. Kalfeur of Co. K died at 4 1/2 A.M. was dying all night. Laid him out & had a very unpleasant job of it. He was buried today, as we are under orders to march tomorrow at daylight. Drew 5 days rations this afternoon. Went to bed at 4 P.M.

Wednesday - December 10th 1862 - Have had everything

ready to pull down - ready to pack - expecting the order would come every moment, but no order has come, unless I except the order to go to bed early as we shall move at 1 Oclock in the night. Something must be to pay - should not wonder if we were on the road to Richmond, but I dont believe we shall get so near it, as we did when little Mac had command of us. Hendricks, one of our Hospt boys arrived in Camp this forenoon from Davids Island, New York with some sick, when we got to Alexandria, last September. He has escaped some hard marches.

Thursday - December 11th 1862 - (Battle of Fredericksburg) - Started on our March this morning at 5 Oclock. Heard the report of Artillery all along our march. Halted at White Oak Church & the Brigade had orders to load their pieces. We arrived at Falmouth & near the Banks of the Rappahannock at 9 1/2 A.M. All day long our Cannon (some 200 in number) kept up their work of shelling the town of Fredericksburg & the works on that side. Several attempts were made to lay the Pontoons, but all proved ineffectual, except the one opposite of where we lay. As soon as dusk our Brigade had orders to fall in. The 2nd Regt land on the lead & the 10th next. We crossed the River, the 2nd deployed as skirmishes, & our Regt supported them. Such a shout I never heard as was then given. We captured some 50 prisoners & then established our pickets. The crossing at Fredericksburg I shall never forget. It was the grandest & most thrilling scene I ever saw or expected to see.

Friday - December 12th 1862 - (Battle of Fredericksburg) - Our forces succeeded in laying Pontoons across the River last night - both at the Centre & Right. We extended our lines & nearly all of Franklins Grand Division crossed. We expect to have an awful fight. The enemy opened on us with their guns but our Batteries fell short of the mark & landed right square in the midst of our Regt, throwing the dirt in masses over us. Heavy firing on the Centre & Right this P.M. Reported that Sumner was repulsed while trying to cross. Hooker has crossed in the Centre & holds the town of Fredericksbury. So far so good. Our Hospital for the Corps is in a large House on the Bank of the River & owned by Alfred Bernard. It was nicely furnished, but now it is all torn to bits. Shells having gone through & through it breaking & smashing everything.

Saturday - December 13th 1862 - (Battle of Fredericksburg) -

The pickets commenced firing this bright & early. Everyone was up & dressed as we knew something was to be done. There was but little going except skirmishing until 10 A.M. when our Batteries opened & such shelling I never heard. On the Centre Hooker was charging his men up St Marys Heights - 3 times they went up & as soon came back again, leaving 2/3 of their member on the ground. It was an awful sight. In our front we charged & drove the enemy over a mile. The 12th Mass. losing 3/4 of their number, we were ordered at 5 P.M. to support the Doubleday Division. Meade in command of a Division had crossed the R. Road & got in the Enemys wagon train, but not being supported was obliged to fall back. We were no sooner in position than the enemy opened on us with 50 pieces. We all lay down under cover of ground & let her rip. Many were killed. Nothing was accomplished by this splurge but our Hospt. Corps of the Division were all sent to the rear. We established a Hospital on the banks of the River & out of danger of many shells. I remained with several others on the bluff to see the performance. It was a grand sight. R. Road Iron & everything under heavens was fired at us, but it done no good. Our Batteries soon silenced them. Were ordered at 8 O clock P.M. back to our old position we held in the morning. It was very cold. Our loss has been immense & cannot see we have gained anything. Many of our best Generals & officers have been killed or wounded. If Meade had been supported as he ought to have been we should have gained a great advantage for the enemys right flank would have been turned. Reported as it always is, in a fight, that Richmond is taken & a force are coming in the rear of the enemy - Who believes it - Answer - Old bullee (?)

  Sunday - December 14th 1862 - (Battle of Fredericksburg) - After quite a comfortable nights sleep in the mud we were aroused by the firing of the pickets. It however soon ceased & soon there were fires agoing & breakfast was getting ready - about 9 A.M. Gen. Burnside made his appearance to examine the position of things at the front. An orderly went on a head to tell the men not to cheer him as it would hinder his movements. The General doffed his hat & every officer & private done the same as he passed by. It has remained quiet all day. Nothing but an occasional shot from the pickets. Prisoners are being brought in every few moments. They say we never can take the heights & I cant say that they tell a lie. Hope they do though. Went to bed pretty early not knowing how soon I might be called up.

Monday - December 15th 1862 - (Battle of Fredericksburg) - We were called up at 2 Oclock this morning, ordered to cook Breakfast & be ready to march at 4. At that time we packed up & went to the front. Our Division relieving the one there. Our Brigade was put to the front on the skirmish line & our Regt to support a light 12 lb. battery. Nothing but occasional picket firing was kept up through the day & no one hurt to my knowledge. The Hospitals were cleared off the wounded & taken across the River & every wagon was ordered to be on the other side by 4 P.M. At 6 P.M. the Hospt Corps of the whole army were ordered across the River, on going to the Division Hospt. I found troops crossing on three pontoon bridges & by 12 M. every man & gun was across except the pickets. It commenced raining about dusk & the mud was very deep & darker than Egyptian darkness. I lay down to rest 1 1/2 miles from the bank of the River. The wounded are sent to Washington.

Tuesday - December 16th 1862 - Our Division being on picket last night they did not recross until 3 oclock this morning. Our Brigade was the last & the 10th Mass the last Regt to recross the River. I was ordered to the Regt at daylight & found the boys all well, but covered with mud & wet through. However they looked no worse than I did & am sure they felt no better or worse either. The mud is very deep. The cannon sinking in up to the hubs. The whole army are encamped on the range of hills just back of the River. The men are all tired & hungry. What the next move will be is not for mortal man to judge. We have in this fight got licked like thunder & all because we have had no good General. When, Oh when will the Authorities at Washington learn something. 18,000 killed & wounded & not a single point gained. A fool could have done as well.

Wednesday - December 17th 1862 - I have felt very uncomfortable all day long being covered with mud from head to foot. I hardly think my most intimate friends at the North would know me could they behold my picture at present. I wrote a long letter to Lucy of the fight - also one to Father. The rest of the day sat shivering over the fire as it was very cold. The Surgeon gave me some of Whiskey. I made me a hot sling & then felt very much better, wish I could have got another one for my bunk mate (Mr Lane). It is reported there is an armistice for 20 days. I rather guess our Generals are satisfied.

Thursday - December 18th 1862 - Orders to pack up & be

ready to fall in at a moments notice, which was done, but we did not fall in for a good number of hours. Troops were passing us continually, & the rest of our Brigade went off, still we remained. Sat around the fire until 3 P.M. when we Fell in line, marched 3/4 of a mile & posted the pickers. Our Hospt boys remained with the Reserve. Kept up a huge fire all night to keep from freesing & on the morning.

Friday - December 19th 1862 - I found one of my blankets nearly burnt up - nothing happened through the day. At 3 OClock P.M. we were relieved from picket. The reserve started in advance of the picket & the (illegible) was, we had to wait nearly 2 hours for them to come in. I thought I should freeze sure pop. We however got in Camp with the remainder of the Brigade. Stacked arms & recd the order to rest which we did of course.

Saturday - December 20th 1862 - Was very busy at work all day - in cleaning up the ground & falling trees, also in pitching the Hospital tents - making beds for the sick & C. Had no time to make a bunk fer myself, so, I must sleep out another night without shelter.

Sunday - December 21st 1862 - Commenced work on a chimiey & a Fireplace fer the Hospital. Our work was harder than yesterday. The Doctors were cross, thinking we ought to have build the whole concern in much less time, about the middle of the afternoon a new Recruit of Co H. was brought to the Hospital in a dying state, with Congestion of the lungs. So one of our boys had to stop work & attend to him & so the chimiey was not finished today.

Monday - December 22nd 1862 - Boys working very hard all day we got things in working order. Boswell from Co. H died this morning at 6 oclock, I performed the work of laying him out. He was buried this afternoon. I built a Bunk for myself this P.M. assisted by Mprs Black & Lane of the Hospt. Corps.

Tuesday - December 23rd 1862 - Up at Revielle & after Breakfast was done away with, I went in the Hospital to nurse the sick & attend to their many wants. I have eight patients today. The other of the Corps are building a fence around our Hospt & making things look nice generally. The officers who sent in their Resignations last September & were Court Martialed have all been dismissed (from) the Service in Disgrace & they started for their Homes today.

Wednesday - December 24th 1862 - I had a very hard time of it last night. Jake Veditto of Co. D. was not expected to live from one minute to another. I had to give him sip of Spirits Fermenti every 10 minutes all night long. Then I had 3 cases besides of Chronic Diarrhea, which kept me on the jump all the time. The patients are better this a.m. Black was my helper last night. Went to sleep in my Bunk after Breakfast & remained there all day.

Thursday - December 25th 1862 - Commenced work on our Cook House & finished the whole thing at dark. The boys in the Hospital are very sick & some of them running over with Lice. They were the dirtiest set of fellows I ever saw. I had nothing good to eat today, it was Christmas, but I live in hopes of better days.

Friday - December 26th 1862 - Went in woods this morning after Brush & fire wood. The boys are fixing up their quarters for Winter, although we have recd no orders to do so. Our Hospt & all its surroundings are fixed up in gay style. Ornaments both inside & outside with evergreen.

Saturday - December 27th 1862 - My turn in Hospital today. Black is with me, have had a very hard time, Eight sick ones & four dangerously so. Reported in camp we are agoing to move to Belle Plain, but I think it is only a Rumor. I have tried to write a letter today, but I had to jump every minute so I gave it up as a bad job - shall be up all night long. Two of my sick ones will not live long.

Sunday - December 28th 1862 - It is Sabbath morning & I have just got from duty in the Hospt. I am very tired, but shall soon go to sleep - The rest of the Boys have got to clean up for inspection. Now at 8 P.M I feel better, have been asleep all day. It has been very pleasant the boys say.

Monday - December 29th 1862 - Another pleasant day, have done but little work. Had a splendid dinner of Baked Beans & pork, finished my letter I began Saturday, also wrote several others. James Robbins of Co G. is dying. His sickness is Chronic Diarrhea contracted while we were on the Penninsula last summer.

Tuesday - December 30th 1862 - I was called up at 2 Oclock this morning to layout the body of James Robbins. He died very easy. At daylight took my turn as Attendant, one of the nurses is sick, threatened with Fever. Robbins was buried this afternoon by his comrades in Co G. It commenced raining about noon & has rained ever since. Shall have to be up all night again.

Wednesday - December 31st 1862 - Was relieved this morning from duty. We were mustered in at 10 A.M. fer our 2 months pay. I have nothing to do, so I shall go to bed as it is now dark & when I wake up I shall be all through with the Old Year. A year of hardships, of trials. A year of sorrow in the death of a Beloved Brother & hosts of Comrades that have fallen in Battle. Peace be to their ashes.

REMARKS FOUND IN BACK OF THE DIARY

Our Regiment has been in the following Battles & Skirmishes the past year. A skirmish at Bottom Bridge, May 20th of two Companies of our Regt. with the Rebels. Again May 26th we were out on a Reconnissance, under heavy Artillery fire for half an hour or more. Drove the enemy, but lost no men. May 31st Battle of Fair Oaks loss 122 killed & wounded. June 25th a skirmish near Fair Oaks. July 1st Battle of Malvern Hills - loss 88. Battle of Antiedam Sept 17th & 18th. Reconnaissance to Williamsport Sept. 20th, drove the enemy across the River. Dec 11th, 12th 13th 14th & 15th at Fredericksburg. also the Battle of Williamsburg, May 5th 1862.

BEREA M. WILLSEY
COMPANY C, TENTH MASSACHUSETTS VOLUNTEERS
ARMY OF THE POTOMAC
CIVIL WAR DIARY
January 7, 1863–December 31, 1863

[NOTE: Entries to the Diary of Berea M. Willsey from January 7th, 1863, through February 11th, 1863, were sent to me by Ann Higgins Cox. She found them in the Willsey Bible belonging to Carrie Willsey Dennis, her paternal great-grandmother.]

Wednesday - January 7th 1863 - Had a good nights sleep although it was as cold as Greenland, after eating Breakfast of Pork & crackers I went to work making a Cook House, finished the building at dusk & was complimented by the Surgeon in doing it so quick. I bought a New York Herald & learned of the success in the South West of our armies at Murfreesboro & Vicksburg.

Thursday - January 8th 1863 - At Reville I was up & had my breakfast nearly finished. Went in the Hospital to nurse the sick, have three convelescent ones to look after. For dinner had Beef Steak, crackers & coffee & fer supper Tea & Toast. Lieut. Eaton was taken sick & admitted to the Hospital. Staid up all night.

Friday - January 9th 1863 - Was relieved from duty this morning. The Regt have gone on Picket - gone for three days. Rec'd a letter from Home & one from I. F. Hurd, wrote Father & then went & took dinner with John Lenoth. Had some slapjacks & fried doughnuts. Bought a Herald & learned that Vicksburg had not been taken as reported. Went to bed at tatoo.

Saturday - January 10th 1863 - After a good nights rest I had a breakfast of boiled potatoes & fresh Pork. Charles Fera of Co. A. came in from Picket shot through the hand accidentally. It commenced raining at 9 A.M. Bought 1/2 lb. of Butter from Bidwell a Pipe & Tobacco for $13.00 A fool & his money are soon parted. Retired at 8 P.M.

Sunday - January 11th 1863 - Had fer Breakfast some slapjacks, sugar & coffee. The day was cold & cloudy. A. S. Kellogg recd a box from home containing a pair of Boots, Cakes, Pies & Cakes - bought his boots for $7.00. Eat so much dinner of pies & cakes I could hardly stir. Had Beans for supper - Retired at 8 P.M. Recd a letter from E. E. Wells.

Monday - January 12th 1863 - Went on duty in the Hospital for 24 hours. Have 8 sick ones. The Regt returned from picket in the afternoon. Had Beans for breakfast, Soup for dinner. Recd 2 papers from I. F. Hurd also the Transcript from Home. The day has been cold & cloudy. No news from the Army in the Southwest.

Tuesday - January 13th 1863 - I was relieved from duty in the Hospital after Surgeons Call. Four of the sick in the Hospital are reported to quarters. I had Beefsteak for Breakfast & dinner. The Regt have been drilling most of the day. We boys in the Hospital Department had a sing in the evening & then some lemonade. Retired at 10.

Wednesday - January 14th 1863 - I got up this morning before Revielle, cooked some slapjacks & Beefsteak fer Breakfast. I then fixed up my tent with Cedar boughs & made a fence. Boiled Rice & molasses fer dinner. The boys are fixing up their tents fer a long stop. Drilling as usual. Retired at Tatoo.

Thursday - January 15th 1863 - Up at Revielle. Had fer Breakfast Boiled Potatoes & Beefsteak. Went to work fixing up the tent belonging to the Hospital. The wind blew a Hurricane all day & I had my hands full in trying to keep things right side up. It commenced raining at 7 P.M. Heard that our Sutler I. H. Bryan was drowned in Chesapeake Bay.

Friday - January 16th 1863 - Beans for breakfast & bully good they were too. Wrote a letter to H Tower of No. Adams. Had biscuit fer dinner, some of my own make. The weather today is pretty rainy, but I suppose it is all right fer the soldier. Recd orders to march in the morning, but they were countermanded until Monday. No letters.

Saturday - January 17th 1863 - After a very cold night I got up, cooked me some potatoes & Pork. Then relieved S. P. Williams from duty, as usual. Had my hair cut & paid 25 cents. Nothing fer dinner. Wrote a letter to Lucy & one to C. C. Wells. Had some slapjacks fer supper. I was sadly disappointed in not receiving letters from home.

Sunday - January 18th 1863 - The day is very pleasant but cold. I had baked beans fer Breakfast, was relieved from duty in the Hospital & then prepared myself fer the regular Sunday morning inspection. Nothing transpired worth of note. Received a letter from Lucy G. which made my heart glad & yet sorrowful in learning of her bad health. Retired at 8 P.M.

Monday - January 19th 1863 - Had boiled potatoes & Beefsteak fer Breakfast. Sent all of our sick to the General Hospital at Aquia Creek. Was told to be in readiness to march in the morning. The day is cold & a fire is very comfortable. Wrote a letter to Father also one to Lucy - Crackers & Pork fer dinner & Beans fer supper. Retired at 7 P.M. as we are to March in the morning.

Tuesday - January 20th 1863 - After eating breakfast went to work packing up. It took us until noon to get ready. Cooked a cup of coffee & then the Regt started. After marching until 5 oclock without stopping to rest, we went into Camp fer the night in a pine woods. Eat supper & then went to bed tired enough. Raining.

Wednesday - January 21st 1863 - It rained all night very hard. I got up at 4 1/2 oclk. Cooked Breakfast. Started on our March at six A.M. Raining all the while, mud knee deep. Pontoons turned over in the road. Halted at 9 A.M. Cooked dinner & at 3 P.M. were ordered to a new camp about one mile from the river. The mud is awful deep. Went to bed at dark. [Memoranda from the rear of this diary written at a later date: On the morning of Jan 21st at six we started on our march fer New River to meet the enemy & to drive them from their strong positions. It had been raining all night & in the morning. The mud was very deep, But not bad enough to stop the grand army. We marched about four mile through mud & water knee deep, raining all the while. Our clothes were wet through, but the loads on our backs & the exercise in walking through the mud kept us from catching cold. We arrived within 1/4 of a mile from the river at nine A.M. We found that the Pontoons were not laid across the river fer us & so we went in camp. While coming along the road we met several wagons of Pontoon Train turned over in the road & others stuck fast. The artillery could not stir with their usual number of horses. One Brigade were detailed to turn out & clear the road helping the caissons & Pontoons along. It was a terrible time & everybody was down on <u>Burnside</u>. We expect to get whipped.]

Thursday - January 22nd 1863 - I got up at six oclk after a very good nights rest. Cooked some coffee & Pork. It rained most of the night & this morning. There is a heavy mist. Were ordered to march at noon, but after getting all packed up the orders were countermanded until the next morning. I retired at 7 PM

Friday - January 23rd 1863 - Got up at 5 A.M. & after eating Breakfast were ordered to march back to our old camp near Falmouth helping the Battery along through the mud. It appears Burnsides movement has not succeeded, got to Camp at 3 P.M. all tired out. A letter from Home.

Saturday - January 24th 1863 - After eating Breakfast I recd another letter from Home date 11th. Went to work fixing up Hospital tent & cook house fences & C. Heard we were going to the West under Gen. Rosencrans. Beef steak fer dinner. Rice fer supper. Retired at 9 A.M. Wrote home.

Sunday - January 25th 1863 - Nothing transpired today worthy of note. The usual Sunday morning inspection. It was indeed a day of rest. I wrote a letter to <u>Lucy</u>. In the evening we had a real old fashioned sing. I often thought of home & of the songs I used to sing with loved ones.

Monday - January 26th 1863 - General Inspection of the whole grand Division & everyone in the Army must be accounted fer. Absentees reported as Deserters & to be treated as such. Gathered a lot of pine boughs fer beds to be used as feathers. Recd two letters one from Father & one from Eddie Turner.

Tuesday - January 27th 1863 - It rained all day, but not withstanding all that I put up a beautiful fence around the Hospital of cedar trees. Made bowers for the entrance. No duties in Camp as it is so rainy. Fer Breakfast & dinner I had Beefsteak & Pork. It commenced snowing at 9 P.M. I turned in

Wednesday - January 28th 1863 - Snowed all night but as it was so warm it all melted. About 11 A.M. it grew colder & now at 3 P.M. it is quite chilly - very nasty under foot. Soup fer dinner. Am in the Hospital as Nurse - have three sick ones. Wrote a letter to Lucy & one to Father. Went to sleep at 9 A.M.

Thursday - January 29th 1863 - Was relieved from duty in the Hospital this morning. Nothing was done in Camp in the shape of drilling. Everyone was shoveling the snow & draining the streets of their several habitations. Beans fer dinner & slapjacks fer supper. Letter from I. F. Hurd.

Friday - January 30th 1863 - I worked at the wood pile all the forenoon. Heard that we were to paid off today, but it appears it was nothing but a report. Lived on Pork & fried crackers all day. Nothing new going on in Camp. Recd 2 papers from I. F. Hurd. Retired at 9 A.M.

Saturday - January 31st 1863 - Reveille found me cooking my Breakfast of Beefsteak & Pork. Done a few light duties around Camp. Had soup fer dinner & I eat my fill. Went in the woods after a few logs fer fire wood. Eat no supper. It has been a splendid day. The sun shining very warmly. The snow has about gone.

Sunday - February 1st 1863 - While eating my Breakfast of Pork & Crackers I recd a letter from Willis E. Coonradt answered his letter after eating my breakfast. Nothing stirring in Camp. All the boys are writing to their friends at home. The day has been very pleasant.

Monday - February 2nd 1863 - Went on duty in the Hospital after the regular morning Surgeons Call. I have one very sick man to take care of. His name is Littlejohn in Co. I My whole time is spent in taking care of him. I had some Beans fer dinner & fer supper. Staid up all night. Sent fer my (illegible).

Tuesday - February 3rd 1863 - After washing all my men I had a good Breakfast of flapjacks & butter. I went to sleep at 10 A.M. & did not get up until 2 P.M. then had another batch of flapjacks. Nothing of interest going on in Camp. It has been an awful cold day

& everybody loves the fire. I dread the cold blankets tonight.

      Wednesday - February 4th 1863 - I got up at 5 A.M. Not being able to keep in bed any longer. I came near freezing. Built a good fire in the Cook-house & cooked my breakfast before the others of the Hospital Corps got up. Roast Beef fer dinner. Tea & crackers fer supper. Had a hot whiskey punch before going to bed.

      Thursday - February 5th 1863 - It snowed all day long. No drills in the Regt. Got a lot of fire wood fer the Hospital & then cooked dinner. In the afternoon Littlejohn of Co. I died & was buried at five oclk. I assisted in robing him fer the grave. Was dissappointed in not receiving a letter.

      Friday - February 6th 1863 - It has been raining all day. The Dr. ordered us Hospital boys out into the woods to get fire wood. We got wet through & then started back to camp. Nothing going on in the Regt. Recd a letter from Father in the evening. Folks all well, went to bed at 10 P.M.

      Saturday - February 7th 1863 - I got up at 4 1/2 oclk AM eat Breakfast & then went on duty in the Hospital. Have five men to take care of. None dangerous. Wrote a letter to Father. I have been very unwell today & feel pretty miserable in spirits. Went to bed at 11 P.M.

      Sunday - February 8th 1863 - Was relieved from duty in the Hospital at 8 AM Our Regt started on Picket to begone three days. I did not go. Beans fer breakfast & dinner. It has been a most splendid day & all nature looks gay. Wrote a letter to W. Retired at 7 P.M.

      Monday - February 9th 1863 - There is nothing today of any importance. Wrote in this anyway. Heard (illegible) be to (illegible)

      Tuesday - February 10th 1863 - (Illegible) Duties very light. It has been a (illegible). Rations yesterday (illegible) Went to my bunk at 9 P.M.

      Wednesday - February 11th 1863 - Was relieved from duty in the Hospital this A.M. The Regt returned from their Picket (illegible).

Thursday - February 12 1863 - (Illegible) fer Breakfast potatoes a Beefsteak. The day unpleasant (illegible) in Camp all day (illegible). Recd a letter from Home (illegible). Mother & all are well. My head is (illegible) in knowing they are well, but I feel (illegible).

Friday - February 13 1863 - Illegible

Saturday - February 14 1863 - Illegible

Sunday - February 15 1863 - The day has been very unpleasant, raining most of the time., No inspection and no duties of any kind. Everybody was sleepy & dull & take it all around. The day passed off very unpleasantly. Expected to hear from Home but was again disappointed. Retired at 9 P.M.

Monday - February 16 1863 - I had breakfast of pork & fried crackers. Split wood most of the forenoon. For dinner had beefsteak & fried onions. Bought six & a half lb. of ham of A. S. Kellogg. It had been very pleasant. Hear that our Brigade are agoing to Baltimore for Provost.

Tuesday - February 17 1863 - Done nothing today but eat Ham & flapjacks as it has been snowing very hard all day. Heard in the afternoon that all newspapers were to be kept out of the Army as there was to much exposure in telling of plans. Wish this Army could go north & clean out this Sesch. Then recd long looked for letter from Lucy.

Wednesday - February 18th 1863 - After snowing all night it turned into Rain this morn. I went in the Hospital as nurse. Have three sick. Wrote to Lucy but after I finished it heard that no mail was to leave the Army for two weeks. A lovely note, I should think. Wonder what will come next. Retired at 10 P.M.

Thursday - February 19th 1863 - S. P. Williams took my place this morning in the hospital. I went to see Lieut Cousens of Co. B. as he had just returned from home on a furlough. Rec'd a small box of Yankee notions from my friend at Home, sent with him to me. Was very much pleased. Raining all day.

Friday - February 20th 1863 - I was up this morning at

Revielle, had beans & pork for breakfast, dinner & supper. I was busy most of the day trying to get a Furlough of 10 days & after some trouble I got one started. Rec'd a letter from Father stating that he was agoing to Hatfield to live in his farm. Went to bed at 10 o'clock.

Saturday - February 21st 1863 - This day is very pleasant. I chopped wood nearly all day for the Hospital. Heard that my furlough had passed Brigade Headquarters, if so, I shall probably get it by Sunday night. Forward fifteen ($15) of O Bidwell in case I should go home. Retired at 10 P.M.

Sunday - February 22nd 1863 - It has been snowing all night & this morning the snow is about 20" deep on the level. It is snowing yet & I guess it will all day long. Salutes have been fired in every Brigade in the Army in honor of Washington's birthday.

Monday - February 23rd 1863 - After Surgeons Call I took my turn as nurse in the hospital. Have three sick ones. It is very cold. Snow is on the ground at the depth of 20 inches. Nothing of any importance here in Camp. Heard nothing from my papers.

Tuesday - February 24th 1863 - Was relieved from duty in the Hospital by Dr. Black. Had flapjacks for breakfast, Bread & Butter for dinner & supper. The day is very pleasant & the snow is leaving the ground rapidly. Retired to my couch at 7 1/2 o'clock.

Wednesday - February 25th 1863 - After eating my Breakfast of flapjacks, I made all necessary preparations for going home as I heard my furlough was coming. In the afternnoon went in the woods & got up two loads of wood for the Hospital. Worked pretty faithfully all day.

Thursday - February 26th 1863 - Rec'd a letter from Father saying he had removed to Hatfield, Mass. & that I must come there if I got my furlough. I have heard nothing more from it yet. I hope to soon. Some writing today as it has been raining out. Retired to my bunk at 8 P.M.

Friday - February 27th 1863 - We had a very severe rain storm last evening & this morning. The snow is about gone. The mud is very deep. Two balloons have been up most all the forenoon from Hookers H. Quarters. The sun shine very warm & all nature looks lovely. Bread & butter for supper.

Saturday - February 28th 1863 - I rec'd a letter this morning from I. F. Hurd. Wrote a letter to Father. After dinner went out in the woods chopping. Got up two loads of good Hickory & then took supper of Bread & Raw <u>onions</u>. I hear nothing of my furlough.

Sunday - March 1st 1863 - I went in the Hospital this morning to look after the sick. Gave them all a good scrubbing over with Mustard water. For dinner had Roast Beef, Fried onions & Baked Potatoes. Was kept busy all day long & night too.

Monday - March 2nd 1863 - Levi Black relieved me from duty in the Hospital this morning. It has been one of the most pleasant days of the season. Most of the boys that went home for furloughs have returned & now I expect my turn will come. How I long to see dear faces of friends at home.

Tuesday - March 3rd 1863 - We had a severe storm of rain this morning. Tents blew down & the wind made some havoc generally. In the afternoon I went out in the woods chopping, got up two loads of wood. Felt very unwell towards night. Took a dose of Hot Whiskey & Quinine & went to bed.

Wednesday - March 4th 1863 - I staid in my bunk most all day, although I felt better than I did last evening. Had some milk toast for supper. It has been very cold & the wind has blown most of the day. Bought of Bidwell 2 lbs of butter at 60 cents per lb. Commenced raining at sundown.

Thursday - March 5th 1863 - Went in the woods chopping for the Hospital. Got up two loads of Hickory wood. As I had not heard from my furlough I concluded I would look it up - found that it had not left Headquarters, & so I am <u>dished</u>. Rec'd a letter from Father. He has gone to Hatfield, Mass.

Friday - March 6th 1863 - It has rained nearly all day & I have kept pretty close in my quarters. The express came this afternoon & my box I found at last. All the eatables were spoilt. My shirts

& other things were in good condition. Sold my boots for $7.00.

Saturday - March 7th 1863 - Went in the Hospital this morning. Have six patients. Wrote a letter to Lucy & one to E. A. Tower. Rec'd a letter at night from Lucy & my heart was made glad. Oh, how I should love to see that dear face once again. Was up all night.

Sunday - March 8th 1863 - Was relieved from duty in the Hospital this morning. After eating my breakfast of Boiled Beans & Pork I went to bed. Slept until three P.M. Had milk toast for supper. Rec'd a letter from Willie Coonradt of No. Adams. Retired at 8 o'clock P.M.

Monday - March 9th 1863 - Had beefsteak for breakfast. Went after wood for the Hospital. Was gone until noon. After dinner cleaned up around the Hospital & choped wood. Had pea soup for dinner & supper. Wrote a letter to Father. Went to bed at 9 P.M. Raining.

Tuesday - March 10th 1863 - It has been very stormy today. Raining & snowing most of the time. I staid in my bunk most of the day reading the papers & all the old books I could get ahold of. Rec'd. a North Adams transcript in the evening. Went to bed after having a good old fashioned sing.

Wednesday - March 11th 1863 - Had breakfast of Boiled potatoes, fried Beefsteak & onions. Dinner of roast beef & supper of tea & toast bread. Nothing was done in camp except a Battallion drill in the afternoon. Rec'd. orders to be ready to march at a moments notice in tight marching order. Wrote to I. F. Hurd. Orders to march.

Thursday - March 12th 1863 - It has been very cold and blustering all day & I have done but little of anything. Commenced writing to Lucy. Had wheat cakes for my dinner & milk toast for my supper. Had a good time in the evening singing & telling stories. Retired 9 P.M.

Friday - March 13th 1863 - After eating breakfast of beefsteak & bread, I went in the Hospital as nurse. Finished my letter to Lucy. Our Brigade were ordered out to be reviewed. Preparation to marching. It has been very cold & windy for this season of the year.

My patients are all doing well. Our Surgeon has been ordered to report at Washington.

Saturday - March 14th 1863 - After Surgeons Call, I was relieved from duty in the Hospital. One of our Boys went to Aquia this morning after medicines for the Brigade & returned at 3 P.M. We had beans for dinner. Nothing going on in camp. Borrowed a book to read of Lieut E. B. Bartlett. Heard that Wm. H. Coop had gone home on a furlough.

Sunday - March 15th 1863 - Everything has been very quiet in camp today. It is very stormy & the first thunderstorm of the season visited us in the evening. Passed away the time in singing, eating & several other things. Had a good fire all day.

Monday - March 16th 1863 - We have one of Co. C nurses in the Hospital (Crazy). It is the first Crazy man I have had to deal with. He keeps a fellow on the grin all the time. It is a splendid day & there is a report that we shall move from here in a week. Don't believe it.

Tuesday - March 17th 1863 - A short time after midnight the Long Roll was beat in the camps off to our right. The Irish Regts had a good time as it was St. Patrick's Day. Very heavy firing was heard all the afternoon off at our right & all are on the tip toes to know what it means. Took a good walk in the afternoon.

Wednesday - March 18th 1863 - The day past off very pleasantly. The different Regts. have been ordered to drill three times a day. Had beans for dinner & supper. Went to Falmouth Station horseback after Medical supplies. Got back at 10 P.M. Heard that Tip Coop had returned from home.

Thursday - March 19th 1863 - After eating Breakfast, I went to see Coop. Was very much please to hear of the folks at home. Went on duty in the Hospital. Wrote to Lucy. Received a letter from Father. Also one from E. E. Graves at Baton Rouge. Got 3 cent postage stamps in the letter from Father. Soup for dinner.

Friday - March 20th 1863 - There has been but Little if anything going on in camp. I wrote a letter to Father. Heard from Rebel sources that our Army in the Southwest had met with defeat. I guess however that the boot is on the other leg. Spent most of the afternoon & evening in reading.

Saturday - March 21st 1863 - When I crawled out of my bunk this morning I found the ground covered with snow. It had stormed all day. At night quite a shower of rain fell, occupied myself in reading. Had company in the evening. Splendid time singing & telling stories.

Sunday - March 22nd 1863 - Very pleasant this morning. Reported that the 6th Army Corps are going to Texas. It beat all, what stories some folks will believe. Gen. Couch has been relieved from duty. Heard Maj. Gen. Sumner died on Friday. Retired at 9 P.M.

Monday - March 23rd 1863 - The day passed as others have. It has been raining some. I worked at the wood pile a good deal of the time. At night I rec'd. a letter from my darling, Lucy. Was very much please to hear from her. I also rec'd. my Transcript. Retired a 9 1/2 P.M.

Tuesday - March 24th 1863 - After eating my breakfast I went in the Hospital to take care of the sick. I commenced writing to Luc but as my patients were very sick I had to pospone operations. Set up all night giving medicine every half hour to Millett of Co. B.

Wednesday - March 25th 1863 - Was relieved from duty in the Hospital. This morn had breakfast of Baked potatoes & Beef steak. Went to bed & slept until one P.M. Then took a walk of far as Divisions H. Quarters to see Corps. Went to bed at sundown but was called up at 7 1/2 P. M. to pay out Millett. He died about 7-40 P.M.

Thursday - March 26th 1863 - It rained nearly all night but this morning it cleared off & the sun has shone very bright all day. Had but very little to do in the way of work. Finished writing my letter to Lute that I commenced on Tuesday. Heard by the papers that our Army were fighting at Vicksburg. All of superfluous baggage through the Army is being turned in.

Friday - March 27th 1863 - Nothing has transpired today of much importance. Apt Surgeon arrived today from Mass. In the evening the guys of Co. E got up a dance & a good time they had of it. The had a banjo & accordian & both were very well played. Rec'd. a letter from Father.

Saturday - March 28th 1863 - Went on duty this morning in the Hospital. Had a very easy time all day. Rec'd. a book though entitled "Prophet In Search Of His Father". It rained all day. A nigger in the 36th New York was accidently shot towards evening. Went to sleep at 10 P.M.

Sunday - March 29th 1863 - Nothing has transpired today. It had been raining most of the time. I wrote a letter to Father in the afternoon. In the evening had a good time singing with Dr J. C. Clark & J. H. Hendrick. Retired at 9 1/2 P.M.

Monday - March 30th 1863 - This morning there was not a cloud to be seen. The sun shone very bright all day. Our Brigade were ordered out to drill in the afternoon. Went over to see them perform & then visited my uncle's in the 37th Regt.

Tuesday - March 31st 1863 - It has been snowing all night long. This evening the snow is four inches deep & commenced raining at daylight. In the afternoon slept. All the snow is gone now & the propect is fair weather tomorrow. —Whiskey punch before going to bed.

Wednesday - April 1st 1863 - The day passed off quite pleasantly. Several good jokes have been perpretrated in honor of the day. Wind is very high. Felt rather lonesome. Thought a good deal of old times, especially of one year ago when my Bro. was with me.

Thursday - April 2nd 1863 - April 2nd has been a day long remembered by me. It had been pleasant & very warm. Fast Day for Mass. Soldiers Division drill in the afternoon. Rec'd. two letters from Westbrook. Retired at 9 o'clk P.M.

Friday - April 3rd 1863 - After eating a hearty Breakfast of Beefsteak, I went in the Hospital to attend to the sick. At 11 A.M. I went over to see Gen. Hooker review our Corps. He attended by his staff & a brilliant affair it was. After coming back I wrote a letter to H.

R. Graves of Hatfield. F. Cooper was admitted to the Hospital sick with fever.

Saturday - April 4th 1863 - Came off duty in the Hospital this morning. Had Beans for breakfast. The day has been very cold & blustering. Done as little as possible in the way of work. Read Gen. McClellen's report of the campaign of the Army of the Potomac from Harrison's Landing until after the fight at Antietam.

Sunday - April 5th 1863 - I found on getting up this morning that the ground was covered with snow, some 4 inches. It has been very disagreeable under foot all day. Cleared off at 3 P.M. Wrote a letter to Father. Rec'd. a paper from North Adams. No news.

Monday - April 6th 1863 - The President arrived at General Hookers H. Quarters this morning. He reviewed all of our Cavalry (25,000) about two miles from our camp. I went up to Division Headquarters & staid until 2 P.M. This day has been very pleasant. Retired at 9 1/2 P.M.

Tuesday - April 7th 1863 - It was reported that the President was to review our Army Corps today. We were ordered out at 8 A.M. for that purpose, but the order was countermanded on account of mud. It having rained all last night. I went in the woods chopping. Our Regts were reviewed by Brig. Gen Devens. B tent burnt.

Wednesday - April 8th 1863 - I was on duty this morning in the Hospital, but as the big review of 4 Army Corps was to take place, I was excused & started for the grounds. I saw the President. This lady Sickles Lieut. Gen. Hooker, Couch, Birny, Bessy, Meade French & many others. Set up all night.

Thursday - April 9th 1863 - All the artillery of the Army of the Potomac have to be reviewed today. It is very pleasant. I had a game of ball & enjoyed myself pretty well. Rec'd. a letter from Father. Expected one from a dear friend, but was disappointed. Retired at 9 A.M.

Friday - April 10th 1863 - Our Regt had to be reviewed today & all answer to their names. The object as to find out how many men we can muster. I went in the afternoon with friend Mason & Hendrick down to the river. Had a very nice time - saw the old battle ground & a lot of Rebels - arrived in camp pretty tired. Lucys Birthday.

Saturday - April 11th 1863 - Went in the woods, in the forenoon choping - got two loads. In the afternoon our Division was reviewed by a Spanish General. It has been very pleasant - the roads are dry & hard & I expect to hear the order, pack up & march before long.

Sunday - April 12th 1863 - Wrote a letter to Father. Our Regt have gone on a three day picket - very warm & pleasant. Think they (illegible).

Monday - April 13th 1863 - Went on duty in the Hospt this morning. Wrote a leter to my Lucy, also one to (illegible) and a letter of Introduction for him to Regt. Recd orders to be ready to march at a moments notice. All of our Cavalry have gone & our forces from the landing are coming up to the front. Silver Set to Lucy cost $40.00.

Tuesday - April 14th 1863 - Eight days rations were given out to the different Regts & all surplus baggage sent away. Prepared myself as well as I could fer the coming struggle & then had a good game of Ball. Commenced raining at dusk & rained all night.

Wednesday - April 15th 1863 - Did not get up until 10 A.M. as it was raining as hard as it could pour - done but a little work. Staid in my tent except to eat my meals. Cleared off about 1 P.M. Fear this rain will retard our contemplated Co. move.

Thursday - April 16th 1863 - The sun is shinning very nicely this morning. All is bustle & reports are flying about in camp in reference to our marching. Two men from our Regt. have been discharged from service & 9 in the 37th Mass. My uncle being one of them - did not see him.

Friday - April 17th 1863 - The rain of Monday has set our marching back. The order is countermanded fer the present, although we are to have eight days rations on hand. Have been busy making a badge in accordance with orders from Head Quarters. Played Muggins.

Saturday - April 18th 1863 - At 9 A.M. Co. E. & K. had a game of Ball. Co. E. proving victorious. Tally 20 -11. In the afternoon Co. F. challenged the Victory. The game commenced at 2 P.M. Co. C. again victorious. Tally 19 -11. The day has been very pleasant. Have recd no letters the last week - some thing to pay, I fear.

Sunday - April 19th 1863 - Was attendant in the Hospt. today. Have three sick. It has been very warm. We had preaching in the afternoon for the first time in four months by a Gentleman from Mass. No letter from home & I feel rather discouraged. Rather poor nights sleep.

Monday - April 20th 1863 - Commenced raining pretty early, but held up at 8 A.M. The 35th New York challenged our boys to a game of Ball. Playing commenced at 9 A.M. In nine innings each party made 18 tallys - It rained most of the time & the ground was very slippery.

Tuesday - April 21st 1863 - It has been very cold & uncomfortable all day. In the forenoon went after a load of wood fer the Hospital. Hear that we are to march tomorrow. The pontoons are to be laid across the River tonight. They all started at sundown from Hiyer camp.

Wednesday - April 22nd 1863 - It was cloudy this morning with signs of Rain. At 8 A.M. it cleared off & another game commenced between the 36th N. York & the 10th. The game closed in favor of the 10th. Tallys - 9 for the 10th & 8 for the 36th. Everything passed off pleasantly. Commenced raining at 9 P.M.

Thursday - April 23rd 1863 - Rained all day so I kept quiet. Wrote in my Diary of last year, in the forenoon. Staid in my bunk nearly all afternoon. Expected letters but was disappointed.

Friday - April 24th 1863 - Went in the Hospital this morning. Read a book called Onyx Stone. Recd a letter from Father & one from Lucy. All well, the paymaster came to H. Q. this afternoon & began to pay off this troop.

Saturday - April 25th 1863 - Was relieved from duty in the hospital. Wrote a letter to Lucy. Then had a nap this P.M. The weather is splendid. W. M. Mason received his furlough & started for home this morning.

Sunday - April 26th 1863 - The paymaster arrived at our Col. Headquarters & commenced paying off our Regt. paid five companies. I wrote a letter to Father. In the afternoon we had a Brigade Dress Parade. The 2nd one since we have been in the service

Monday - April 27th 1863 - Took my turn in the Hospt. this afternoon. I recd my pay 82 dollars, settled up all my accounts & sent to I. F. Hurd 40 dollars by Rev. Mr <u>Souruse</u> (?) of Shelburne Falls. Orders came to send off our sick in the morning General Hospital.

Tuesday - April 28th 1863 - Our sick were all sent off at 6 A.M. in Ambulances to Potomac Creek. I went to Corps & then the H Q of the Army fer a pass to Washington fer our Lieut Col. & Mr. Loomis. Rode the Doctors Horse. Orders to March at 3 P.M. Left our old camp & marched to the River. [<u>Memoranda</u> from the rear of this diary written at a later date: <u>April 28th</u> We left our Camp of the past winter fer a summer camp. The day has been quite rainy. We marched within one mile of the river & encamped fer the night.]

Wednesday - April 29th 1863 - The day is cloudy, very misty, with rain. Up at 4 1/2. Started for Battle at 7 - Gen Russells Brigade crossed the river at the same place of Dec 17 at 1/2, Gen Reynold Corps crossed one mile below at 10 A.M., fighting all the time, while moving. It has rained nearly all day & this evening it fairly pours. But little fighting has been done today. Our troops are in position ready fer attack - rained - go to bed at dusk by Gen. Hooker. [<u>Memoranda</u> from the rear of this diary which was written at a later date: At 3 oclock morning of the 29th our army commenced laying pontoons. The Rebels were taken by surprise & we met with little resistance. Gen Russells Brigade crossed at 8 1/2 A.M. Got in position awaiting the movements of other parts of the army. Gen. Reynolds Corps crossed at 10 A.M. one mile farther down the river. Considerable firing from our men & artillery. Slackened up at 11 A.M. Gen. Butterfield (Chief of Hookers staff) with Gen. Fogliardi & just passed down the lines at 11 A.M.]

Thursday - April 30th 1863 - Orders came at four A.M. to be ready in 3/4 of an hour fer marching, but on account of rain, we did not go, at 9 A.M. it looked some like fair weather. Orders come at 10. Then an order was recd from Gen Hooker saying in consequence of the success of our army in the past three days we had got the Rebels so they would have to fight upon our ground. Great enthusiasm prevails among the soldiers. Cannonading commenced at 6 P.M. through the evening & lasted 2 hours. No damage done. [Memoranda from the rear of this diary which was written at a later date: At daybreak of the 30th we were ordered to move, but as no demonstration was made, we remained in readiness. Our forces advanced from their position on the other side. Heavy cannonading commenced at 6 P.M. from the Rebels, our artillery replied, several excellent shots were made on both sides.]

  Friday - May 1st 1863 - (Battle of Chancellorsville, Virginia) - It is a fine morning. All last night rations were dealt out to our troops Artillery moving & C. Heavy firing has been heard all day in the Rebels rear & large forces of enemy have been on the move over the mountain. Orders to march at 1/2 A.M. Went across the road & halted fer half an hour. Great cheering was heard from our troops on the other side of the river. After marching awhile we went back to camp at 11 1/2 P.M. [Memoranda from the rear of this diary which was written at a later date: May 1st, Friday, was very splendid. Firing has been heard all day. Reported that our forces are At Gordonsville & are driving the enemy. No firing from the enemy opposite our corps.]

  Saturday - May 2nd 1863 - I was up at 4 1/2 A.M. orders to pack up & ferm in Line of Battle, at 7 A.M. The ball opened with the enemy attacking us at 7 1/2. We marched down to the left where the Pontoons were laid & rested under a hill until 3 1/2 P.M. We then went back to our camp of the morning & staid until near dusk. Orders came again to pack up as the enemy were skirmishing. Went across the river at 10 P.M. [Memoranda from the rear of this diary written at a later date: Today Saturday we marched & countermarched nearly all day. Crossed the River at 10 oclock in the evening. Heard that Gen. Hooker had driven the enemy, & so our Gen. Sedgwick made preparations to carry the Heights. Heavy cannonading commenced on the right at 10 1/2 PM & lasted 1 1/2 hours. We started on our march at 12 (midnight) & marched all night long, got the distance of one mile from where we started from, in direct route, but travelled 12 mile. All strategy I suppose.]

Continuing with Colonel Joseph B. Parson's address delivered April 3, 1901:

"Sunday, May 3d, occurred the battle of Salem Heights, in which the regiment suffered severely. It lost in killed and wounded 66. Among the number were three officers. On Saturday, June 3d, the Tenth regiment recrossed the river from Fredericksburg to Falmuth, and was the last regiment of the army before it was taken up to cross upon the pontoon bridge."

Sunday - May 3rd 1863 - Marched & countermarched nearly all night long, got no sleep. In the morning found us at Fredericksburg under the Batteries of the Rebels. They opened fire on us as light. No damage done, until 11 A.M. when our Brigade made a charge & carried the Height; capturing lrg cannon & some 500 prisoners. The 7th lost 50 in wounded. The 36th & our Regt lost 100. The fire was very severe. Worked hard all night. [Memoranda from the rear of this diary which was written at a later date: At daylight of Sunday the 3rd we were attacked & I went by the Doctors orders to look fer a place fer the wounded - found one in the Bank of the River. No damage done until 10 A.M., although there was very heavy firing all the time. The 7th Mass & 2nd R. Island supporting Batteries & the 37th Mass acting as reserve carried the Heights, capturing lots of (illegible), 6 cannon, == loss in killed & wounded about 800. Worked very hard all day in dressing the wounds of the sufferers. Our Corps advanced five mile & there met the enemy - a hard fight ensued. Our Regt lost two in killed, wounded, missing. I came up with the Regt at 11 P.M. all tired out. Got our wounded aboard Ambulances fer Fredericksburg.]

Monday - May 4th 1863 - I started fer my Regt last night & arrived at Midnight. They were five mile from Fredericksburg. Our Regt. had a terrible fight yesterday & so did our whole corps. We were outnumbered by the enemy in the afternoon & nearly taken prisoner, but by snit (?) of good luck, we got out of the scrape. Arrived at Banks Ford & drew up in a line, ready for a fight with secesh. [Memoranda from the rear of this diary written at a later date: On Monday morning our Corps were all in line of Battle all day, at (illegible) the Rebels flanked us, & came over cutting us off. It was the most exciting time I ever was in, yet I had no fears about myself.

It is reported that we are defeated because the 11th Army Corps failed in doing their duty. They having run at the first firing, but can't believe it. I think we have worsted the enemy, at least I know that our Corps have. <u>We are going back to our old Camp & so ends Hookers first Campaign.</u>]

Tuesday - May 5th 1863 - Crossed the River at Banks Ford (2 A.M.) A good many of the stragglers were left behind & they have been swimming the River all day. Some were taken prisoner. Although we had a hard fight & a pretty narrow escape of it we came off beat. 4 men from the 57th & five from the 7th, died suddenly of exhaustion last night. Rumors are afloat of every kind. Things look dubious. Raining very hard.

Wednesday - May 6th 1863 - We are encamped about one mile from Banks Ford. It has rained all day & it is very cold. The boys are pretty well tired out & a few sick. Gen Hooker has retreated from the other side of the River & I suppose we have suffered another defeat. I hope & pray it is not so. The 11th Corps, broke & run & fer this reason Hooker has failed in his plans. It is to bad.

Thursday - May 7th 1863 - It has been raining all day & I have done but very little except to eat & drink & give out medicine to the sick. Reports are flying around in camp about Hooker being defeated, yet I dont believe it, although every thing goes to show different, as his troops are all marching back to their old camp. Oh dear what is to pay.

Friday - May 8th 1863 - We left Banks Ford this morning at 8 oclock, marched until 2 P.M. when we halted & went into Camp, one mile farther down the River from our old camp of last Winter. Put up a Hospital Tent & then went to my own bunk. It commenced raining at sundown. A letter from L - F home.

Saturday - May 9th 1863 - It is very pleasant day. I have been to work nearly all the time at our tents & policing the ground & getting things in shape. Commenced writing a letter to Lucy. Recd letter from Home. Bought a paper & read that we done better than Burnside.

Sunday - May 10th 1863 - Done some work this morning

about the Hospital. It is very warm & uncomfortable yet I have to keep around; Had a nap in the afternoon. We had preaching at 3 P.M. I did not go as I felt very unwell. I have got an attack of Chronic Dysentary, took some medicine & then went to bed.

Monday - May 11th 1863 - Didnot feel much better this morning, yet I have been at work all day, policing our grounds, fixing beds in Hospital. It is very warm. Recd a paper from No. Adams. Had another nap this P.M. Bought a Washington Chronicle but read no news. All quiet along the lines.

Tuesday - May 12th 1863 - We finished cleaning up our Hospital grounds this morning. It has been a hard & nasty job. I wrote a letter to Father. It has been another very warm day. Went to Division Sutlers - bought a (illegible). There has been no mail today.

Wednesday - May 13th 1863 - Done but a very little of anything today. From the papers I learn that Stonewall Jackson died last Sunday. There is a scruff around Camp that Halleck has taken command of the Army of the Potomac, & that we shall soon be on the move again.

Thursday - May 14th 1863 - Nothing stirring in Camp - everything is quiet as can be. Had a very hard shower in the afternoon accompanied with thunder. Feel very unwell.

Friday - May 15th 1863 - The day has passed the same as yesterday with the exception of rain - I expected letters from Friends, but was sadly disappointed. Our Surgeon Col Chamberlain has resigned & will leave soon to occupy a higher position.

Saturday - May 16th 1863 - The Adut. Surg. A. B. Robinson gave orders to fix up the Hospital - make a fence of Cedar boughs & C. Have been at work all day doing my best to please this man. I fear we shall not stay to enjoy the work. Heavy cannon are being planted on the heights about Fredericksburg.

Sunday - May 17th 1863 - I helped police our Hospital grounds & there staid in my bunk. It was very warm. In the afternoon I received a visit from friend Charles Barker of So. Adams now in the 9th New York. Recd a letter from my friend Lucy.

Monday - May 18th 1863 - Went on duty in the Hospital this morning. Have three sick. I wrote three letters today, one to Lucy, one to Father, one to I. F. Hurd.

Tuesday - May 19th 1863 - Our Regt are detailed to go on Picket. Hayward & myself had to go too. We went five mile from Camp to the rear of our picket line is in our old Camp of last Dec. We had our quarters in an orchard near a large house - everything looks pleasant & I mite expect a nice time.

Wednesday - May 20th 1863 - Didnot sleep very well as there were so many <u>Bugs</u> crawling around. Had some Bread & Milk fer Breakfast. Milk cost 30 cents per quart. Bought 4 eggs & had Ham & Eggs fer supper. It is very warm. Our Boys went on the Picket post this evening.

Thursday - May 21st 1863 - Hayward went in Camp this morning fer a supply of food. He got back at 3 P.M. bringing some Whiskey, Oysters & C. I bought some milk & had some <u>oyster stew</u> fer supper. It has been very (illegible) the house & near us is inhabited by about 2 dozen niggers all near the age of 60.

Friday - May 22nd 1863 - Had a very comfortable night - got up at 5 OClock, packed up - ready to go back to Camp - Started at 11 oclock. It was the hardest March I ever had. I was wet through with sweat. Found on getting into Camp - everything packed up ready to leave.

Saturday - May 23rd 1863 - We moved our camp 1/2 mile. Worked very hard until noon. Had a blow up with Col Parsons, and was relieved from duty in the Hospital. I expected orders to report to my company but they did not come.

Sunday - May 24th 1863 - Done nothing today. In the afternoon had a talk with the Dr. & then Col. Parson. Was told to stay at the Hospt. Had a perfect understanding all around. Went to see Tip Coop at H.Q in the evening. He came near being killed by some of the Battery Boys Saturday night.

Monday - May 25th 1863 - Worked very hard all day cleaning up the grounds around the Hospital. Gen. Newton & our Col

Eustis visited the Hospital today. It is rather cold & wet. Think we shall (have) some rain. Official Despatches from Grant came to H. Quarters of the capture of <u>Vicksburg</u>. Went to bed feeling unwell.

Tuesday - May 26th 1863 - Did not sleep but a very little. Had a <u>chill</u> & then a severe headache all day long - with a good deal of fever. Dr. Giilman prescribed fer me & Mr Lane tended to my wants. Felt better at night.

Wednesday - May 27th 1863 - Rested pretty well through the night. Feel better this morning. Took medicine all day. Mr Maders has been detailed to Potomac Creek so we are short another nurse.

Thursday - May 28th 1863 - I went on duty in the Hospital as there was to much to do out of doors. Wrote a letter to Father. Heard that a certain young Widow had given birth to a fine <u>bouncing boy</u>.

Friday - May 29th 1863 - Done nothing to day as I felt pretty miserable. Had some greens for supper. Bought a paper - hear that Grant is doing well - near Vicksburg.

Saturday - May 30th 1863 - Went to work this morning cleaning up. Worked hard all day - at night was taken sick again with Fever & Chills. Had a hard time of it. Mr Lane took care of me.

Sunday - May 31st 1863 - I felt no better this morning. Had a very severe headache. Took a dose of Salts & Quinine. Felt better towards night. Recd a letter from my friend Lucy that made my heart rejoice-

Monday - June 1st 1863 - After eating a slight meal I took short walk. Found I was very weak - took several doses of drugs during the day. Wrote a letter to my Lucy - Read a Transcript & letter from I. F. Hurd, with a receipt fer money.

Tuesday - June 2nd 1863 - I remained in my bunk nearly all day - feeling very weak & indisposed - occupied myself in reading various books & the wind has blown very hard all day & now at dusk it looks very much like rain.

Wednesday - June 3rd 1863 - Did not feel much better this

morning yet decided I would go to work thinking I would feel better. Have four sick to look after. It had been quite cool with some rain. Recd in the afternoon a letter from my cousin Kate of Pittsfield.

Colonel Parsons continued his narrative of the Tenth Regiment: *"It started Sunday night, June 4th, and brought up at Gettysburg July 2, 1863, where the second division, to which the Tenth belonged, was ordered into battle about 4 o'clock in the afternoon at Little Round Top."*

Thursday - June 4th 1863 - It has rained some today. Dr. Robinsons wife came to Camp today & visited the Hospital. Recd a letter & 4 books from New York. No news, although it is expected we shall move soon.

Friday - June 5th 1863 - Staid in my bunk nearly all day reading, orders came to be ready to March at 1 P.M. The 2nd Division in our Corps have gone down to the River. They crossed at 5 P.M. Very heavy cannonading fer 2 hours. Took 200 prisoners. 8 days rations dealt out.

Saturday - June 6th 1863 - Recd orders to march at 10 A.M. Marched to the River at Franklin Crossing. It is very warm. Heavy showers in the afternoon. Gen Shaters Brigade in our Division, were ordered over the River In Picket. It is expected that the enemy will attack us & try to drive us in the River. I have no blankets fer night. [Memoranda from the rear of this diary written at a later date: Saturday - June 6th - We the 6th Corps broke Camp & crossed the river at Franklins Crossing. Remained over there 8 days under fire nearly everyday. One man wounded from Co. G while on picket. Recrossed the River on Saturday evening. Found that our Army were moving towards the old Bull Run battle ground. We marched Sunday morning & arrived at Stafford C. House at 12 N. Bivoucked until 10 PM marched all night & at noon of Monday arrived at Dumfries. Bivoucked until 2 AM of Tuesday & then started again, arrived at Fairfax Station. Staid there until Thursday morning marched to the C. House. Rebel prisoners were brought in also wounded men from the front. A Cavalry fight took place near Aldie & Snickers Gap.]

Sunday - June 7th 1863 - No alarm through the night

although the enemy were pretty bold. No excitement through the day. The Rebels have been busy digging Rifle pits & building Redoubts fer cannon. At 5 P.M. our artillery opened fire & drove the Rebels away (from) a position they had - Fine sight.

Monday - June 8th 1863 - Our Brigade went over the River last night & dug Rifle Pits 1 1/2 mile long - 3 feet wide & 3 feet deep. We have an excellent position to defend. The enemy are strongly fortified & with great strength. Went in swimming this A.M. Firing by our artillery commenced at 5 1/2 P.M. Lasted 15 minutes. Rebel sharpshooters are very busy.

Tuesday - June 9th 1863 - (Battle of Brandy Station) - Our sharpshooters went over the River last night & today they have been popping nearly all the time doing good execution. The Rebels opened with their Artillery at 5 P.M. throwing spherical case promiscuously amongst us - wounded one of Co. G. named Whitmore - slight fire was returned - our Bands played until 10 P.M.

Wednesday - June 10th 1863 - The night passed very quietly, but this morning the sharpshooters commenced again & have been firing all day. Orders to pack up at 5 P.M. & go on picket over the River. The Rebels are very near us - Parker from Co. G. was wounded through both thighs, while going to his post - one sharpshooter of ours killed.

Thursday - June 11th 1863 - Was relieved from picket at 8 A.M. The Sharpshooters let us have it pretty hot - but no one wounded. The place is very well fertified. We are stationed near the Rifle Pits - orders came to pack up & be ready to fall back at any time in case the enemy opened on us with his artillery. They did not do it & so we staid all night.

Friday - June 12th 1863 - 40 of Berdoms Sharpshooters came over last night. Rifle pits were dug fer them & this morning they are giving the Rebels jessie. We have been on the left all day occupying the pits & supporting a Battery. The Rebels opened on us at 5 1/2 P.M. & our siege guns on the opposite side of the River replied. The wind blows hard & looks like rain.

Saturday - June 13th 1863 - The Regt. came in from the Pits

at 3 1/2 A.M. Had my breakfast out of the way at daylight. The Rebs opened on us with their guns at 4 P.M. making some splendid shots. Our artillery replied, but a severe shower put an end to that contest. Orders to retreat at 9 P.M. our Regt. were rear guard. Wrote a letter to Lucy.

Sunday - June 14th 1863 - Laid down to rest at midnight - our pickets are all safe, although the Reb Cavalry followed us pretty close - up at daylight & on the march fer Dumfrees - 5 mile from here on the Road to Washington. Saw Old Joe but would give more to see little <u>Mac</u> and a thousand like him. Halted at Stafford until 10 P.M. - 11 mile.

Monday - June 15th 1863 - Marched all night long - but very slowly as the artillery took up the road - crossed over the three streams of considerable depth - arrived at Dumfries at 11 1/2 A.M. We went over the road as if we had been sent for, since daylight. Rations given out for three days. Report says we are to march at 4 1/2 P.M. for Fairfax C.H. Dont believe it as we are all tired out - not having had any sleep fer nearly 3 days.

Tuesday - June 16th 1863 - We were ordered to march at 1 A.M. this morning. Marched 17 mile and crossed Occoquan Creek at 12 M. Rested two hours & started fer Fairfax Station - arrived there at 6 P.M. Marched 23 mile. Hear the Rebels are all over & through Maryland & into Penn. Ordered to march fer Alexandria at Midnight.

Wednesday - June 17th 1863 - Orders to march countermanded. Remained in the woods all day. Had rations fer two days given out to us. It is very warm & we ate all tired out. Bought a Beef tongue & cooked it for a march - Nothing very exciting in the way of news. The 36th N. York Regt. were put under arrest for laying down their arms.

Thursday - June 18th 1863 - We started this morning at 6 oclock on our march. Passed through Fairfax C.H & encamped about 2 mile on the road towards Germantown. Marched 6 mile. The 36th N. York was returned to duty. Rebel prisoners were brought in from <u>Snickers Gap</u> or <u>Aldie</u>. Report says our forces are victorious & are marching on.

Friday - June 19th 1863 - Received a letter from Home this morning - after eating breakfast, I wrote a letter to Lucy. We were ordered to pack up at 3 P.M. but at 4 the order was countermanded & we had a general inspection. Can't hear anything about the Rebels - where they are or what they are doing - Raining.

Saturday - June 20th 1863 - It rained very hard all night & I got wet through & was very chilly - orders came to reduce our Hospital stores & all our goods. Recd letters from my very dear Lucy. This morning one Division of our Corps has moved to the point, today nothing exciting is on going on & we remain inactive - Rain.

Sunday - June 21st 1863 - At 7 oclock this morning cannonading commenced at the front & has kept up all day. Report says our Cavalry drove the enemy 8 mile capturing a lot (of) prisoners. Troops have been passing all day going to the front, one corps still remain at Fairfax C.H. Recd a paper from Adams - One year from today our time will be out.

Monday - June 22nd 1863 - We moved our camp this morning a few rods to a better locality. I wrote a letter to my friend Lucy, in the afternoon cannonading commenced about 3 P.M. in our front but didnot last long. New report is that our Division or Corps will stay here in place of the 8th Corps.

Tuesday - June 23rd 1863 - A detail of 100 men was made from our Regt this morning to guard a train of cars loaded with rations to Gainesville for the 2nd Army Corps. They returned at dusk having seen nothing, but a couple of Quaker Guns. A (illegible) from Co. A. was arrested & dismissed from Service this forenoon. Pleasant day.

Wednesday - June 24th 1863 - Felt very unwell this morning & eat but little. We recd orders to pack up & march at one P.M. Marched at 2 & arrived at Centreville - distance six mile, at five oclock saw a good many Rifle pits thrown up by the Rebels & here at Centreville, there are 6 ferts. We have a fine view - our camp being on the hill back of the village. Letter from home.

Thursday - June 25th 1863 - After eating breakfast I went 1/2 mile & had a good swim - then wrote a letter to Father. After dinner orders came to change our camp. We moved in our old Camp formerly used by the 126th N. York. They moving to Gum Swamp - Reported that we move tomorrow. Raining.

Friday - June 26th 1863 - Last night the Rebs made a Raid on Fairfax Station capturing several car loads of ammunitions. We recd orders to pack up at 8 this morning - but did not march until 9. Passed Broad Run at 12 (noon) passed Hermon & crossed the R.R. at 3 & arrived at Drainsville at 6 P.M. We marched in all 22 mile. Rations delivered.

Saturday - June 27th 1863 - Broke Camp at Drainsville at 4 1/2 AM - worked our way towards Edward Ferry on the Potomac - we arrived there at 11 A.M. but didnt cross the river until 2 P.M. Found that our whole Army had crossed here during the past two days. Two Pontoon Bridges were laid down - hear Lee crossed with his Army yesterday morning at Williamsport.

Sunday - June 28th 1863 - Hooker relieved from the Command. Started from near Poolerville at 4 A.M. passed through the Village at 5 & through Barnsville at 9. Halted for 2 hours & near took the road to Frederick - turned off the road to that place fer New Market - passed through Hyattsville & halted 4 mile from the village at 5 P.M. - 25 mile.

Monday - June 29th 1863 - Our Regt. detailed as rear guard. The line commenced to move at 4 1/2 A.M. but we did not get underway until 10 A.M. Passed through Monrovia, New Market, Ritzville, Mt Pleasant & halted at Hams Creek at 1 1/2 A.M. having marched 27 miles. I never was so tired in my life. My feet are very sore. I am near played out.

Tuesday - June 30th 1863 - Line was formed at 7 1/2 A.M. & we started for Westminister where we arrived at 11 A.M. Report says 20,000 rebels passed through this place last evening. Our advance guard captured, in the morning, several officers that were eating. We then took our way towards Manchester, halted within 2 miles of the town fer the night - 17 miles.

The regiment had been marching to Gettysburg and on the move since June 3rd!
Colonel Parsons continued: *"The Sixth Corps, to*

which this regiment belonged, was placed on the reserve next day and was ordered from point to point as the necessity of the case required. After Pickett's Charge, the Sixth Corps was brought to the front, and the Tenth Regiment was detailed for picket duty."

Wednesday & Thursday - July 1st & 2nd 1863 - (Battle of Gettysburg) - We remained in our camp all day - Heavy firing had been heard most of the afternoon in Pennsylvania. Our baggage train are burnt by the Rebels thus checking one advance but our men have nearly rebuilt. Wrote 3 letters - orders to march at 8 P.M. Marched all night & all the (illegible) distance 35 mile arrived at Gettysville at 2 P.M. The Rebs are in big force - fighting all day yesterday. Gen Reynolds of the 1st Corps was killed. Cannonading commenced at 4 P.M. Our men yesterday drove them 2 mile - The enemy advanced & our corps went to the front - terrible battle.

Friday - July 3rd 1863 - (Battle of Gettysburg) - Longstreet wounded & prisoner & firing commenced at daylight (illegible) of musketry & artillery & was kept up all day our <u>Brigade</u> was held as in Reserve. Have had to march from one end of the line to the other one. The double quick 4 or 5 times. We were in heavy artillery fire several times. One man wounded in our Regt. Brigade lost - nearly 40 - Our forces have gained a great victory - capturing 1500 men.

According to Colonel Parsons summary, "About 3 o'clock in the morning on the 4th a sergeant and six men from the Twenty-second Virginia approached the line. They were halted and ordered to advance . . . they wished to give themselves up as prisoners and desired good treatment. I interviewed the sergeant and was informed by him that the Confederate Army had all withdrawn . . . . After verification they were sent to headquarters and advised they had given true information voluntarily . . ."

"On July 5th we started about noon to follow up the retreating army. Dead men, dead horses, guns, equipments, caissons, shot and shell, and all the paraphernalia of the battlefield scattered and

shattered in wild profusion. Every barn on the line of march was filled to overflowing with rebel wounded, the dying and the dead. A large group of tents to the right was visited by my surgeon and he informed me that there were over 8000 wounded men in those tents. Everything along the route showed conclusively that the enemy had been badly whipped and that they were retreating as fast as possible."

Saturday & Sunday - July 4th & 5th 1863 - This morning our Brigade went to the front. The enemy has fallen back & nothing but skirmishing is going on advancing our lines all along during the day. Rebel wounded have been brought in & the dead are being buried. A very hard shower at 3 P.M. Regt went on Picket at night. Stept on a rebel & was as wet & cold as could be. Our lines advanced but no rebels could be found. We were relieved from picket in the morning & returned (illegible).

Monday - July 6th 1863 - Up at 3 A.M. The rebels are in full retreat 1/2 mile from our advance. We captured part of their train. (illegible).

Tuesday - July 7th 1863 - Illegible

Wednesday - July 8th 1863 - Illegible

Thursday - July 9th 1863 - Left Middletown at 6 A.M. Marched through Poolivar at 10 A.M. through the South Mountain Gap at 11. Cannonading is heard at the front. Our Cavalry is hard at work at the enemy's rear. A few wounded have been brought in. We encamped fer the night at Boonsboro. Went in swimming.

Friday - July 10th 1863 - Started this morning for the front to support our Cavalry. Skirmishing has been going on all day & we drove the enemy about 2 mile, but 5 wounded in the Cavalry. Had a good supper of boiled chicken & crackers. Went to bed at 8 P.M.

Saturday - July 11th 1863 - Remained in our forest position all day. Everything is quiet, but very little firing has been going on. I recd a letter from I. F. Hurd & wrote a letter to my friend Lucy.

Sunday - July 12th 1863 - We left our position & marched to the front as the Rebels have fallen back. Some three mile - passed through Funkstown at 9 A.M. found the enemy in force 1 mile from town. Our forces are in line of Battle ready for any emergency. The 10th all in front.

Colonel Parsons continued, *"We dallied along day after day and arrived in Williamsport Monday, July 13th, and there threw up rifle pits. Upon the arrival of Gen. Meade he called a council of war of his corps generals, of which Gen. Sedgwick was one, thought it best to wait until the next day, and then throw out a heavy reconnaissance and feel the enemy. While these officers were in deliberation the enemy including its 25 miles of wagon trains loaded with their wounded, were crossing the river, and the next day . . . about 10 in the morning, the rebel army had entirely disappeared. Gen. Meade had lost the opportunity of destroying Lee's Army and thus being the greatest general of the war."*

Monday - July 13th 1863 - It has been raining quite hard. Reinforcements have come from Newburn (?) & Ft. Monroe - We have thrown up Breastworks & are now all fixed fer a fight, our Brigade had a skirmish & lost some men.

Tuesday - July 14th 1863 - This morning found the enemy falling back & our Division were ordered to reconnoiter in front - Found that the Rebels had left - our Cavalry captured near 2000 of their rear guard. We arrived at Williamsport about 3 P.M. & halted fer the night.

Wednesday - July 15th 1863 - We were on the March at 3 A.M. bound fer Boonsboro on the way to Berlin. It was very warm & I came the nearest being played out that I have since I have been in the service. Distance 14 mile - News of the surrender of Port Hudson - & 18,000 prisoners.

Thursday - July 16th 1863 - We left Boonsboro at 4 oclock this morning & got to Berlin at 12 noon. We are awaiting the

Pontoons. Have recd a supply of clothing & rations sufficient fer the next three months. My feet are in a bad condition.

 Friday - July 17th 1863 - It has rained most of the day & as there has been no movement I have staid in my bunk most of the day. I read (illegible) & hear our country (illegible) making (illegible) May & June.

 Saturday - July 18th 1863 - Recd a letter from Home & I. F. Hurd. No movement today by our Corps, although it was reported that we should move at 5 P.M. I hear that our army is crossing into Virginia & that our Cavalry hold all the passes in the South Mountains. Wrote a letter to Father this A.M. Feel well rested.

 Sunday - July 19th 1863 - We were ordered to pack up & march at 7 A.M. We crossed the River at Berlin, MD at 9 A.M. passed through Lovettsville & Wheatland, - encamped fer the night one mile from the latter place. A large barn was set on Fire & a splendid sight it was at 9 PM.

 Monday - July 20th 1863 - Left our camp near Wheatland at 10 A.M. passed through Parcellville at 1 P.M. - eat dinner at 2 then marched fer Aldies Crossroads - where we arrived at 7 P M after crossing two branches of Goose Creek. Reported that Charlestown is ours.

 Tuesday - July 21st 1863 - Wrote two letters this morning one to Lucius & Hurd & one to Lucy - We remained in our Camp all day. It is very warm & I have kept myself under the shade trees most of the time. Hear that the draft has taken many of my friends. 9 officers from our Regt. started for home this A.M.

 Wednesday - July 22nd 1863 - Wrote a letter to Father this A.M. We had orders to pack up & march at 1 P.M. Passed through Union at 3 & halted fer the night some 4 miles beyond. It is very warm. Reported that Ft. Darling is in our possession.

 Thursday - July 23rd 1863 - We marched this morning from Upperville to Rectorstown. We put up our tents, but at one were ordered to pack up again. Marched fer Barbies Cross. We passed through Salbin on the Manassis Gap RR at 3 P.M. At 11 oclock P.M.

we turned in fer the night all tired out.

Friday - July 24th 1863 - Up this morning at 3 A.M. packed up & started on our march fer Manassis Gap as the enemy were in force here yesterday & our men had a brush with them, driving them some distance. We arrived there at 11 A.M. At one P.M. we retraced our steps passing Barbies Cross roads to Orleans.

Saturday - July 25th 1863 - We started for Warrenton at 5 A.M. The men are all out of rations & we are pretty well played out. We forage a good deal. I eat dinner of Berries which I found in great abundance. We passed through Orleans & arrived at our destination at 4 P.M. Rations were issued.

Sunday - July 26th 1863 - We remained in our Camp all day. I slept most of the time. Had a hard shower of rain that was very acceptable - took a good wash in the brook close by our camp.

Monday - July 27th 1863 - I started this morning bright & early after berries - get five quarts. Had a good supper & dinner of scouce made from the berries. The boys are bringing in sheep, beef, fresh pork in abundance which they have stolen from the Farmers - 2 papers from home.

Tuesday - July 28th 1863 - We are still in our Camp & report says we shall remain some time. A fight occured between our forces some distance on our right. The 2nd Division have retraced their steps & gone to protect the Gaps of the Blue Ridge.

Wednesday - July 29th 1863 - Nothing stirring in camp. All the boys are out foraging for sheep & Pigs. I wrote a letter to Lucy.

Thursday - July 30th 1863 - Went out this morning after Berries - got 5 quarts. I then wrote a letter to Henry Manchester of Hatfield. The 37th Regt have left us & are ordered to report to New York on a secret expedition I guess.

Friday - July 31st 1863 - Recd a letter from Lucy saying all her upper teeth were extracted. Dear one, I am sorry. Wrote a letter to Colista, also one to her friend Lute. Retired at 8 1/2.

Saturday - August 1st 1863 - It is very warm today. No news of importance from any part of the armies. Wrote a letter to cousin Kate. Reported we are to move our camp tomorrow. Had a Berry pudding which was very nice.

Sunday - August 2nd 1863 - At 8 oclock we recd orders to pack up & move our camp. Have been busy all day. Have been busy all day fixing up our Hospital tent. Never came so near to playing out with the heat as I have today. Had a swim in a brook close by & then retired.

Monday - August 3rd 1863 - This morning I went in the Hospital to care fer the sick ones. Have five to look after, but more very sick. Recd a paper from Adams in the evening. Found 85 men had been exempted from the Draft. Got a letter from I. F. H.

Tuesday - August 4th 1863 - Wrote a letter to I. F. Hurd & one to Father. At 4 P.M. we had a severe storm of wind & rain. The wind blew our tents all down, in fact all the tents in the Division, our sick got wet through & we had a rough time generally. Got the sick in a house.

Wednesday - August 5th 1863 - Have been all day fixing up our Hospt. tent & drying blankets & other things belonging to the Hospt. Hope never to see another such a time. Reported that Brigadier Gen. Terry from Port Hudson takes command of our Division tomorrow.

Thursday - August 6th 1863 - We moved our sick into the Hospt. from the house. I was on duty. We had a fine shower this afternoon. It has been very warm.

Friday - August 7th 1863 - The weather is almost intolerable, went in the evening to see Tip Coop - had a good visit & returned in time to save a good soaking as it commenced raining very hard.

Saturday - August 8th 1863 - Wrote a letter to Henry P. Goodrich, this P.M. No news & no nothing. It is exceedingly warm. Can hardly stand the racket. Put up beds in the Hospt which was very warm work.

Sunday - August 9th 1863 - On duty in Hospt - Have 4 sic all convelescing. Another shower this P.M. Recd a visit from Ti Coop.

Monday - August 10th 1863 - Got a paper from Nort Adams, our sutler arrived in Camp bringing a load of tobacco & othe trash. The boys have been as thick as bees around him.

Tuesday - August 11th 1863 - Wrote a letter to Lucy. Nothin going on - 50 men from our Regt went on picket to be gone 3 days.

Wednesday - August 12th 1863 - Nothing going on.

Thursday - August 13th 1863 - Nothing going on.

Friday - August 14th 1863 - Recd letters from I. F. Hurd & from my friend Kate & Colista. Orders to be ready to March at any time.

Saturday - August 15th 1863 - Everything quiet.

Sunday - August 16th 1863 - Everything remains quiet alon the lines.

Monday - August 17th 1863 - Our Paymaster has arrived & commenced paying off. I recd $76.34 fer my four months pay & las years clothing.

Tuesday - August 18th 1863 - Wrote a letter to I. F. H. & sent him $6.50 also wrote a letter to Father sending him $60.00.

Wednesday - August 19th to Tuesday August 25th 1863 - A quiet along the lines. Nothing to write about.

Wednesday - August 26th 1863 - Went to Corp Headquarters. Gen. Sedgwick was the recipient of a present Hors accoutrements, sword & belt

Thursday - Friday - Saturday - August 27th, 28th & 29th 186 - All quiet.

Sunday -August 30th 1863 - Brigade inspection this A.M. & Brigade Dress Parade this evening.

Monday - August 31 1863 - Received a letter from my Uncle T. Cousins living in Hatfield, Mass.

Tuesday - September 1st 1863 - Wrote a letter to my Uncle Henry Manchester.

Wednesday - September 2nd 1863 - Nothing -

Thursday - September 3rd 1863 - Capt. Ives of Co A. Officer of the Day of Picket Post was taken prisoner at 2 oclock P.M.

Friday - September 4th 1863 Brigade Dress Parade this evening. Recd a letter from A. S. Kellogg at Gettysburg.

Saturday - September 5th 1863 - Recd a letter from my friend Lucy.

Sunday - September 6th 1863 - Wrote letter to Lucy & Kellogg. Recd a paper from Adams.

Monday - September 7th 1863 - A Raid was made inside our lines by Guerrillas this morning about 2 A.M. capturing 26 Cavalry Horses.

Tuesday - September 8th 1863 - Wrote a letter to Father while on duty in the Hospt. Have 5 sick.

Wednesday - September 9th 1863 - Took a walk over to the 3rd Brigade to see my friend Tip Coop. He is on (illegible) in a Sutlers Shop. Had a good time. Recd a letter from E. C. Graves of Florence.

Thursday - September 10th 1863 - On duty in the Hospt. Recd a letter from Wm. Mason at Gettysburg.

Friday - September 11th 1863 - Went to the 3rd Brigade again. Bought a Hatchet & frying pan. A letter from A. S. Kellogg.

Saturday - September 12th 1863 - Had a very severe storm of wind & rain. Our Hospt. tent blew down & we had a rough time generally.

Sunday - September 13th 1863 - Orders to March or be in readiness to march at a moments notice.

Monday - September 14th 1863 - The same orders were given today as regards marching.

Tuesday - September 15th 1863 - Sent our sick off to Alexandria. Otis of Co. I. is very sick & will not live. We left our Camp at 4 P.M. & marched 7 mile to Sulphur Springs. Bivoucked at 7 1/2 P.M.

Wednesday - September 16th 1863 - Started this morning at 5 1/2 A.M. for Stone House Mountain. After a very fatiguing (march) of 20 miles we arrived at our destination at 8 oclock P.M. I was completely played out as I had a very heavy load. The Maj. let me ride on his horse.

Thursday - September 17th 1863 - Up this morning at 4 A.M. & the Regt. stood under Arms until 9 o'clock. We are three miles west of Culpepper C.H. on the road to Staunton. Our pickets are out several mile.

Friday - September 18th 1863 - While going to the wagons I came across my friend Tip Coop & found him very sick. I got the Dr. to see him & then nursed him up a little. Fear he will have a fever. Heard firing all day off on our left front.

Saturday - September 19th 1863 - My friend Tip is no better. Staid with him nearly all day. Our Brigade have moved their camp half a mile & are now in regular line of Batle. Firing heard today - Slept very cold last night.

Sunday - September 20th 1863 - Have been at work all day quite hard on pitching our Hospt. tent & making bunks for the sick. Coop is some better tonight & is glad he has a friend to look after him.

Monday - September 21st 1863 - Admitted 4 men in Hospt. No news to write. Recd a paper from Adams.

Tuesday - September 22nd 1863 - Heavy firing heard in the vicinity of Rapidan. Hear that a large body of Cavalry have gone on a Reconnnaissance. The papers tell of a fight between Rosecrans & Braggs.

Wednesday - September 23rd 1863 - Put a floor in our Hospt tent - Orders to be ready to move. Terrible fighting between Bragg & Rosencrans.

Thursday - September 24th 1863 - Had a picture taken. Orders to be ready to move packed up our baggage at 3 P.M.

Friday - September 25th 1863 - Orders Countermanded for the present. Reports flying in every direction about Marching. The 11th & 12th Corps have gone to reinforce Gen. Rosencrans.

Saturday - September 26th 1863 - Nothing but rumors afloat & everything is upside down. Wrote a letter to Henry W. Coops Father.

Sunday - September 27th 1863 - The same today. A letter to a friend in Greenbush.

Monday - September 28th 1863 - Orders this evening be ready to march at a moments notice.

Tuesday - September 29th 1863 - The same orders today.

Wednesday - September 30th 1863 - Wrote letter to Lucy & Colista, both friends of mine.

Thursday - October 1st 1863 - Playing Ball all day. Orders to be ready to march at a moments notice - packed up & started from our Camp at 11 1/2 P.M.

Friday - October 2nd 1863 - Marched all night & all day until 4 1/2 P.M. It has rained all day - very hard - passed Culpepper Station - Brandy, Rappahannock & Bealeton Stations. Encamped fer the night 1/2 beyond the last named place.

Saturday - October 3rd 1863 - Left our camp near Bealton at 8 A.M. passed Warrenton junction at 10 1/2 arrived at Catletts Station 1 P.M. took dinner & started for Bristol Station - arrived here at 5 P.M. The 3rd Brig. are at Rappahannock Station, 1st at Catletts & the 2nd (ours) at Bristol.

Sunday - October 4th 1863 - Have been hard at work all day in putting up the Hospt. tent & our own bunks. Built our bunks of sheet iron. Trains are passing all the while. Mail came in, but I got no letters. Have not heard from any of my dear friends for 5 weeks.

Monday - October 5th 1863 - At work fixing up our tents all day.

Tuesday - October 6th 1863 - The Regt. went out to did Rifle pits on the Hill overlooking the depot. I went to Manassas Junction after a load of boards.

Wednesday - October 7th 1863 - Busy all day at work in the Hospt. Wrote a letter to Mr Coop - recd a letter from Father.

Thursday - October 8th 1863 - Everything is quiet.

Friday - October 9th 1863 - The same today. Wrote a letter to Lucy.

Saturday - October 10th 1863 - Report in Camp that our Army have made a move towards Gerdonsville.

Sunday - October 11th 1863 - Hear that Lee has been trying to outflank us - & that our Army are falling back.

Monday - October 12th 1863 - Heavy firing all day. Recd orders to march at midnight. Heard that our forces have been repulsed.

Tuesday - October 13th 1863 - Marched this morning at 4 A.M. Went to Warrenton Junction found our whole army in line of Battle. No attack being made our forces fell back to Kettle Run Encampment at 3 A.M. of Wednesday.

Wednesday - October 14th 1863 - At daylight we started on

our March fer Centreville. Arrived there at 3 P.M. Heavy firing in our front from that time until after dark. Our Rear Guard are holding their position. Received a letter from the Beaver. Very bad news.

Thursday - October 15th 1863 - Orders to March at 8 A.M. Arrived at our destination three mile from Centreville near the Chantilly grounds & fermed in line of Battle. Heavy firing of cannon & musketry has been heard at our left. The Hospt. Corps of the brigade went to the rear & established Hospt.

Friday - October 16th 1863 - News came this morning that Capt. Barton of Co. I. 10th Regt & A.A.A. Gen. Lt Gen Eustis was taken prisoner by Gurillas last evening on his way from Fairfax C. House to the front. Rifle pits are being dug & everything goes to show we are in fer a fight. Hard rain.

Saturday - October 17th 1863 - Wrote letters to Calista & Mollie of N. Adams Skirmishing at the front but no egagement. Received letters from Father & cousins Mother is very unwell.

Sunday - October 18th 1863 - The enemy have retreated & we are to follow them up. Recd a paper from Adams & found one of my letters published (Letters & Obituaries, p. 177).

Monday - October 19th 1863 - Illegible

Tuesday - October 20th 1863 - Illegible

Wednesday - October 21st 1863 - Illegible

Thursday - October 22nd 1863 - Recd orders to march at 12 M. fer rear camp.

Friday - October 23rd 1863 - Pitched our Hospt tent & policed the grounds

Saturday - October 24th 1863 - Rations were issued also clothing. I got a pair of pants. Orders to march at a moments notice. More Rain.

Sunday - October 25th 1863 - Very cold & no news.

Monday - October 26th 1863 - Wrote to Father this forenoon - orders to be ready to March at a moments notice.

Tuesday - October 27th 1863 - Recd a paper from Adams. Wrote a letter to Nellie Cornadt at Boston Harbor.

Wednesday - October 28th 1863 - Very pleasant today. Put up beds in Hospt.

Thursday - October 29th 1863 - Wrote to my Cousins Jane & Althea. It is reported that the 6th Corps are agoing to join the Army of the Cumberland.

Friday - October 30th 1863 - No news. A few of the Sutlers have arrived in Camp & the boys are going in fer Tobacco as they have been without it fer sometime. I bought 2 lbs. of butter.

Saturday - October 31st 1863 - Took a walk to the Sutlers of the 139th Penn. Saw my friend H. had a jovial time & a good dinner of Spiced Oysters & other et ceteras

Sunday - November 1st 1863 - The wind was very high last evening blew our fly down & shook up things generally - No Mail came yesterday & none today. Expect the cars will come in Warrenton tonight.

Monday - November 2nd 1863 - Grand review of our Division today by Brig. Gen Terry. Went & got a lot of logs fer my bunk.

Tuesday - November 3rd 1863 - The 37th moved Camp today near Gen Sedgewick H. Quarters. Two of his orderlies were taken prisoners by Mosebys Men. Recd a letter from Father written at Adams - folks are better.

Wednesday - November 4th 1863 - Wrote a letter to my folks at Hatfield Had Roast & stuffed Turkey fer supper.

Thursday - November 5th 1863 - Wrote a letter to David Clegg at No Adams

Friday - November 6th 1863 - Recd orders to be ready to

March tomorrow morning at daylight. The wind is very high & our tents are being torn. Rations issued fer 8 days.

Colonel Parson's narration continues, "We left Williamsport July 15th, marched through Funkstown, from there to Berlin, from there to Warrenton, thence to Culpepper and on Saturday, Nov. 7th, arrived at Rappahannock station. The Tenth and Seventh Massachusetts regiments were ordered to report to Gen. Shaler whose brigade was already formed in two lines of battle in the rear of four batteries."

Saturday - November 7th 1863 - Marched at daylight for Rappahannock Station arrived there at 3 P.M. fermed in line of Battle with the 5th Corps & advanced on the enemy - at night we were in possession of the works with 1600 prisoners & 4 guns 2 of our men wounded.

Sunday - November 8th 1863 - Our forces advanced & drove the enemy past Brandy Station. Half of our division went to Kellys Ford our Regt crossed the River at the Station & occupied a Fort. Smith of Co I died from his wound.

Monday - November 9th 1863 - We were relieved at 1 P.M. by the 1st Chassuers & marched to Kellys Ford where we joined the rest of our Division. Very cold all day. Commenced snowing this evening.

Tuesday - November 10th 1863 - Nothing going on. Remained in Camp all day.

Wednesday - November 11th 1863 - A brigade of the 5th Corps came to relieve us from duty at the Ford. Orders fer us to join our Corps at Brandy Station in the morning.

"November 12th the Sixth Corps to which the Tenth regiment belonged, went into camp on the plantation of John Minor Botts at Brandy Station, who was a distinguished Southern statesman and whose sympathies were always with the Union, and *remained there during the winter to drills and picket duty."*

Thursday - November 12th 1863 - Started at 7 Oclock A.M. & at 10 A.M. found us at our destination. Having marched 11 mile in 3 hours. Orders to build Winter Huts. Received a letter from my friend Lucy.

Friday - November 13th 1863 - Put up our Hospt. Tent this A.M. Recd orders to be ready to march at a moments notice.

Saturday - November 14th 1863 - Visited my friend Henry Coop at the Sutlers of the 3d Brigade. Had a nice time.

Sunday - November 15th 1863 - Inspection this morning by Capt. Young of Gen. Eustis Staff. A hard thunder storm in the evening. Heavy firing took place at daylight near Culpepper Corners.

Monday - November 16th 1863 - Ball playing all day.

Tuesday - November 17th 1863 - The same today.

Wednesday - November 18th 1863 - Went this morning some 8 mile after pine brush to build a fence around the Hospt. Made the fence - a difficulty took place between the Officers & the privates of the Regt in regard to Ball playing.

Thursday - November 19th 1863 - Nothing stirring in Camp. Paymaster has arrived & commenced paying of the 37th Mass.

Friday - November 20th 1863 - Went to the 139th Sutlers. Recd letters from D. Clegg & I. F. Hurd. Wrote to Father - having heard that Mother was seriously ill.

Saturday - November 21st 1863 - Rec'd a letter from Lucy & one from Calista. Both are well. Orders to march at any moment.

Sunday - November 22nd 1863 - Our Regt were paid off today, except five Companies. The officers & privates are pretty well set up -

Monday - November 23rd 1863 - Express came for the Regt this morning - Recd my pay $26.00 this forenoon. Orders to March tomorrow morning at daylight.

Tuesday - November 24th 1863 - Up at 4 oclock A.M. Had everything packed up & loaded at daylight when the order was countermanded fer a time as it was raining quite hard & the roads were bad.

Wednesday - November 25th 1863 - Orders to march at early daylight tomorrow morning. No rain today but quite cloudy. Sutlers came to the Brigade. Recd a letter from E. E. Graves.

"On Thursday, November 26th, before dawn, reveille sounded and the great army was moving in three columns towards the Rapidan. At dusk we entered a wilderness of almost interminable length, and on November 29th at daylight the Third Division to which the Tenth belonged, was ordered to report to Gen. Warren . . . they assembled upon the plank road and took a forced march to the Rapidan and returned to camp at Brandy Station. Here it at once commenced to build winter quarters."

Thursday - November 26th 1863 - Up at 3 1/2 A. M. this morning. All ready to March at Sunrise. Were all day reaching the Rapidan - Crossed the River at Jacobs ferd at 9 P.M. A hard fight took placed at Raccoon ferd with Bufords Cavalry.

Friday - November 27th 1863 - Fighting all day in our front. The 2nd & 3d Corps were the only troops engaged until evening when the 3rd being hard pressed at Division of our Corps. - 6th were sent to their support & drove the Rebels several mile.

Saturday - November 28th 1863 - Ordered up at 2 A.M. Started the march fer the front - as I supposed, but at daylight found us through the woods called the Wilderness where Hooker was outflanked last Spring. - Commenced raining - Skirmishing all day.

Sunday - November 29th 1863 - Had a very uncomfortable night. Our Division were detached & sent with the 2nd Corps to flank the enemy. Marched until near night & done our duty. We (illegible) the Cavalry a (illegible) miles - formed a line of Battle & then rested on our ground & then rested on our arms. Very cold all night.

Monday - November 30th 1863 - Advanced about a mile. Our Brigade were at the front & skirmished all day - The enemy have a good position. Several wounded in our Brigade. Bitter cold all day & no fires allowed. Were relieved from the front by a Division of the 2nd Corps & went to Warrens H. Quarters.

Tuesday - December 1st 1863 - Very cold all night. Were in Reserve until night when we were put on picket. The Army fell back, at 8 oclock P.M. & orders were fer us to march at 3 A.M. tomorrow morning.

Wednesday - December 2nd 1863 - Started at 3 A.M. fer the Rapidan. Marched 17 mile in 4 1/2 hours crossed the River at Culpepper Mine Ford - 4 mile below Germania Ford. At 8 A.M. rested 1 1/2 hours & then started fer Brandy Station but could not get there.

Thursday - December 3rd 1863 - Started fer our old camp beyond Brandy Station at 8 A.M. - arrived in the Camp at 1 P.M. all tired out. Hear that our movement was only a diversion in favor of Grants forces in the Southwest & that Grant has done wonders.

Friday - December 4th 1863 - Recd two letters from Home. Wrote to Father & Lucy - also sent a paper. Orders to pack up after I had got to bed, but they were soon countermanded.

Saturday - December 5th 1863 - Bought some bread & oysters - Orders again to be ready to March at a moments notice. Hear that the enemy have crossed the Rapidan.

Sunday - December 6th 1863 - Orders countermanded again as the enemy only made a flying visit. Preaching by our Chaplain in the Afternoon. Wrote a letter to Father asking him to send me a box the 15th of this month.

Monday - December 7th 1863 - Nothing stirring in Camp today.

Tuesday - December 8th 1863 - Went out in the woods beyond our pickets to get wood to build winter quarters. Got two loads fer the Hospt & fer our use.

Wednesday - December 9th 1863 - At work all day on the Hospt tent.

Thursday - December 10th 1863 - The same today. Recd the Presidents message in the Army today.

Friday - December 11th 1863 - Commenced work on my bunk today.

Saturday - December 12th 1863 - Finished my bunk - fireplace & all this afternoon. It has rained nearly all day.

Sunday - December 13th 1863 - Very wet under foot. Preaching by our Chaplain.

Monday - December 14th 1863 - Built a fence around our Hospt & policed the ground inside the fence. Wrote a letter to Lucy.

Tuesday - December 15th 1863 - Went out some 2 mile after wood to burn. Wrote a letter to Father. The corps was reviewed by Gen. Sedgwick & the Russion Naval Officers at 4 P.M.

Wednesday - December 16th 1863 - Built on an addition to my chiminey this A.M. Expected letters from Adams & Hatfield, but was disappointed.

Thursday - December 17th 1863 - Rained all last night & today. Nothing going on in Camp. Went to Corps HQ. Had supper with S. P. Williams.

Friday - December 18th 1863 - Everything quiet in front. Went to the 2nd Division & saw two men executed. It was a sorrowful sight - they were from the 2nd & 8th Vermont. The first execution I ever saw & the last one I ever wish to see.

Saturday - December 19th 1863 - Was out all day in getting one load of Wood. Henry Gray was the teamster. We had a new team. Recd a letter from Home & one from Lucy.

Sunday - December 20th 1863 - Very cold - Wrote a letter to Lute - Preaching this P.M.

Monday - December 21st 1863 - Wrote a letter to Father. Orders have come to make ourselves comfortable fer the Winter. - 65 have reenlisted from our Regt.

Tuesday - December 22nd 1863 - Was out nearly all day chopping wood to burn & make a bunk - very cold.

Wednesday - December 23rd 1863 - Snowed last night - very cold & strong So. East wind - Bought potatoes of the commissary - Ground the Axe - & done other little chores.

Thursday - December 24th 1863 - Done but very little today - Wrote some in my last years Diary. My Box arrived from Home this P.M. - chocked full of every thing that was good. Now fer a Christmas dinner.

Friday - December 25th 1863 - Busy all the morning in arranging things for a good Dinner. Invited all the Hospt. Corps & Dr. Robinson. Our Dinner was oysters both fried & stewed, Tom & Jerry - Apples - Cake & pies & lots of other things.

Saturday - December 26th 1863 - This morning started for the woods - Got up two loads of wood. Had Tripe for dinner, Mince pie & C. Commenced raining this afternoon.

Sunday - December 27th 1863 - Wrote a letter to Father & Lucy. Recd a letter from Calista. Quite pleasant but very cold. A good many are reenlisting in the Regt. Preaching this P.M.

Monday - December 28th 1863 - Commenced raining this morning - & rained hard all day. Have staid in my bunk all the while reading & writing. Reported we are to move the 1st. Long Island were sworn in the Service today they having reenlisted.

Tuesday - December 29th 1863 - Went after one load of wood, then worked in the Cook House. It rained quite hard this afternoon. The boys in our Regt that have reenlisted were sworn in the service this afternoon.

Wednesday - December 30th 1863 - Went after two loads of wood. Nearly finished the cook House. The roads are in a horrible condition. I got covered with mud from head to foot. It looks like rain again.

Thursday - December 31st 1863 - Commenced raining this morning & has kept up all day. Our Regt were mustered in fer 2 months pay this A.M. We have a Turkey & other fixing for tomorrow New Years.

****

<u>Memoranda</u>
A wife full of Truth, innocence & love
is the prettiest flower a man
cherishes next his heart.
A wife full of truth, innocence & love
is the (illegible)est flower a man (illegible) his heart.

****

On the morning of <u>Jan 21st</u> at six we started on our march fer New River to meet the enemy & to drive them from their strong positions. It had been raining all night & in the morning. The mud was very deep, But not bad enough to stop the grand army. We marched about four mile through mud & water knee deep, raining all the while. Our clothes were wet through, but the loads on our backs & the exercise in walking through the mud kept us from catching cold. We arrived within 1/4 of a mile from the river at nine A.M. We found that the Pontoons were not laid across the river fer us & so we went in camp. While coming along the road we met several wagons of Pontoon Train turned over in the road & others stuck fast. The artillery could not stir with their usual number of horses. One Brigade were detailed to turn out & (illegible) the road helping the caissons & Pontoons along. It was a terrible time & everybody was down on <u>Burnside</u>. We expect to get whipped. <u>April 28th</u> We left our Camp of the past winter fer a summer camp. The day has been quite rainy. We marched within one mile of the river & encamped fer the night. At 3 oclock morning of the 29th our army commenced laying pontoons.

The Rebels were taken by surprise & we met with little resistance. Gen Russells Brigade crossed at 8 1/2 A.M. Got in position awaiting the movements of other parts of the army. Gen. Reynolds Corps crossed at 10 A.M. one mile farther down the river. Considerable firing from our men & artillery. Slackened up at 11 A.M. Gen. Butterfield (Chief of Hookers staff) with Gen. Fogliardi & suit passed down the lines at 11 A.M. At daybreak of the 30th we were ordered to move, but as no demonstration was made, we remained in readiness. Our forces advanced from their position on the other side. Heavy cannonading commenced at 6 P.M. from the Rebels, our artillery replied, several excellent shots were made on both sides. May 1st, Friday, was very splendid. Firing has been heard all day. Reported that our forces are At Gordonsville & are driving the enemy. No firing from the enemy opposite our corps. Today Saturday we marched & countermarched nearly all day. Crossed the River at 10 oclock in the evening. Heard that Gen. Hooker had driven the enemy, & so our Gen. Sedgwick made preparations to carry the Heights. Heavy cannonading commenced on the right at 10 1/2 PM & lasted 1 1/2 hours. We started on our march at 12 (midnight) & marched all night long, got the distance of one mile from where we started from, in direct route, but travelled 12 mile. All strategy I suppose. At daylight of Sunday the 3rd we were attacked & I went by the Doctors orders to look fer a place fer the wounded - found one in the Bank of the River. No damage done until 10 A.M., although there was very heavy firing all the time. The 7th Mass & 2nd R. Island supporting Batteries & the 37th Mass acting as reserve carried the Heights, capturing lots of (illegible), 6 cannon, == loss in killed & wounded about 800. Worked very hard all day in dressing the wounds of the sufferers. Our Corps advanced five mile & there met the enemy - a hard fight ensued. Our Regt lost two in killed, wounded, missing. I came up with the Regt at 11 P.M. all tired out. Got our wounded aboard Ambulances fer Fredericksburg. On Monday morning our Corps were all in line of Battle all day, at (illegible) the Rebels flanked us, & came over cutting us off. It was the most exciting time I ever was in, yet I had no fears about myself. It is reported that we are defeated because the 11th Army Corps failed in doing their duty. They having run at the first firing, but can't believe it. I think we have worsted the enemy, at least I know that our Corps have. We are going back to our old Camp & so ends Hookers first Campaign. Saturday - June 6th - We the 6th Corps broke Camp & crossed the river at Franklins Crossing. Remained over there 8 days under fire nearly everyday. One man wounded from Co. G while on picket. Recrossed the River on Saturday evening. Found that our Army were moving towards the old Bull Run battle ground. We marched Sunday morning & arrived at Stafford D. House at 12 N. bivoucked until 10 PM marched all night & at noon of Monday arrived at Dumfries. Bivoucked until 2 AM of Tuesday & then started again, arrived at Fairfax Station. Staid there until Thursday morning marched to the C. House. Rebel prisoners were brought in also wounded men from the front. A Cavalry fight took place near Aldie & Snickers Gap.

Cash Account January 1863

Date		Paid
1	Herald & Chronicle	.25
3	One Ambrotype	1.00
4	One Chronicle	.10
6th	One Herald	.10
6th	6 apples	.50
7th	One Herald	.10
8th	2 lb Sugar	.25
9th	One Herald	.10
10th	1/2 pound of butter	.25
10th	5 apples	.25
10th	Pipe & tobacco	10.00
10th	One Herald	.10
11th	1 pr. Boots	8.00
15th	1/2 pound of butter	.25
17th	Cutting hair	.25
18th	1/2 pound of butter	.25
18th	25 Ginger Cake	.50
18th	5 apples	.25
24th	2 1/2 sugar	.25
25th	15 cakes	.35
28th	1/2 bottle ink	.05
29th	1 1/2 butter	1.50
30th	Dr. to Bidwell	8.50
		$33.15

BEREA M. WILLSEY
COMPANY C, TENTH MASSACHUSETTS VOLUNTEERS
ARMY OF THE POTOMAC
CIVIL WAR DIARY
January 1, 1864—June 24, 1864

Friday - January 1st 1864 - The sun came out this morning bright & the clouds have all disappeared after a very stormy night of Rain. The Express came from the north this morning & we have all had our fill of Turkeys, Mince pies & cakes. Had a splendid dinner & I partook very bountifully. Went to the 37th Mass in the afternoon. Recd orders to be ready to march at a moments notice. The 3rd Brigade of our Division took the cars this A.M. fer Harpers Ferry.

Saturday - January 2nd 1864 - The day has been very pleasant & cold. Hendrick, Kellogg & myself went out some 2 mile after wood with our Hospital Team. We brought in one large load of Walnut. Cut enough firewood to last over the Sabbath & then cleaned up things generally around the Hospital. It is the coldest day we have had this winter & it is with difficulty that we keep warm. Fared sumptuously on the good things from Home.

Sunday - January 3rd 1864 - Very cold this morning. The regular Sunday morning Inspection took place at 9 1/2 A.M. I did not attend as I had work to do. It is a fact not to be disputed that we have more work to do on any other day. I worked on the chimney of our Cook House until noon. Preaching at 2 A.M. by the 2nd R. Island Chaplain & prayer meeting. This eve. orders again to be ready to march at a moments notice.

Monday - January 4th 1864 - After a good Breakfast of Potatoes & Onions I went to work in our Cook House & at 3 P.M. had all the work finished. It is very cold & looks like a storm overhead. Wrote a letter to Father this morning very early & one to my <u>kind friend</u> at North Adams. Orders came this evening that we shall march before daylight tomorrow & take the cars for Harpers Ferry. Have got everything packed & ready for a start. Commenced snowing at 9 P.M.

Tuesday - January 5th 1864 - I didnot rest very well last night in thinking of moving, besides it stormed very hard all the time. I was busy all day in plastering up the holes in our Cook house & laying stone for the fireplace. It was very disagreeable work & I suffered considerably with the cold. I got the cook House all done at 4 P.M. The 1st Brigade have recd orders to march tomorrow morning to the station & there take the cars for H. Ferry, Va.

Wednesday - January 6th 1864 - The 1st Brigade (Gen Shaler) started this morning at 2 A.M. The boys in the Regt there got up & commenced work in getting wood, boards & C fer their bunks. I got several loads, but at daylight, guards were put in the old camps to prevent anything being taken away - as the Brigade will come back soon. Went in the woods after a load of logs - this P.M. The men that have reenlisted in one Regt. were paid off today & they expect to go Home tomorrow on a Furlough - It has been very pleasant all day.

Thursday - January 7th 1864 - Commenced work this morning about the Hospital & then fixed up the fireplace, put in a floor in my tent & C. We were then ordered to collect a lot of boards from the deserted camps of the 1st Brigade for a floor in our Hospital Tent - worked hard all the afternoon in hauling wood & boards to our camp. It is said that the 3rd Brig have lost 17 men from exposure on the night of Jan. 5th. I recd a paper from Adams. I am learning of the marriage of several of my acquaintances.

Friday - January 8th 1864 - The first thing I observed this morning was that we had been visited during the night with a large fall of snow. Our tents were nearly crushed with its weight. Helped our Cook all the forenoon in preparing the dinner. Had Roast Beef & other fixins. In the afternoon, read the story called, Ranger of Ravenstream. It has been a beautiful day. Have recd no mail at our Brigade fer 3 days. The 1st Brigade are at Sandersky City guarding prisoners.

Saturday - January 9th 1864 - This morning after eating Breakfast I went in the Hospital to care for the sick. One Cassidy of Co. D. is very sick with Chronic Diarrhea. Have had to watch him closely all day long & expect to all through the night. Have read a book entitled, "Gambling Unmasked," by J. H. Green. In the evening recd a letter from my friend Lucy & was of course made happy. My thoughts are continually dwelling on the happy moments I have enjoyed with her & expect to enjoy in the future.

Sunday - January 10th 1864 - I was relieved from duty in the Hospt this morning by Kellogg. I had a very hard time all night long. Have done nothing today but eat & sleep. Tried to write a letter this afternoon but feeling so much like a fool I gave up the job until I felt different. Inspection & C took place as usual. 9 new recruits came to the Regt. yesterday. Had some good baked beans fer dinner. Preaching this afternoon by our Chaplain. Recd paper from Adams.

Monday - January 11th 1864 - It was quite cold last night & still colder all day. Have done but very little work of any kind. Finished writing my letter to Lucy & then spent the rest of the day in reading. No news or rumors are afloat now, instead everything is quiet all along the lines & in the Army. Gen Eustis moved his Hd Qrts today. A deserter from Co. A. was brought to the Regt this evening.

Tuesday - January 12th 1864 - After eating a good nice Breakfast, I relieved Joe Hendrick from tending to the sick in the Hospital. James Cassidy is very sick & I have had to look after him very sharp. Expect to be up all night with him. One of the new recruits that came to us on Sunday is having his discharge papers made out on account of Hernia. It is strange what people will do fer a little money. I bought a coat of Mr. Lane fer $6.20.

Wednesday - January 13th 1864 - I was relieved this morning by Kellogg after a very fatiguing nights work. My patient was troublesome. Fear he will not live. I help put a floor in the Hospt then went to Bed. Slept until noon. Had Roast Beef fer dinner. Went in the afternoon I had my picture taken & a miserable thing it is. If the original looks one half as bad I fear there will be no chance fer me with the gals.

Thursday - January 14th 1864 - After eating Breakfast I took a ride to the Ambulance park then started fer the woods with Henry Gray - we brought in a load of logs. The mud is quite deep, as the frost is nearly out of the ground. Recd a letter from Cousin Jane this evening. All are well at Home. Had an excellent game of whist with Warner, Kellogg & Cady - before going to Bed. Mr Lane is quiet, oh be joyful this evening having imbibed rather to freely of the stuff.

Friday - January 15th 1864 - This morning I again took my turn in the Hospital. The sick are improving so I have had a pretty easy time. Wrote three letters today, one to Lucy & sent my picture, one to Father & the other to E. C. Graves of Florence, Mass. In the afternoon recd a visit from Albert Field of the 7th Mass. Had a real good time in talking over matters & things that interested us very much. No mail tonight.

Saturday - January 16th 1864 - I slept most of the night so I feel quite cheerful this morning. The team had to go in the woods again today. Hendrick went with it. I helped our cook prepare the dinner. Had a Roast Turkey, apple pie & gingerbread. It is quite pleasant overhead but very disagreeable under foot, as the mud is very deep. Spent the evening in reading the "Springfield Republican" of Wednesday the 13th.

Sunday - January 17th 1864 - I recd a letter from Father this morning that set my heart at rest, as I had not heard from him in nearly four weeks. I went to the 7th Mass. in the Afternoon also to the Co. The day has been very pleasant, but Muddy. Read the papers most of the day & evening. Preaching this P.M. & prayer meeting this evening. Heard that Aaron Dickinson's Wife of Westbrook was dead. Sent an order tonight fer the wagons in the morning.

Monday - January 18th 1864 - This morning I again took my relief in the Hospital. My patients do not get any better very fast. Have most of the day been reading the "Wavery Magazine" & solving the Enigmas. It has rained most of the day, yet our wood pile has been replenished & yard fixed up, or rather decorated with Serpentine walks made of yellow pine sticks 2 feet long - Big Thing.

Tuesday - January 19th 1864 - As I had but very little medicine to give last night I slept most of the time. Went this forenoon over to the 7th Mass & had a good time playing at Backgammon. I again went over in the evening with Hendrick & had a game of Eichne (?) Received my "Hooser Valley News" this evening from Adams & read it through before going to bed.

Wednesday - January 20th 1864 - The day has been quite pleasant & the mud has dried up considerable & the frost has come out of the ground. Went to the Woods twice after a load of logs. Had baked Beans fer dinner. Spent the Evening at the Sutlers. No mail as there was another accident on R. Road. Had Oysters & Lobsters before going to bed, as much as I could eat.

Thursday - January 21st 1864 - This morning before eating Breakfast I cut a pile of wood fer the Hospital tent as it was my turn on duty. Have seen quite busy, as one of my patients is very sick. The Surgeon has but little hopes of him. Have been reading a book entitled, "Shoulder Straps." I received a letter this evening from I. F. Hurd which was indeed a rich treat, not having heard from him in a good while before.

Friday - January 22nd 1864 - After being relieved from duty in the Hospital I went to work in cleaning & fixing up things around the premises. Done some carpentering, Masonry & Blacksmithing. Expect if I keep on that I shall be a Jack of All trades in a short time. Heard that the 32nd Mass. had reenlisted, & had met with a glorious reception at Boston, also the 19th & 29th Mass. A few more from our Regt have reenlisted today.

Saturday - January 23rd 1864 - This morning all hands turned out to build Corduroy roads or walks in our Hospital yard. Had quite a job in bringing wood fer that purpose, as it is quite scarce around these parts. Finished about half what we got to do. Shall leave the rest until Monday - as we then have a leave. Had a good time over to the 7th Mass Hosp. playing Dominoes & Eichre (?) - lost this Diary while there.

Sunday - January 24th 1864 - Cut up more wood this morning fer the Hosp. My patients are better so I shall expect to enjoy myself today - wrote a letter to I. F. Hurd of So. Adams, also one to Father. It has been very pleasant & this evening I remained out of doors to enjoy myself. I thought of Home of friends and wondered if I should every be permitted to see the forms of loved ones again.

Monday - January 25th 1864 - This morning after Breakfast all hands commenced work fixing up the Hosp Chimney, as it has become disarranged. Had it fixed by noon & a rousing fire in it. The team has gone after wood again today. The weather is very fine and the mud is drying up. Had a ride on the Dr's Horse to Division Hd Qrts. Recd a paper from North Adams. Played at Dominoes this evening.

Tuesday - January 26th 1864 - I worked very hard all the forenoon in excavating the earth in a central portion of the yard for the slops we make, fixed up the fence & cleaned up generally. Had a splendid game of Dominoes in the afternoon & evening. Albert Field of the 7th Mass came over & we had a good time. The day has been warm & spring like. The frost is entirely out of the ground.

Wednesday - January 27th 1864 - This morning I again went in the Hospital. The sick ones are very much better. As the day has been so pleasant, I opened the tent & gave the boys a whiff of fresh air. Read the book called the "White River" in the afternoon. Had Beans & a splendid baked pudding fer dinner. Our Col. has returned to the Regt. from a ten day leave of absence. We are all glad as the Major is very disagreeable.

Thursday - January 28th 1864 - The Major was admitted to the Hospital. He being quite unwell with a cold. The boys are very glad he is sick & they hope he will never get well again. Everyone has been raising the old Harry all day & this evening the Line Officers are in fer their share. The Sutler has come up with a load of stuff & all are drunk on stout cider ale & poor whiskey can make them.

Friday - January 29th 1864 - The Major entered a complaint this morning against the officers fer getting drunk & disturbing the camp after Taps. Took a ride with Surgeon Robinson & Kellogg to the 3rd Division, 3rd Corps - to see a couple of Guerrillas hung, fer some reason the execution was postponed & we rode back, had a splendid time. The day has been very beautiful & as warm as a July day.

Saturday - January 30th 1864 - This morning I again took my turn in the Hospital. The Major is very nervous, & awful mean to take care of. He wants everything to _eat_ & _drink_ that he not ought to have. Wm. W. Mason of our Hospital Corps. came back to us this evening from Gettysburg having been gone 7 months or more. All were glad to see him & to hear his voice again.

Sunday - January 31st 1864 - This morning Surgeon Robinson took his departure from the Army on a 10 day leave of absence to his home in Mass. After dinner Mason & myself took the Doctors Horses & went to the Depot as Mason expected Dr Chamberlain (our old surgeon) would arrive on the train from Washington. He came & I rode with him to Army Headquarters. Then took the horses & started fer Camp on a Run. Recd a paper & letter from Home.

Monday - February 1st 1864 - It has been very wet & disagreeable all day. The boys have been at work all through the Camp, also at work finishing up the Church or Chapel, fer our Regt. It is to be dedicated tonight. Surgeon Chamberlain came to see us today. He will go to the 1st Corps as Medical Inspector. Several more of the Regt. have reenlisted today making in all 135 men that are called Veterans. Bully fer the Veterans.

Tuesday - February 2nd 1864 - After breakfast I relieved Joe Hendrick from duty in the Hospital. The sick are very much better. Had an easy time all day. Wrote a letter to Father. This P.M. a squad of recruits passed by our Regt today on the way to the 1st Division. Several Rebels came in our brigade today & gave themselves up. This morning was rainy - cleared off at 11 A.M. very pleasant until 7 P.M. then we were visited by a Thunderstorm. Meeting in our Chapel, couldn't go.

Wednesday - February 3rd 1864 - It has been very cold all day with high winds. Cleaned up the ground around our Hospital & carried the dirt away. Went in the woods with Henry Gray after fire wood. Had some difficulty with the detail send in the woods to chop, but as I had the law on my side I came out first best. Our chapel was dedicated this evening. Preaching by the Rev. Mr. Robertson of the 4th Vt. Vols. The General & his lady were in attendance, as well as his staff & their ladys.

Thursday - February 4th 1864 - Very pleasant all day, but cold, our Sutler had 3 loads of stuff arrive this P.M. The officers & privates made a grand rush for his Cider & ale so that this evening the Camp is quite noisy. There is a Lyceum started this evening. The question for Debate is "Whether the present commitation Law is a benefit to the country or not." Next meeting a week from today.

Friday - February 5th 1864 - Very warm & pleasant all day. Relieved my friend Joe from duty in the Hospital. The Major has gone to a Mrs. Lewis to stay until he gets well. My duties have been very light. Had all the Cider I could drink & all the walnuts I could eat. Reported that we are soon to move. The Veterans are returning from their furloughs & those in our Regt who have reenlisted expect to go home soon.

Saturday - February 6th 1864 - Orders came to march this morning at 8 oclock. Fermed in line ready to go, when they were countermanded for a time. Firing all day long on the Rapidan. Report says we have captured a Brigade of prisoners & that our forces are driving the enemy from their works on the other side of the River. We can hear the musketry very plain. Took a ride to the Depot this P.M. everything is packed up ready for a move. Recd a letter from my dear friend Lucy - then wrote in return.

Sunday - February 7th 1864 - I expected certainly that we should have to move this morning - but it seems that the present movement is only a Reconnaisance. Reports are flying around of lots of prisoners being taken & C. Wrote a letter to Father. Went to meeting this afternoon & heard an excellent discourse from our chaplain. Recd a paper from North Adams. The day has been rather unpleasant.

Monday - February 8th 1864 - This morning I started with our Hospt Wagons fer the woods - as we were entirely out of Fuel. The drive was quite cold & I pretty got well chilled enough before getting to our destination. The troops that went in the late reconnaisance are all safely back to their old camps. Only the 2nd Corp met with loss. Went to the Spelling School this evening, had a good time & spelt the whole school down.

Tuesday - February 9th 1864 - After splitting up a good quantity of wood I took my turn at nursing. Patients quite well & but little to do. Wrote to I. F. Hurd this P.M. for pictures of himself & wife. The boys have been playing at Ball nearly all day as it has been pleasant. The reenlisted Veterans received their furloughs this evening & a happier set of boys cant be found in this Army. Prayer meeting this evening.

Wednesday - February 10th 1864 - Didnot rest very well as the boys in Camp felt to joyful. They all started fer the Depot this morning feeling as happy as larks. More are expecting to go tomorrow. The Colonel tried to have them stay until three, but they would not do it. Surgeon Robinson came back to the Regt from a visit at his Home of 10 days. The officers of the Regt recd their furloughs this P.M. fer 35 days. They are to go in the morning.

Thursday - February 11th 1864 - This morning 8 of the officers started for their Homes. I have felt quite Blue all day - being disappointed at the way things have gone in our Department. I went to the Sanitary Commission this P. M. fer articles that we needed in the Hospital. Got a couple of gallons of oysters. Had a good supper & felt better. Recd a letter from E. E. Graves of Florence. Went to Lyceum in the Evening - a poor affair.

Friday - February 12th 1864 - This morning I again took my turn in Hospital as one of the Nurses being detailed to act as Steward while Warner is away on Furlough. Have done nothing inside & dont mean too. I shall hereafter do as little as I can help - fer the more a fellow does - the less he is though by the officers that run this Machine. If I live shall tell them plain truths that will make them cringe. There was singing school this evening.

Saturday - February 13th 1864 - After eating Breakfast, I started for Culpepper on the Doctors Horse. I put in a pass last night but it was not approved - so Mr Lane gave me his & I went on that. I saw friend Coop & had a good visit with him. Went all through the town & came back at dusk in company with Mr. Ecclestis, found on arriving two letters fer me, one from my friend Lucius and the other from my Lucy. She wants me to reenlist & come home for awhile.

Sunday - February 14th 1864 - I done nothing today but write letters. I hardly knew what to think of my Lucys letter, but finally concluded she did not mean what she said, so I wrote I would not reenlist. I recd a letter from Home this afternoon, folks are all well, except Father. He has cut his foot. The Band from No. Adams arrived this evening at Brigade. H. Qrs. meeting this evening. It has been quite blustery all day.

Monday - February 15th 1864 - I went on duty in the Hospt.

this morning. The boys are quite smart. There was a Brigade Review & our new Band were in attendance. Gens. Sedgewick, Talbot, O'Neal & Eustis were there. It is quite cold & snows a little. I recd another letter from my Lucy this evening. She is sorry she wrote me the other letter & has suffered a great deal, wrote an answer immediately. Wish I could see the dear creature.

Tuesday - February 16th 1864 - It has been very cold all day. The wagon from the ambulance train brought us two loads of wood. I have spent most of the day in visiting with my old friends of the Band. They all look natural & were very glad to see me. They played for Gen. Eustis this afternoon & this evening we all had a splendid time in singing. Some friends brought over a Banjo.

Wednesday - February 17th 1864 - Very cold & blustering dont know as I ever suffered with the cold so much as I did last night. Visited the Band again & took over some Medicine for Burdick Stewart as he has a very sore throat. The Band went to Brig. H. Qrs. & played a few times. Went with them & I enjoyed myself nicely although it was very cold, think it is the coldest day of the season.

Thursday - February 18th 1864 - This morning I again went in the Hospital. The boys are gaining rapidly. Read all the papers & books & I could find. The wind blows terribly & my chimney has smoked me out several times. Went to the Lycium this evening. There was quite a spirited debate & everything passed off pleasantly & profitable to all concerned - very cold all day.

Friday - February 19th 1864 - After being relieved from duties in the Hospt. I recd a visit from several of the Band boys. Our Regt. presented a nice Sword & Sash to Gen. Eustis, formerly our Col. I was with the Band, & of course I had my fill of the good things. Beautiful music was discoursed & the presence of ladies made it seem home like. The leader of the Band is not well yet, although he does not complain of any pain.

Saturday - February 20th 1864 - This morning the Doctor thought he would bring Stewart to the Hospital, as the boys were to move their Quarters. We got him to the Hospital at 2 P.M. & at 5 1/2 P.M. he died. I never was more surprised in my life. He died without a struggle & even when none of us expected it. He said he felt better

& we all thought he would soon be up. The Doctors call it Typhoid Fever with Heart disease. Surely in the midst of life, we are in death.

Sunday - February 21st 1864 - I watched with the dead from midnight. His Brothers & comrades feel very much afflicted. Prayer was had at 11 A.M. & he then was taken to the Embalming Rooms near the station preparatory to being sent Home. I went to the rooms with the Body & saw the operation. It was a source of much gratification to me. Came back at 5 P.M. & then took my turn as nurse again for the remainder of the day. Recd a paper from Adams.

Monday - February 22nd 1864 - Was relieved from duty this morning by Mr. Mason. After eating Breakfast I went to the Depot with Henry Stewart to see his Brothers body. I also went to Christian Commission & got several articles fer our Hospital. We had a splendid ride & I enjoyed myself nicely. It has been a beautiful day. The boys have had a match game of Ball today. Went with the Band to serenade Capt. Baldwin.

Tuesday - February 23rd 1864 - Another splendid day. Our Corps were reviewed by Gen. Russell & Sedgwick this A.M. A great many officers with their Ladies were in attendance & take the performance all through it was a brilliant affair. Company drills & Inspections are now the order of the day. We have but little to do in our Corps. Wrote a letter to my dear friend Lucy. Spent the evening with some of the boys of the Band.

Wednesday - February 24th 1864 - This morning I again took my turn in the Hospital. I had nothing to do as my patients are well. Read all the papers I could get hold of. There is a sham Battle to take place between the 1st & 2nd Corps at Culpepper fer the edification of the ladies now in the army. Big thing fer I cant see it, but paymaster has arrived & will commence paying us off tomorrow. A Splendid day.

Thursday - February 25th 1864 - After eating a good Breakfast I went & signed the payrolls. We were paid off fer two months. I recd $26.00, paid my debts & then went a visiting. The officers & men are on another drunk, so that I could not bear to stay in camp. The Band have been playing at Brigade Headquarters all day. The weather is fine & all seem to enjoy it. Took a ride on the

Surgeons Horse with Mr. Lane.

Friday - February 26th 1864 - The day has passed off in the usual manner. Drills inspection & officers being drunk. Had a peck of Walnuts this evening to eat or rather half eat. We recd orders to be ready to march at daylight tomorrow morning on a Reconnaisance as the enemy are supposed to be making a movement. Recd a letter from my brother George. The first one he ever wrote & I was highly delighted.

Saturday - February 27th 1864 - Was up bright & early this morning, ordered to stay in Camp while the Regiment was gone to look after things & take care of the sick. The Corps marched at 9 oclock & left all their tents & all the sick. It is a splendid day. Wrote a letter to my brother. Reported that Butler is making another raid to Richmond & we are working in his favor. Hear at 9 P.M. that our Corps have crossed the Rapidan, but dont believe it.

Sunday - February 28th 1864 - Another splendid day, but oh how lonesome I have been. Very anxious all day about our Regt. Have heard no firing at all, yet report say the corps are at Grange Co House. The 3rd Corps started this morning for the front & the rest of the Army are under orders Several of the stragglers from the Regt came back to camp this evening. Have but little to do as there are but three sick in camp. The pickets are doubled day & night.

Monday - February 29th 1864 - And yet another lonesome day. Can hear nothing reliable from our Corps. Reports say they are at Gordonsville one minute & another that they have gone no farther than Cedar Mountain. Saw a Squad of 15 prisoners coming from the front. Can hear no firing as yet. Either the enemy have retreated or our Corps have not crossed the river. Recd a paper this evening by mail. More stragglers have come back to Camp.

Tuesday - March 1st 1864 - Have spent the day the same as yesterday. No news from the Corps. We are left without rations & what to do we do not know. Recd a "Springfield Republican" this evening by mail. Hear our reenlisted men will not come back to us, but will join Gen. Burnside. Hear also our forces have met with defeat in Florida. It has rained all day.

Wednesday - March 2nd 1864 - This morning the sun shines brightly, but the ground is frozen & covered with snow. The trees are so loaded they nearly break with the weight. The Regt & Corps came back this evening all tired out & covered with mud. They marched from Madison C. House a distance of 24 mile in mud 8 inches deep. They had a large ration of Whiskey on their return.

Thursday - March 3rd 1864 - Was up bright & early preparing fer the days labors. Everything must be cleaned as there is to be an inspection. The boys are nearly worn out. A host of negroes were brought in Camp & in fact that was all the fruits of the expedition, as yet to be seen. No loss of men on our side. Took some 80 prisoners. Kilpatrick with 5000 picked men has gone to Richmond, but dont think he will succeed.

Friday - March 4th 1864 - It has been rather a dreary day looking very much like rain all the time. The boys are getting better from their late march. No news from Gen. Kilpatrick as yet. I recd a letter from I. F. Hurd this evening. Had a good game at cards with some of the Band boys & then listened to several pieces of excellent music.

Saturday - March 5th 1864 - This morning I went in the Hospital. Have two sick ones to look to. The day has been quite warm & springlike. Recd a visit from Joe Mysick & Gerold of the 3d VT Vols this evening. Had a good time. The papers say Kilpatrick has been heard from in Gen. Butlers Department & that he went inside the first line of fertification around Richmond.

Sunday - March 6th 1864 - It has been a very pleasant day & as I had nothing to do I visited numerous places. In the afternoon Henry Stewart & O. Warren paid me a visit. Recd a letter from my dear friend Lucy & I must say I was very much pleased, also recd a paper from North Adams.

Monday - March 7th 1864 - Nothing unusual has transpired today - in fact nothing but the regular daily routine of Camp duty. Everything & everybody is dull & at times I am heartily sick of soldering. Wrote a letter to my soon to be Frau then paid a visit to Band Quarters. They went to serenade the 2nd R. Island. We had beer & cider to drink.

Tuesday - March 8th 1864 - It has rained all day & I was on duty in the Hospital. I didnot care. Read a borrowed book & wrote a letter to I. F. Hurd of S. Adams. I have felt very lonesome, but the thoughts that I had, but 3 1/2 months longer to serve before seeing Home & friends caused only to keep within bounds. Oh how anxious I am to meet my dear friends once more. Our Major has gone on a 4 day furlough.

Wednesday - March 9th 1864 - The rain all cleared off last evening & this morning it was like Spring. The birds are beginning to come around & it makes life more pleasant. H. Rand & H. Stewart came to see me this P.M. & took Supper with me. Recd a letter from D. D. Graves of the 32nd Mass. stationed at Liberty, Va near Bealeston Station. This evening it looks like rain.

Thursday - March 10th 1864 - It has rained all day long very hard keeping most everyone in doors. I was at the Sutlers all the forenoon reading a story called Seth Soberday. This P. M. staid in my tent & cracked & ate about two qts of Walnuts. Read over the old letters I recd from Home & friends & tried to pass the day as well as I could. Received a letter from Home - was pleased to know that my people were all well.

Friday - March 11th 1864 - I had to stay in the Hospt. last night as the Rain drove me out of my tent. Have been in the Hospital all day. We have no sick. Wrote letters to my Father & Brother. We have had two very hard thunder storms - the hardest I every knew. Lieut. Gen. U. S. Grant is at the Army Hd Qrts. Hear that the 5 Corps of the Army are to be reduced & made in three Corps or grand divisions.

Saturday - March 12th 1864 - My bunkmate was again obliged to stay in the Hospital as the blankets were very wet. The sun has been out all day & the mud has dried up very much. It is reported we are soon to go in the defences of Washington, as the 8th Corps are arriving in the field. The Band paid us a serenade this eve. The officers treated with Ale, apples & A'jars. A nice time was had.

Sunday - March 13th 1864 - The spree did not break up until 3 A.M. The Major had to speak to the officers & send them to bed.

Did not sleep but very little as so much noise was made. Preaching this P.M. & prayer meeting this evening. Had dress parade. It has been a beautiful day. Spent the evening at the Band Quarters. Our old Surgeon C. N. Chamberlain & Lady visited us this aforenoon.

Monday - March 14th 1864 - I went on duty this morning. The Hospt. was free from sick ones, but in the afternoon a patient was admitted - complaint Sore Eyes. Had but very little to do. Wrote a long letter to my kind friend Lucy. Drills by the Regt have been agoing all day. The wind blows quite hard & it has been almost impossible for me to stay in the tent as it smoked so badly.

Tuesday - March 15th 1864 - It has been a very cold & blustering day. We had quite a snow storm about noon. Went to the Band Quarters this forenoon & had my Whiskers colored. The whiskers look like the old Larry, or else I do not know which. Some of our Veterans came back nearly killed, as the cars run off the track near the Station upsetting things generally.

Wednesday - March 16th 1864 - We have had a beautiful day, but some wld have had but very little to do. Great excitement in Camp this P.M. on account of a foot race between our Regt & 2nd R.I. a great many dollars were bet & we had a good deal of fun. Our men came out victorious. A new match is being got up. More of the Veterans have come back. We expect them all tomorrow. Another call fer 100,000 men.

Thursday - March 17th 1864 - Have been quite unwell all day from a severe cold, yet I have not kept myself from work, but Division was reviewed by Gen. O'Neal this A.M. Mr. Lane went to the Depot with the horses after the Doctor & Warner, none but Warner came however. The rest of the boys staid over in Washington. Had a good time this evening in talking over matters & things with John as he lives near my own people.

Friday - March 18th 1864 - My cold has been some better today. Spent the forenoon quite merrily in seeing the return Veterans. Went this P.M. to the Depot as the remainder of the Vets were expected. They all came in the 2 1/2 Oclock train. The Surgeon also arrived. Expected to receive a letter from No Adams, but was sadly disappointed. The Band came down this Evening to serenade the

Colonel & all had a lively time. Cider, Beer & Whiskey was there too.

Saturday - March 19th 1864 - Have done little or nothing today, as I am about used up having so severe a cold. The wind has blown very hard all day. We have recd an addition to our Regt by the arrival of two new men. They enlisted fer Regts in the 3rd Brigade, but as they are not here we are to keep them until the Brigade returns. Went to the Band this evening with Joe Hendrick. They came at Tattoo to serenade the 7th Mass.

Sunday - March 20th 1864 - Have been sick all day, caught more cold yesterday & now I am in fer it. Took some medicine, but I had about as leave have the cold, as to take the stuff. High winds all day. Orders to be ready fer the grand review to come off Tuesday. White gloves fer the whole army were the orders. Received a paper from No Adams this afternoon. Prayer meeting this evening but I could not attend.

Monday - March 21st 1864 - Went in the Hospital this morning. 2 of the new recruits were admitted at Surgeons Call, pretty busy all day. Wrote a letter to Father this afternoon. It has been a beautiful day, & the Regt have been trying to enjoy it. The new recruits have been hard at work building huts with our boys helping them. The Major, Capt Bishop & Wife started fer Mass. this morning. The Maj says he means to revel in natures charm fer 6 days, sure.

Tuesday - March 22nd 1864 - Was relieved from duty this A.M. Two more of the recruits were admitted this morning. One of them is quite sick with Chronic Diarrhea. Have no hopes of him. Hear Lieut. Eaton of Co F is dead. He went Home on ten days furlough got blew up in a Cartidge Factory, dying in two days after. Have been very lonesome all day, been in my bunk most of the time thinking of somebody I think a great deal of. Expect a letter this week - sure hope.

Wednesday - March 23rd 1864 - It commenced snowing last evening at dark & this morning we found it 8 inches deep, more snow fell this time than all the other times put together during the winter. It has been very warm all day long. Have done little or nothing in work. The team has been out after two loads of wood for us. Hear that the grand review will come off tomorrow. Gen. Grant, Halleck & a host of

Indian Chiefs are to be in attendance.

Thursday - March 24th 1864 - Very pleasant all day. The snow has melted fast. Worked about half the day in throwing the snow out of our yard. The Regiment have had a jolly time in snow balling each other. I recd a letter from Father this evening. Learn that he has sold his Farm & all his stuff, except a Colt. He is very anxious that I should be at Home. Folks are all well. Visited the Band Quarters this evening.

Friday - March 25th 1864 - Went on duty this morning in Hosptial. We have but one sick one. We sent two sick, to the Gen Hospital at Washington this morning early. commenced raining about noon & kept it up all day & night. Recd a letter from my friend Lucy this evening. Wrote a letter to Father & my Bro George also one to Goodey Two Shoes. A good many of the boys are on a drunk this evening.

Saturday - March 26th 1864 - Found all the snow gone this morning & quite muddy. Have done nothing today in the way of work. The express came this afternoon & our Steward having received a Box we all had a jolly good time. Cakes & meats of several kinds. Whiskey - Gin & Wine to wash it down. A few boys got laid out. Had considerable fun. We are permanently attached to the 2nd Division being the 4th Brig.

Sunday - March 27th 1864 - The boys looked pretty hard this morning from their carousal last evening - but it soon wore off. The day has been very pleasant. Went this afternoon to the 3d Vt Vols with A. S. Kellogg & this evening to the Band Quarters. The 98th Penn came back to their old quarters this afternoon. They belong to the 3rd Brigade & have been at Harpers Ferry. The rest of the Brig are on their way back to us.

Monday - March 28th 1864 - Very Pleasant all day. Have had but little work to do. The Surgeon & Mr. Lane went to Culpepper this P.M. Wheatons Brigade came back to their old Camp this evening - had a very good time & was entertained with high honors by (illegible) Steward Rarid Warren.

Tuesday - March 29th 1864 -All our new recruits left us this morning to join their Brigade which came yesterday. Had a very hard storm of wind & Rain all day. We admitted one patient to the Hospital this afternoon. Was on duty, but had little to do, except keep warm. We had a load of wood brought to the Hospital, but do not expect to ever be able to cut it up.

Wednesday - March 30th 1864 - We had one case of Erysiphlas admitted to the Hospital this morning. Was relieved from duty by Joe Hendrick. It has rained all day quite hard, yet I could not stay indoors. Went to the band quarters had a Bully good dinner of Fried Oysters. Gen. Eustis came back to Head Quarters from a 10 day leave of absense. They are serenading him in fine style.

Thursday - March 31st 1864 - Very pleasant all day. The boys have been having a Game of Ball. Went this afternoon to Corps H. Quarters to see a Big Horse race fer 1000 dollars a side between a horse from our Corps & one from the 2nd Corps. Our Corps won the race by several rods. The Paymaster arrived at the 7th Mass this evening. Also two of our officers that left us on recruiting service last Fall.

Friday - April 1st 1864 - Another great game of Ball this forenoon in our Regiment. No news stirring in the Army that I can hear of & we are all as lonesome as we can be. Commenced raining this afternoon & now at night it is very muddy. Received a paper from my Cousin Clara of Whately. Have been reading stories most all day.

Saturday - April 2nd 1864 - It snowed quite hard last night & this morning it is awful going. Had to chop a lot of wood fer the Hospital as it is my turn on duty. A large detail went on picket from our Regt this morning. It is storming very hard & everybody in under cover. The Paymaster has got through with the 7th Mass & will now pay off the 37th.

Sunday - April 3rd 1864 - No rain today, yet the clouds are heavy & dull. The mud is quite deep & we all go out as little as possible. I went to Brigade Head Quarters this afternoon & had a good visit. Hear that our Army will be strengthened by 60,000 additional troops this coming week, also that the 11th & 12th army corps are on the way to Penninsula under Gen. W. F. Smith.

Monday - April 4th 1864 - Another rainy day - yet we received two months from our Paymaster (Major Dixon). Recd a visit from Wm H. Coop & went with him to the 3rd Brigade Sutlers. The place where he stops. Came back in the Evening & found a paper & letter for me from I. F. Hurd. Recd three pictures in the letter of his little Boy.

Tuesday - April 5th 1864 - It rained all last night & all day. The Regt are nearly out of fire wood & yet we cant get any as the mud is so deep. Wrote a letter to my friend Lucy - sending the pictures I received yesterday. Hear no news of any description. Chopped up a lot of wood fer the Hospital, as it is my turn on duty tomorrow. Our Sutler has had a load of goods arrive this evening.

Wednesday - April 6th 1864 - The weather is quite clear & pleasant this morning after raining incessantly fer over 4 1/2 hours. My patient in Hospital are gaining rapidly. Sam Williams fermerly one of our attendents was admitted this P.M. to the Hospital. He is threatened with fever. Have had several good drinks of our Sutlers Ale.

Thursday - April 7th 1864 - Was up nearly all the night with the sick. Went visiting around the different camps. Hear the Sutlers are ordered to leave the Army before the 16th of this month. The roads & bridges are being repaired throughout the Army. Had a game of Ball this A.M. Spent the evening at the 7th Mass. Received a letter from Father.

Friday - April 8th 1864 - It has been a beautiful day, but looks like rain this evening. Recd a letter from Lucy. Hear that we shall move by the 16th for Richmond, but fear it will end like all our other movements, yet shall hope fer the best. The Band played fer the 7th Mass at Dress Parade this evening. They are expecting to visit our Regt tomorrow.

Saturday - April 9th 1864 - Have kept in my Bunk all day writing letters. It has rained very hard all the time. Hear that the R Road bridges are washed away by the late rains between here & Alexandria. Sent a birthday present to my fair friend & then retired early.

Sunday - April 10th 1864 - Have been on duty in the

Hospital today. It rained most of the time, yet I have managed to keep dry & warm. Have thought of Home & friends most of the time. It is the only way I can enjoy myself these lonesome days. This is the Birthday of a friend uppermost in my thoughts. No mail today as communication is cut off fer the present.

Monday - April 11th 1864 - It has been a very pleasant day & the mud has dried up quite fast. There is nothing new stirring in Camp. We had a Dress Parade this evening & our Band done the agreeable. Everything passed off pleasantly. We have recd no mail as the bridges have not been repaired.

Tuesday - April 12th 1864 - I have done nothing today, but eat, sleep & walk around. Have felt very lonely. It rained again this afternoon. The Sutlers are selling their stuff very fast, not being very anxious to make a great deal. Recd a mail this evening. Orders came to be ready to send off all our sick at a moments notice.

Wednesday - April 13th 1864 - It has been a nice day. Everyone seemed bound to enjoy it. We had a match game of Wicket ball with the 37th Mass. Our boys beat & have challenged the Brig. I bought 2 lbs of Butter of Coop as the Sutlers will leave in a few days. Saw the 37th go through their Dress Parade. Split up a lot of wood fer Hospital.

Thursday - April 14th 1864 - Have been on duty in Hospital today. Could not do a great deal as I am troubled with one of Jobs Comfortors on my wrist. Have felt very much used up as I am in a great deal of pain. The Sutlers are selling out at auction & will leave the Army tomorrow.

Friday - April 15th 1864 - The Sutlers have been selling off at cost and the boys are loaded down with stuff. A good deal of excitement & fighting has been on the troops from bad whiskey, but Quartermaster auctioneered off the 7th Mass Sutlers goods this evening. My arm is very painful and fear I shall not be able to sleep much.

Saturday - April 16th 1864 - Have done but little today. Nothing to do & no desire to do that. Our Sutler sold out today & will leave for Washington tomorrow. We had a Dress Parade at which the

Band done their best & everything passed off well. Had a visit from H. C. Rand this evening. Wrote a letter to Lucy this afternoon.

Sunday - April 17th 1864 - After raining all night it cleared off this morning & we had a nice day. Went to hear the Rev. Mr. Buddington from Brooklyn preach this P.M. Had a visit L. Rand this A.M. Recd a paper from Home this evening. Took a walk after sundown to Brigade Head Quarters. Hear that we are to be reviewed by Lieut. Gen Grant tomorrow.

Monday - April 18th 1864 - Went on duty this morning. Had considerable to do in fixing up the Vets as some of them are pretty bad off. The Review came off at 12 N. I went to it, but did not see Gen Grant until after the review was over. He passed through our Camp together with Generals Meade & Sedgewick & their Staffs. Hear that the mails are not to come to us after the 20th of this month. Match game of Ball between the 2nd R.I. & the 6th.

Tuesday - April 19th 1864 - Have been doing a little of everything today. Two loads of wood were brought to the Hospital & I had a good time in working them up. Went to the 37th Mass this evening to see them on their parade. Hear that the 2nd Corps were reviewed today by Gen Grant. Heard of the Massacre at Fort Pillow (Tenn) in todays paper.

Wednesday - April 20th 1864 - A great match game of Ball came off today between the 7th & 37th Mass. The fermer beating 40 tallies. It has been very cold & quite uncomfortable. The papers speak of another reverse to our armies in the Southwest, that 26 pieces of Cannon were captured with 2000 prisoners. Recd a letter from Father & my Brother George.

Thursday - April 21st 1864 - It has been a beautiful day & I have enjoyed myself accordingly. Went to the Band Quarters this afternoon & saw all the Boys. The Band came & serenaded our Regiment this evening. Expected to receive a letter from Lucy, but was disappointed. Had a game of Quoits after eating a good supper.

Friday - April 22nd 1864 - Chopped up a lot of wood fer the Hospital before breakfast & then relieved the nurse from duty. Wrote a letter to Father this forenoon. It has been a splendid day, but commenced raining at dark. Was disappointed again in not receiving a letter from the woman.

Saturday - April 23rd 1864 - The dust has been flying in clouds all day, yet it didnot prevent the game of Ball from being played. Our boys were opposed to the 37th Mass at a game of wicket making 337 tallies, while the 37th only made 200. Wrote a letter to my brother George. Went to the 3d Vt. Vols.

Sunday - April 24th 1864 - It has been very warm all day. Have done but little. Spent the day with Wm. H. Coop & I enjoyed myself nicely. It is said that we shall move by Tuesday, yet I cant believe any of the yarns. Hear that our troops at Annapolis are being put on Transports as fast as possible, also that our Army in No Carolina is being hard pushed.

Monday - April 25th 1864 - Another very pleasant day. Have been in the woods all the forenoon working at hauling in wood. Got several loads enough to last us while we remain here. Joe & Mason have got in a mess of greens this P.M. Have picked them over & washed them up ready to cook. Recd a paper from Adams.

Tuesday - April 26th 1864 - Have been on duty today in Hospital. The sick are nearly well. Another match game of Ball between our Regiment & the 2nd R. Island. Our boys made 15 tallies & the 2nd only 7. Our boys have challenged the New Jerseys Brigade to play tomorrow. Hear that Plymouth 32 C has been surrendered to the enemy with 2500 men.

Wednesday - April 27th 1864 - It has been a very pleasant day and I tried to enjoy myself accordingly. The 2nd Corps have changed their camp today. We expect to move in a few days as everything is cleaned out & Everybody is ready. Our boys did not play with the Jersey Regiment, but will do it next Saturday.

Thursday - April 28th 1864 - Another pleasant day. Went to see my friend Coop & this A.M. at the Sutlers of the 139th Penn. Vols. found him quite unwell with congestive fever. Tried to get him to the Regiment, but could not succeed. Received a letter from my dear friend Lucy which made my heart rejoice.

Friday - April 29th 1864 - Went this forenoon with Wm. Mason to see Coop & again, find him much worse, staid with him several hours & had a good time. Regimental drill this afternoon & Dress Parade with the 7th Mass at which the Band presided. Hear that Gen Burnsides 9th Army Corps are on the March to Brandy Station.

Saturday - April 30 1864 - Orders came to send off our sick. Sent off all in Hospital. Went to see Coop & fixed him up. Our Regt had a game of Ball with the 1st Jersey, tallies 15 & 13 our boys beating two tallies. We have never been beat. Hear that the Sutlers shop of Coop & has been closed by the Provost Marshal also that Coope will be down here tonight. Commenced raining at 3 P.M.

Sunday - May 1st 1864 - Troops have been coming in all day to Brandy Station & all East of the R.R. is covered with Men. Coope sent fer me to come & see him this P.M. He is much worse. Got the Surgeon to go up & see him. Recd a paper from Adams. Had two friends come to see me.

Monday - May 2nd 1864 - Staid with Coope all last night & until 4 P.M. Hear that we will soon move & I guess it is true. Had a hard shower & storm of wind and rain this evening. Rations were issued fer 6 days. No letters are allowed to leave Washington from the Army.

Tuesday - May 3rd 1864 - Started this morning to see the 32nd Mass in the fifth Corps found them & saw the boys I was looking after. They came back to camp with me. Orders came at noon to March at 4 oclock tomorrow morning. Packed up all our Hospital stuff this P.M. & loaded it, also got everything ready belonging to ourselves. Do not know where we shall go—.

"May 4, 1864, the whole Army of the Potomac broke camp, and made a severe march to the Rapidan. Nearly all the men started with shelter tents, rubber and woolen blankets, and overcoats, five days rations and 60 rounds of ammunition. Long before they reached the ford they had relieved themselves of one or more of these articles. Gen. Eustis' brigade led the Corps, the Tenth regiment in the lead. I was detailed Brigade Officer of the Day after establishing my picket down through the interminable wilderness, I reported to headquarters for orders. I learned that the army with all its transportation had crossed the river and it was the general impression that we had come over to stay.

"The army moved at daylight, Eustis' brigade being in the rear of the sixth corps, and the Tenth regiment the rear of the brigade. When the Second Division, commanded by Gen. Getty, reached the old Wilderness Tavern, couriers reported that Hill's troops were coming down the Brock road.

"I was ordered by Gen. Eustice to throw our skirmishers to cover his whole brigade, which was formed in two lines, the Tenth Massachusetts and the Second Rhode Island on the front line, Thirty-seventh and seventh Massachusetts forming the rear.

"The firing now being terrific. Men who had been in all the battles of the war up to this time say they never saw anything like it. It seemed to come from two or three lines of battle, one above the other, a perfect hail of balls . . . . Men dropped like the leaves of autumn, Still the line wavered not. The ground was literally covered with the wounded, the dying and the dead. Col. Edwards of the Thirty-seventh gallantly moved his regiment forward and assisted the Rhode Island and the line was soon established."

Wednesday - May 4th 1864 - Was up this morning at 1 1/2 A.M. broke camp and started on the march at 5 1/2 A.M. passed through Stevensberg at 8 A.M. & crossed the Rapidan at 1 P.M. at Germania Ford. Our Cavalry charged across the river this morning at 4 o'clock & took the enemy by surprise. We marched about six miles after crossing the river & encamped on the plank road running between Culpeper & Fredericksburg. Am completely worn out - 18 mile.

Thursday - May 5th 1864 - (Battle of the Wilderness) - We were up at 4 1/2 oclock this morning. Marched to the Orange C

House & Fredericksburg plank road where we fermed in line of battle and at 2 1/2 P.M. we had a <u>terrible</u> <u>battle</u>. Neither side gaining any advantage. Our Regiment lost very heavily & I had all I could do to keep me busy until midnight. Have had nothing to eat & feel about used up.

> Continuing Colonel Parson's report: "The following day, May 6th, we were called up before daylight. The enemy had retired about half a mile during the night. We were placed in the second line of battle and moved as occasion required. There was a continuous roar of musketry all the day each side in turn gaining a slight advantage . . . . We marched out of the Wilderness starting at 9:30 in the evening, marching with occasional halts all night, making a journey of five miles . . . . towards the new field of operation at Spottsylvania Court House.
>
> "The march was resumed towards Spottsylvania where the enemy were found in force in strong position. We arrived in front of the enemy early in the afternoon . . . . It was nearly dusk when the order "forward" was given. The general commanding the brigade having been informed that there was still another line in advance of the one we connected with, ordered his front line to take the double quick which we did for nearly a quarter of a mile . . . . the line of battle had been driven back."

Friday - May 6th 1864 - (Battle of the Wilderness) - Firing commenced at daylight & our forces drove the enemy considerably, but soon they drove us back & we had to try it over again. The 9th Corps came to relieve us about noon but they hardly got engaged before they broke & run. The action nearly proved a disaster but new recruits cant be expected to do what is right. They were finally rallied & our Division acquitted themselves nobly. We were ordered to report to our Corps at 9 1/2 P.M.

Saturday - May 7th 1864 - Had a good nights sleep yet do not feel very much refreshed. Ordered up at day light & put in position fer fight. The wagon trains of the whole Army passed by last night fer U.S. Front. We were ordered from our position on the right flank at 12 M - went to the front where we expected a sharp fight, but the rebels left our front & the army was put under marching orders. Started at 8 1/2 P.M. as rear guard of the army having under our charge 2500 prisoners.

Sunday - May 8th 1864 - (Battle of Spotsylvania Court House) - Marched all night long not stopping long enough to eat Breakfast until 9 1/2 A.M. There has been heavy firing going on ever since day light & I should think by the operations each Army was trying to get to a certain destination. It is very warm & sultry & has been fer the last week. We passed through Chancellorville at 11 A.M. then halted until 1 P.M. when we were ordered to the front near Spotsylvania & our Brigade supported a charge about dusk losing several.

Monday - May 9th 1864 - (Battle of Spotsylvania Court House) - Had a very poor night as the firing was kept up about all the time between the pickets. Found our Brigade this morning close to the front building breastworks. The Sharpshooters were very busy picking off our men. Gen Sedgwick of our Corps was instantly killed by one of them. All our sick & wounded are being sent off to Fredericksburg. There to go via Aquia Creek to Washington. Our forces advanced their pickets. This evening nothing but skirmishing going on today. Very warm.

"The next day we were moved into rifle pits a little distance to the left, where Gen. Sedgwick was killed by a sharpshooter, while directing the position of artillery. There was sincere mourning throughout the army and especially in the Sixth Corps. "Uncle John," as he was familiarly called, was loved and revered as only soldiers love a true, brave and heroic man."

Tuesday - May 10th 1864 - (Battle of Spotsylvania Court House) - We again advanced our skirmishers this morning & have been in front of the enemys rifle pits nearly all day. A dispatch was read to the troops that Johnstons Army was badly whipped at Tunnel Hill & Dalton that Butler had taken Petersburg & was marching toward Richmond. We made a charge this evening & captured 1000 prisoners, very heavy cannonading was kept up & the enemy were pretty well shelled. Five or six wounded in our Regiments.

Wednesday - May 11th 1864 - (Battle of Spotsylvania Court House) - Orders were given this morning to the army to rest, but to hold themselves in readiness to repel any attack that might be made. The Sharpshooters have been at work in some parts of the line yet nothing has happened until near evening when we heard that the enemy were moving away to our left. Gen Auger will be with us tonight. We are under orders to march. Had a fine shower this P.M.

> "May 12, 1864, Hancock with the Second Corps was ordered to capture the works since known as "The Bloody Angle." The Sixth corps was ordered the night before in a position to give Hancock their assistance . . . . The brigade moved out by the right flank, Edwards on the right, next to the Second Rhode Island, then the Tenth Massachusetts. The Seventh Massachusetts was on picket line.
> "We moved out through the woods, filed to the left, passed the line of prisoners, and came out into the open field . . . . We moved across in line of battle, down the ravine, which was about 10 rods from the works. The Tenth regiment being on the extreme right came up beyond the line of works and engaged the enemy in the rifle pits beyond. After delivering our fire there being no time to load, we had a hand to hand contest with the enemy, using the bayonet and clubbing with the musket. A force of the rebels scaled the works and poured a terrific fire into the right flank of the regiment and drove us back beyond the knoll in rear of the Second Rhode Island."

Thursday - May 12th 1864 - (Battle of Spotsylvania Court House) - Our Corps marched this morning at 4 1/2 oclock to the left. The 2nd Corps made a charge capturing one division of Rebels with 35 pieces of artillery. Our Corps relieved the 2nd & were fighting hard all day for possession of the enemys forts. Our Regt lost 8 officers & 50 men wounded besides a number killed. It is reported that Burnside captured as many more of the enemy as we did. Our

Cavalry are in the rear & have broken the communicatioon of the Rebels. Capturing 10,000 men - some of our prisoners.

Friday - May 13th 1864 - (Battle of Spotsylvania Court House) - It was reported that the enemy have fallen back from our front, but after sending out skirmishers we found them in abundance. We hold the enemys pits & have driven them several miles. All the wounded have been brought in & our lines very much strengthened. Our Division has been in reserve today & this evening we were placed in position ready to repel or make an attack. It has been raining all day. Our Order from Gen Meade congratulating the troops was read to us.

Saturday - May 14th 1864 - (Battle of Spotsylvania Court House) - Up at 3 1/2 oclock. Commenced marching at 6. Very muddy & raining quite hard. Marched until 10 A.M. & halted for Breakfast. A brigade of the 1st Division was sent out some two mile in picket without support. The consequences being that they were nearly all taken prisoners. Our Corps then marched to the place, sent out skirmishers & drove the enemy. Reinforcements have arrived from Washington. Reported by a Captain of a Gunboat that Butler has taken Richmond.

Sunday - May 15th 1864 - (Battle of Spotsylvania Court House) - There has been but very little going on today. The army are resting from their labors. Preaching & prayer meetings are being held. It has been a great deal more pleasant than yesterday. The mud having dried up a good deal. I sent a letter to Lucy the first one I have had a chance to send since we started on our campaign. Hear that Gen Grant has gone to Butlers Department. Several men have joined our Regt. that have been home. Rifle pits have been thrown up & our Cavalry are reconnoitering.

Monday - May 16th 1864 - (Battle of Spotsylvania Court House) - We were up at 3 oclock and stood under arms until daylight to prevent a surprise. It has been very foggy & damp. Stragglers are coming in & our army is again itself. 7000 new men have been added to each Corps & 20,000 more are on the way to us. We are to stay here until supplies can reach us. It is reported that our loss in this campaign amounts to 32,000 in killed, wounded & missing. There is no enemy in our front for several miles. Saw a paper of the 11th —.

Tuesday - May 17th 1864 - (Battle of Spotsylvania Court House) - Up again at 3 oclock, at daybreak our Regiment had orders to pack up, we moved at 8 oclock with two other Regiments from our Division on a reconnaisance. Our Regiment deployed as skirmishers & drove the enemy within 3/4 of a mile of Spotsylvannia C House. Our pickets advanced & we retired to Camp. found our Corps ready to march to the extreme right. We marched all night long over the same road we came down. I didnot get a wink of sleep.

Wednesday - May 18th 1864 - (Battle of Spotsylvania Court House) - At daylight our Corps advanced & drove the enemy from three of their pits. The firing was quite heavy & our Regiment lost five officers & several men besides a dozen prisoners. We then fell back leaving the 2nd Corps to hold position. Marched back to the extreme left & halted for the night with orders to be ready at a moments notice fer any attack. Burnside has advanced his lines today, in the (illegible) are about used up.

Thursday - May 19th 1864 - (Battle of Spotsylvania Court House) - Orders to move at daylight to the front. Advanced about 1 1/2 miles. We are on the flank of the enemy. Have been hard at work all day in building breastworks & making slashings finished them this evening. We recd a large mail today. I got two letters & papers. Some firing on the extreme right this evening, but on our front nothing but the occasional crack of the musket has been heard. Several showers of rain. Our loss so far in this campaign is 35 killed, 137 wounded & 38 missing.

"Time will not permit a detailed account of the scenes of the week. . . . The fact that in eight days the Army of the Potomac lost 30,000 men, demonstrates beyond question the most terrific fighting that ever occurred in the world within a similar time.

"Of all the battles of the war, the "salient" at Spottsylvania stands out the most desperate and bloody. The next morning I went over the ground, and had an opportunity of witnessing the effects of the terrible struggle which occurred between the two *armies, to gain possession of that vital point in the line."*

Friday - May 20th 1864 - (Battle of Spotsylvania Court House) - Wrote a letter to Lucy. Heard this morning that the firing on the right was occasioned by the Johnnies coming to get our wagon train. They were repulsed with fearful loss. Our Pioneers have been hard at work slashing down trees in our front. But very little firing except from our sharpshooters. An order from Gen Meade was read to the troops & this evening concerning those that desert our colors in the time of engagement. Also an order congratulating the new troops engaged yesterday.

Saturday - May 21st 1864 - (Battle of Spotsylvania Court House) - We received orders to be ready to march at a moments notice this morning, but did not start until 2 P.M. We then moved back 1/2 mile to another line of pits. Two corps of our army have gone to Guiney Station. The enemy pressed our lines about 6 P.M. & quite a little skirmish took place. We repulsed the enemy & at 10 P.M. started to join the rest of the army. Grant is cornering a flank movement on Lee & we are on fer Richmond.

Sunday - May 22nd 1864 - We marched all night long & at 8 1/2 A.M. reached Guiney Station. The country is very beautiful where we have passed through. We halted at Guiney until 3 P.M. when we started for Bowling Green. Gen Hartack & his Corps arrived there this morning & just as the enemy were getting into position he opened on them & drove them forth with. We marched within 5 mile of the place & halted fer the night. Army Headquarters at B. Green.

Monday - May 23rd 1864 - (Battle of North Anna River) - Our Regiment has been the advance guard of the Corps. Started on the march fer North Anna River at 9 A.M. Skirmished all the way until 2 P.M. when we run on to the 5th Corps. Heavy firing commenced soon after & we put sticks the best we knew how until 8 1/2 PM when we reached the scene of action, but our forces drove the enemy & then crossed the river. There was alot of prisoners taken. Marched today about 16 mile. Am very tired.

Tuesday - May 24th 1864 - (Battle of North Anna River) - We were routed up at 4 1/2 A.M. & marched across the river fermed in line of Battle in rear of the 5th Corps. A great many prisoners have been taken today coming in our lines in squads of 20 to 100 — Recd orders to rest as much as we could today. The enemy have fallen back & the 5th Corps are in pursuit. Saw E. H. Graves. Recd a letter from Father. Heavy firing off in our left all day. The prisoners say the enemy will drive us in the river tonight, but we cant see it around our lines this evening.

Wednesday - May 25th 1864 - (Battle of North Anna River) - We were up at 5 1/2 oclock but found the enemy had fallen back. We started immediately in pursuit & found the Rebs at <u>Little River</u> some two miles south of the junction. Our forces have been destroying the R Road & all the public property. Hear the Burnside has got in a tight place & cant get out. A division of our Corps was sent to help them. Wrote a letter to Father. Reported at Head Quarters that Fort Darling is ours. Severe skirmishing has been going on all the afternoon.

Thursday - May 26th 1864 - (Battle of North Anna River) - Skirmishing going on all day. The enemy tried our lines this P.M., but soon got sick of the affair. I wrote a letter to Lucy this forenoon. Bought a Beef tongue & boiled it today. Orders came at 1 oclock to be ready to march at a moments notice. Hear that we are going to the White House. We left our Breastworks at Dusk and marched all night long recrossing the North Anna. It was the hardest march I ever done, the mud being so deep.

Friday - May 27th 1864 - At daylight we arrived at Chesterfield Station on the F & Richmond R. Road. One days rations were issued to us, when we again took up our line of March fer the White House. We passed many fine plantations. The country being very beautiful, passed Concord Church at 1 P.M. & arrived at Taylors Ferd on the Pamunkey River at dusk having marched 20 mile since daylight, am very tired. Sent off the letter I wrote yesterday.

Saturday - May 28th 1864 - Ordered up at 5 1/2 oclock this morning & started on the march immediately. Went down the river some 6 mile & then crossed on the pontoons. We marched some 2 mile after crossing & fermed in line of Battle. The whole army crossed the River today and all the troops are now hard at work throwing up Breastworks & Redoubts. We had a skirmish with the enemy this afternoon & captured a few prisoners. Our Cavalry started fer the White House this P.M. Had a good wash this evening - feel much refreshed.

Sunday - May 29th 1864 - After sleeping until 7 oclock I got up feeling very much refreshed. Eat breakfast & attended Surgeons Call then went to Division Hosp after some medicines. Could not find my knapsack & fear it is lost with all its contents. Wrote a letter to Father this fernoon, yet donot know when I shall be able to send it. We are all of us out of rations some of the boys not having had anything to eat fer several days. At Sundown recd orders to march. Went to Jones Church near Hanover CH to support the 1st Division at midnight.

Monday - May 30th 1864 - At sunrise took the advance and started to find the enemy. Arrived at Peakes Station on the Va Central R. Road at 6 oclock. Plenty of <u>Pigs</u> & <u>Chickens</u> are to be found. The Station is 15 mile from Richmond. We remained here until 3 P.M. when we fell back destroying the R. Road. Depot & other public buildings. Our Regt fermed the rear guard & we skirmished all the way until dusk. We halted fer the night near an old mill & had 3 day rations issued to us. We also recd a mail, but I got nothing. Sent off my letter that I wrote yesterday. A hard fight has been going on fer the last 3 hours on our left.

Tuesday - May 31st 1864 - (Starting of Battle of Cold Harbor) - Remained in the same position all day. We are on the extreme right flank of the army guarding of the road that Stonewall Jackson flanked our army on two years ago. Heavy Artillery firing on our left all day. We can hear no news & we have made up our minds to rest contented. Have had several good naps & feel very much refreshed. It has been very warm all day but still we try to keep cool. Nothing to be seen in our front, but a few Rebel cavalry. Have had a nice time for once.

"June 1st we made a forced march to Cold Harbor, some 15 miles. It was excessively hot, the roads very dry and dusty, and it was a wearisome march. Before we got near the battlefield we could hear a tremendous roar of artillery and we knew that something had got to happen.
". . . . Those of you who were at Cold Harbor

will agree with me that it was the worst position that the regiment was ever in. The next morning we joined the Sixth corps . . . . On the morning of the 3rd a charge was ordered of the whole army; no resources were left anywhere; each corps rushed in. The assault did not last over 10 or 15 minutes, but it is said that there were more men killed in that 15 minutes at Cold Harbor than in any other 15 minutes in the whole rebellion. In the succeeding 10 days there was constant firing day and night, with casualties occurring all of the time, and then began the race between Grant and Lee to see who could reach Petersburg first. We arrived in time to take part in the unsuccessful series of assaults to gain possession of that city."

Wednesday - June 1st 1864 - (Battle of Cold Harbor) - Orders to march came to us at daylight. We marched 8 mile without stopping to rest. Then halted to let the ambulance train pass us. Left old Church at 9 A.M. and after suffering untold hardships arrived at Cold Harbor. After resting a few hours we fermed in line & marched against the enemy. A severe engagement took place and ended at night by our force driving the enemy and capturing some 1000 men. The 18th Corps joined us tonight. Our Regt lost 3 men wounded.

Thursday - June 2nd 1864 - (Battle of Cold Harbor) - The army have been fighting all day fer positions. We lost no men in our Regiment. About 12 M we moved from our position of the morning being relieved by the 2nd Corps & went to the Right. Very heavy fighting commenced on the extreme right at 4 P.M. The 18th & 5th Corps being engaged. Commenced raining at 3 P M had a nice shower. The dust was very thick & the Brooks were dry. Ration were issued to us fer two days. We all expect a great Battle tomorrow as it is anticipated that we are to attack.

Friday - June 3rd 1864 - (Battle of Cold Harbor) - Was up very early, eat my Breakfast & prepared for the duties of the day. Cannonading commenced at daylight along the whole lines. At 9 A M we were in possession of one line of pits belonging to the enemy. Our Brigagde was the next to line of Battle. The Regiment had lost seven in killed & wounded & yet they have not fired a shot. After dark the enemy made a charge on our left, but were handsomely repulsed by Hancock & driven from their own works. Hendrick found his Brother of the 27th Mass. mortally injured & will stay with him tonight.

Saturday - June 4th 1864 - Hendricks returned to us at 10 A.M. after burying his Bro. Orders have been given to the army that no more charging shall be done and more firing unless attacked by the enemy. The enemy sharpshooters have been busy at work & ours also. We have had 12 wounded & 1 killed since coming to this place, all from stray bullets. Rations fer 3 days were issued. Recd a mail of our paper. Some of our slightly wounded have returned, also Capt Barton. Quite an artillery duel today.

Sunday - June 5th 1864 - Heavy skirmishing has been kept up all day, our Regt have not lost any although they have been in the front line all day. The enemy made an attack tonight but were repulsed. The 2nd R. Island Regiment started fer Home at 2 oclock today, their time being out. They had two men killed in the forenoon. I wrote a letter to my friend Lucy & sent it off. Recd another mail today. The troops are busy at work digging out the Rebels & making Forts.

Monday - June 6th 1864 - Nothing new stirring today. The same firing of skirmishers & of artillery has been kept up. Gen Niel sent out a Flag of truce, but the enemy would not recognise it, as it did not come from a Maj Gen. The Pioneers are hard at work building works both fer offensive & defensive assaults. We recd another mail again today. Had a letter from Father. The Regiment were relieved from the front this afternoon for 24 hours. Some shelling by the enemy this evening from a new Battery came very near our Hospital.

Tuesday - June 7th 1864 - The enemy opened very early this morning with Howetzers. The shells exploding right in the midst of us. Had the narrowest escape from death I ever had, one shell exploding not a foot from me while eating my dinner, throwing the dirt all over me. Had orders to entrench ourselves & by evening had a very formidable breastwork. Another flag of truce went out this evening. We are in a strong position & nearly ready to commence our siege. Feel very tired & sore. Recd a mail again today but nothing from Lucy.

Wednesday - June 8th 1864 - There has been very little firing in our front today. The sharpshooters agreed not to fire on one another unless there was an advance. Quite heavy firing has been going on at our left, both of musketry & artillery. Everyone is entrenching himself in view of the coming conflict. Several of our Forts have been finished today & the Guns mounted. A correspondent of the New York Herald was escorted through our lines with placards on him as a (libeller ?) of the press & C.

Thursday - June 9th 1864 - The Sharpshooters have been very busy today. We have heard their popping continually. An Uncle of mine (John Vining) a sharpshooter from the 37th Mass was mortally wounded this P.M. I dressed his wound & have got the bullet that was extracted from his neck. He was sent to Corps Hospital at 9 oclock P M. Cheering commenced along our lines at 3 oclock & every Band in our Army struck up the National aire. Cannot hear what should occasion it, although it is reported that Fort Darling is captured.

Friday - June 10th 1864 - Went this morning to Corps Hospital to see my Uncle, but he had been sent off the White House before I reached there. Wrote a letter to Father after returning from my walk. Hear that part of the Army are going to move this evening. The 2nd & 5th & part of the 9th Corps. It has been very warm & I have done little else but eat Baked Beans. The Sharpshooters have been busy at work again today, but I have seen no casualties. More of our slightly wounded have returned to the Regiment today.

Saturday - June 11th 1864 - Rations were issued this morning for four days & Potatoes, 2 apples & whiskey. The teams are all ordered to the White House & it is rumored that we are to move again. Some say that the 5th Corps has gone to the James River & others that it has not. The enemy opened their Howitzer again this P.M. the shells bursting very near our Hospt. A heavy detail from the Corps & are at work digging breastworks in our rear. Cant imagine what it is for.

Sunday - June 12th 1864 - Troops were moving all last night & have been all day. Our corps covers the movement. It is said we are to go to Charles City, CH & there cross the River. Had orders to be ready to march at Sundown. The enemy have been quite troublesome today in our front, but the Sharpshooters have given them as good as they sent. More of the Mortars have visited us today, making things quite lively around the Hospital. We moved from our position at 8 oclock & formed in line a mile to the rear.

Monday - June 13th 1864 - Marched all night & all day to crossing the Richmond & West Point RR at Dispatch Station at 8 1/2 A.M. We halted on the same ground where we encamped some two years ago fer Breakfast. We then marched down the River & crossed the Chikahominy at long bridge or Jones Ford about sundown & then halted fer the night after securing a position. We are 6 miles from Charles City C House having marched 29 mile without sleep or rest. Never felt any worse used up & after getting in Camp had to draw rations which took me until midnight.

Tuesday - June 14th 1864 - Ordered up at 4 oclock & started immediately on the march fer Charles City. Encamped fer the day on the same ground we encamped on the first night after leaving Harrisons Landing & remained the rest of the day & night. The 7th Mass were relieved from duty in the Army & ordered to report to the Mustering office at Boston. They will start in the morning. We are 2 mile from Charles City and are to remain here until the Army Supply train passes us. The Bands are playing this evening from all the Head Quarters.

Wednesday - June 15th 1864 - The 7th Mass left us this morning for the James River & at 8 oclock our Corps immediately had orders to pack up & make a new line nearer the River. We encamped in a large corn field & pitched tents. Rations were issued to us this P.M. for four days. The supply train has been passing all this afternoon. The 9th Army Corps is encamped on the left. The Gunboats are passing up & down the River continually. Our Cavalry found the enemy in force at Malvern Hill today. Heard some firing.

Thursday - June 16th 1864 - We changed our position this morning & moved to the River, our Regt eating on the bank. We all had a nice swim & enjoyed ourselves amazingly. A Pontoon bridge is thrown across the River, nothing but the Wagons to cross. The troops are conveyed in transports. Steamers & Gun Boats are going by all the time. Never enjoyed myself better in my life. Everything is perfectly splendid. Heavy firing is heard up the River & report says

Butler is engaged. We crossed the River on Pontoons at sundown. 101 Boats, Marched all night - Petersburg has fallen.

Friday - June 17th 1864 - Marched all night long. Rations fer one day were issued to us this morning. The day has been very warm & the troops have suffered a good deal. We are guard fer our wagon train. The 1st & 3rd Divisions took the transports last night fer City Point & found them to Petersburg. Heavy firing is agoing on all the time & we have done some tall marching, arrived at or near Petersburg about 4 P.M. having marched some 22 mile. We hear Petersburg is not taken, although the city is being shelled. A hard fight took place this morning.

Saturday - June 18th 1864 - Our Brigade was sent to the front at 7 oclk. We advanced slowly all day long driving the enemy before us. I had a splendid view of the skirmishing & of the operations of the enemy. We had 5 wounded in our Regt. Petersburg is almost within a stones throw of our lines. Our artillery throws solid shot at the cars as they came in knocking things around us in fine style. Saw the nigger troops make a charge & I must say they are perfect bricks & make splendid soldiers. They take no prisoners.

Sunday - June 19th 1864 - Considerable sharpshooting in our front today, but no advance has been made. The boys have been well protected by earthworks & we have had none wounded. The artillery have done considerable firing. Petersburg can be seen very easy. Our Regiment were relieved from the front at dark & were ordered to Div. H. Quarters, when they arrived there they were ordered back to the front, but Col Edwards, Commanding one Brigade, sent them to the rear on his own responsibility, about 10 oclock. Heavy firing on the left both ours & musketry.

Monday - June 20th 1864 - We were up at 5 oclock A.M. Cooked our breakfast - then waited for orders from Division Head Quarters to go to the rear. At 9 oclock the enemy commenced firing on us & at the Fort killing our Sergt Major <u>George</u> Polley. At 10 A.M. we started fer the Wagon Trains where we arrived at 4 P.M. Rations were issued for two days & lots of Whiskey. The rolls seperating the veterans from those who are to go home were made out. Coop came to see me & we concluded to keep together for the rest of our time.

Tuesday - June 21st 1864 - Time out today. We left the train at 7 oclock & marched to the landing at City Point. Attended the funeral of Polley & then went on board the Tom Powell (the mail boat from City Point & Washington) Started at 10 AM passed down the River & arrived at Fortress Monroe at 4 P.M. Left the Fort at 5 PM the water being very heavy & the swells running high. Expected a rough time & was not disappointed. The boat struck three times & I thought we were done. Reached the mouth of the Potomac at (illegible).

Wednesday - June 22nd 1864 - Sailed in the River until 1 oclock A.M. & anchored until daylight, at 4 A.M. started again & passed Spauldings Point at 4 1/2 AM & the mouth of the Aquia Creek at 5 AM. The water is not so rough as yesterday. Could not sleep last night. Passed Alexandria at 10 oclock & arrived in Washington at 10 1/2. Marched down to Soldiers Rest & there remained the rest of the day. Eating all we wanted of Ham & Bread. Have cleaned myself up as well as I could. H. I. Graves made us a visit last evening.

Thursday - June 23rd 1864 - Visited the Capitol this fornoon, also passed up Pennsyvania Ave with Coop & at 12 M we were loaded on a lot of freight cars & started fer Home. Got in Baltimore at 3 oclock. Marched through the city & then took another lot of cars at 6 oclock we started arriving in Wilmington at 9 PM & at Philadelphia at 11 P.M. Took supper at the Cooper House resting for several hours. We also passed through (illegible) New Jersey crossing the (illegible) in a large boat. Have had issued (illegible) rations fer (illegible).

Friday - June 24th 1864 - We left Philadelphia at 5 oclock this morning. Had very good accommodations, took the R Road from Camden to So Aubrey, from there we took the Steamer to New York City where we arrived at 11 AM We were taken to the Soldiers Rest & at 3 PM we took the Steamer fer Hartford going on Long Island Sound. Mr. Brayton of No Adams called to see me while at the Soldiers Rest. He leaves fer Home tomorrow. We shall have to (illegible) him all night.

"At Petersburg, the time of the regiment expired and bidding goodbye to the Thirty-seventh, the only regiment left of the old brigade, we started for home.

"Such in brief is the record of the Tenth Massachusetts, made up of the most intelligent and loyal citizens of this commonwealth, who endured the hardships of the grand old Army of the Potomac and kept the white flag of Massachusetts unsullied."

APPENDIX

NAMES OF MEN MENTIONED IN BEREA M. WILLSEY'S DIARY

RANK AND COMPANY TAKEN FROM
THE TENTH REGIMENT MASSACHUSETTS
VOLUNTEER INFANTRY 1861–1864
By Alfred S. Roe (A Veteran of the Civil War)
Published by the Tenth Regiment Veteran Association,
Springfield, Mass., 1909

COMMISSIONED STAFF - CO. C

Lieutenant Colonels

Decker, Jefford M., b. Wiscasset, Me; 47, M; hotel-keeper, Laurence; June 21, 1861; his skill and ability as drillmaster were of great service to the Regiment in its earlier days; while at Brightwood he was in command of the 7th Mass. for several months, filling the position with credit and satisfaction; suffering from chronic rheumatic attacks, he could not endure the exposures of active service and consequently resigned, July 17, '62; a resident of Lawrence, Col. Decker had been at the head of the Tenth Regiment Militia, before that having served for some time as Captain of a Lawrence Company; in organizing the new Tenth he took the second place; subsequent to his service in the Tenth, he became First Lieut. and Adjutant of the 52d Mass., thus having a nine months experience in the Department of the Gulf; d. Jan. 1, 1870, Salem.

Parsons, Joseph B., from Captain Co. C., July 15, '62; in this capacity, Col Parsons commanded the Regiment after the promotion of Col. Eustis, the numbers in the ranks being so far below the minimum that an officer of higher rannk could not be mustered; through always with his men in the thickest of the fray he was not wounded after assuming command; M. O. July 1, '64; subsequently to the War, he commanded the Second Regiment M. V. M. several years; in 1888, he was appointed State Pension Agent, holding the position at the time of his death; no man held a higher place in the affections of his men than their Lieut. Colonel; when Northampton celebrated her 250th anniversary, she called home, as orator of the occasion, Jos. B. Parsons and he gave the address on the grounds that had been in his family for a quarter of a millennium; b. April 29, 1828, he died June 4, 1906 in Winthrop, though his residence had been in Roxbury for some time. For a more extended estimate, see p. 307.

Majors

Marsh, William R., b. Walpole, N. H., Jan 26, 1828; 33, M.; hotel-keeper, Northampton; June 21, '61; had served ten years in the Militia, Tenth Regt., rising from Fourth Lieut. to command of Co. C; naturally a prominent place fell to his lot in the newly organized regiment; res. June, 14, '62.

Miller, Ozro, from Co. H. June 15, '62; commanded Regiment July 1, '62 and was shot in the neck by a Rebel sharpshooter; falling into the hands of the enemy he was carried to Libby Prison, Richmond where he died, July 15, '62; on the fourteenth of the following September, funeral services were held in Shelburne Falls by the united three congregations in the Baptist edifice, the eulogy being pronounced by the Rev. G. H. Deere; Messrs. Loomis and Gray followed in addresses directed more especially to the Masonic order and the citizens and soldiers present; an adaptation of "The Vacant Chair," then in its first year of popularity, was rendered in a most impressive manner. The closing paragraph of Mr. Deere's eulogy follows: "In closing, allow me to say that this loyal man, - who was so compassionately mindful of you whose kindred were in his care, so considerate of the welfare of his men in camp, so pleasantly calm and nobly brave, powerful and controlling in battle, and whose heroic death closed so enviable a public career, - was, in private life, the blameless son and brother, the tender father, the faithful and affectionate husband, the industrious and scrupulously honest business man, the public-spirited citizen, a man whose intimate friendship was not cheaply purchased, but 'the friends he had and their adoption tried, he grappled them to his soul with hooks of steel.' and, touching all the mournful keys of our bereavement, the words of God's providence sweep over our bowed souls; "He shall return no more to his house, neither shall his place know him any more.'"

Parker, Dexter F., b. Aug. 2, 1828, Boston; 34, M.: mechanic, Worcester; Aug. 12, '62; wd. May 12, '64, Spottsylvania; a Minie ball hit and shattered his right arm, eight days later amputation was necessary, and he did not rally from the shock, dying May 30, '64; his remains were sent home to Worcester where a public funeral was accorded him, the services being held in the First Unitarian Church of which he was a member; addresses were given by the Pastor, Dr. Alonzo Hill and Dr. M. Richardson of the Salem Street Congregational Church; the burial was in Rural Cemetery; early orphaned, the subsequent officer by perseverance and diligence soon demonstrated the possibilities of American living; at fourteen he was self-supporting and, besides, able to pay his own way through several terms of academy study; from 1850 onward, he was a citizen of Worcester, during the earlier years a workman in a boot-shop; a studious reader, an ardent advocate of all reformatory measures, eloquent and ready in speech, he soon became a prominent figure in local affairs; of strong literary tastes, he was a contributor to *Hunt's Merchant' Magazine* and in 1856 was elected to the lower branch of the Legislature, returning there in 1858 also; in 1859 and 1860 he represented the city in the Senate and 1861 found him again in the House; the firing upon Sumter found the man ready who, as a boy, had failed in his efforts to enlist for the Mexican War; joining the Light Infantry, Sixth Regt., in Washington, he was later promoted Fourth Lieut.; from subsequent Quartermaster and Staff service he was advanced to his final position in the Tenth.

Quartermasters

Howland, John W., 43, M.; hotel-keeper, Pittsfield; June 21, '61; res. Sept. 29, '62, to be commissioned Captain, Assistant Quartermaster, U. S. Vols., Sept. 30, '62; in 1873, resided near Great Barrington.

Surgeons

Chamberlain, Cyrus N., b. West Barnstable; 30, S.; physician, Northampton; June 21, '61; as an expression of the good will of fellow citizens the surgeon carried away with him from his city, a surgeon's sword and sash with a brace of Smith and Wesson's revolvers; dis. April 13, '63 to be appointed Surgeon of Volunteers; was in continuous and active service in the field until Aug. 1, '64, save the winter of '63 and '64, when he was in Philadelphia at work; in Aug. '64 he was ordered to Worcester to organize the Dale U. S.

Gen'l Hosp., continuing there till his M. O. Oct. 7, '65; bvt. Lieut. Colonel, U. S. Volunteers, Oct. 6, '65; in 1875, physician and surgeon, Lawrence; d. 1900.

Robinson, Albert B; May 15, '63; M.O. July 1, '64; later surgeon, 42d Mass., 100 days' service; M.O. Nov. 11, '64; in 1875, physician, Boston Highlands; was prominent in medical, Masonic and Grand Army circles; d. Mar. 29, 1908, Roxbury, aged 73 years; bur. Holden.

Assistant Surgeons

Jewett, George, b. Ridge, N. H., April 28, 1825; physician, Fitchburg; Jan. 21, '62, prom. Surgeon, 51st Mass., Nov. 4, '62; M. O. July 27, '63; in 1875, physician Fitchburg; d. Dec. 16, 1894.

Gilman, John H., b. Sangerville, Me., Feb. 24, 1836; physician, Lowell; Mar. 18, '63; educated at public schools and Phillips-Andover; M. D. Harvard, 1863; had served in the Sanitary Commission gratuitously in the campaigns of McClellan and Pope; M. O. July 1, '64; later entered the service as Acting Asst. Surg., U. S. Army, remaining until the end of the war; in 1869 and 1870 was City Physician, Lowell; d. 1890.

Chaplains

Bingham, Adoniram J., pastor of the Central Baptist Church, Westfield, was commissioned Aug. 13, '62; his infirm health would not admit of his long stay in the service; res. Jan. 16, '63.

NON-COMMISSIONED STAFF - CO. C

Sergeant Majors

Polley, George F., from Co. C.; Feb. 9, '63; re. Dec. 22, '63; prom. First Lieut. May 6, '64; it does not appear that he was assigned to any company in the Tenth, a transfer to the 55th Mass. being in transit when he was killed, June 20, '64, in front of Petersburg.

Hospital Stewards

Wells, Charles C., b. Port Gibson, Miss.; 21, S.; clerk, Northampton; dis. Oct. 17, '62, disa.

Warner, Jonathan D., from Co. C; Oct. 10, '62; re. Dec. 21, '63; Trans. June 20, '64, 37th Mass.; dis. as Hosp. Steward, Tenth Regt., Nov. 16, '64; in 1872, resided Hatfield; dead.

REGIMENTAL BAND

Clark, Francis L., b. North Adams; 23, S.; shoemaker, North Adams; June 21, '61; M. O. Aug. 11, '62; re. July 26, Co. E., 3d Mass. Heavy Artillery; dis. Dec. 12, '64, disa.; in 1872, boot and shoe dealer, North Adams; d. Jan. 4, 1876.

Stewart, Burdick A., 24, M.; engraver, Adams; June 21, '61; M. O. Aug. 11, '62; in Jan. 1864, reorganized the old band, adding new men where necessary, and reported to the Brigade which included the Tenth; within a few hours after his arrival at Brandy Station, he suddenly died; Chaplain Perkins of the Tenth conducted his funeral services; the body, embalmed, was sent home to Adams for burial.

Stewart, Henry C., b. North Adams; 24, M.; engraver, Adams. June 21, '61; M. O. Aug. 11, '62; later was in Eustis's Brigade Band; in 1873, glove stitcher, North Bennington. d. Aug. 18, 1884.

COMMISSIONED OFFICERS - CO. A

Captains

Ives, Ralph O., b. New York City; 22, M.; attorney, Great Barrinton; June 14, '61; in winter of '62-'63, served on staff of General Wm. H. Emory, in Louisiana; in Sept. '63, while brigade officer of the day, was captured by guerrillas and sent to Libby prison, Richmond; dis. Sept. 19, '64; in 1873, broker in Cal.; since d.

First Lieutenants

Cady, Henry, b. Lee; 20, S.; baker, Lee; June 21, '61; M. O. July 1, '64; in 1872, living in New Milford, Conn.

COMMISSIONED OFFICERS - CO. B

Captains

Smart, Elisha, b. Stamford, Vt.; 37, M.; carpenter, Adams; June 14, '61; k. May 31, '62, Fair Oaks; had served in the regular army, 2nd U. S. Dragoons; two and a half years in Florida War, finished enlistment in Fourth Artillery; afterwards had been active in the militia.

Traver, Samuel C., June 1, '62; cashiered, Nov. 25, '62; letter Adj't. Gen'ls Office, Washington, Dec. 10, '62; d. Hymore, Hyde Co., South Dakota, 1907.

First Lieutenants

Traver, Samuel C., b. Dutchess Co., N. Y.; 24, M.; merchant, North Adams; June 14, '61; prom. Captain.

Wells, David W., June 1, '62, disa. in retreat from Harrison's Landing, by loaded ammunition wagon running over right foot; some time in Chesapeake hosp.; came back to Reg't. at Drownsville, Md., and again at New Baltimore, in both cases, unable to march, whereupon he res. and was dis., Nov. 28, '62; from '63 to '75, Kansas City, Mo.; manager of Santa Fe Stage Line; in 1875, moved to Chicago; member, Geo. H. Thomas Post 5, G. A. R., and Illinois Commandery, Loyal Legion; d. Mar. 16, 1908.

Cousens, Wm. H.; May 22, '64; trans. June 21, '64, 37th Mass.; wd. July 12, '64, Fort Stevens, D. C.; M. O. as supernumerary, Nov. 26, '64; in 1869, lumberman, Adams.

Bartlett, Edwin B., Sept. 29, '62; (F), prom. First Lieut.

NON-COMMISIONED OFFICERS AND PRIVATES CO. B

Amidon, Lewis F., b. North Adams; 24, S.; carder, North Adams; June 14, '61; wd. right leg, Fair Oaks, May 31, '62; dis. Oct. 31, '62, disa.; later in First Mass. Cav. till close of war; wd. Wilderness, captured and held in Richmond, four months; 1909, No. Adams.

Blais, Napoleon P. A., (First Sergt.), b. Canada; 27, M.; carpenter, North Adams; June 14, '61; prom. Second Lieut.

Cooper, Ferris A., (R), b. New York City; 19, S.; bookkeeper, Adams; Aug. 29, '61; trans. June 21, '64, 37th Mass.; dis. Aug. 23, '64, ex. of s.; in 1869, bookkeeper, Cincinnati, Ohio; d. 1890, St. Louis, Mo., bank teller.

Haskins, Adelbert A., b. North Adams; 21, M.; molder, North Adams; June 14, '61; wd. hand, May 31, '62, Fair Oaks, and shoulder, Malvern Hill; trans. V. R. C., Sept. 1, '63; dis. June 21, '64; in 1869, marble business, South Adams; 1909, No. Adams.

Joy, Edward S., b. South Adams; 24, M.; painter, Pittsfield, June 14, '61; dis. July 23, '62, disa.; had suffered from typhoid fever, sick a year after return home; served a year's enlistment in 61st Mass., becoming Principal Mus.; M. O. June 4, '65, ex. of s.; in 1869, painter, Independence, Iowa; d. Mar. 19, 1908.

Millett, Samuel, (R); 43, M.; laborer, North Adams; June 14, '61, wd. May 31, "62; d. Mar. 25, '63, Falmouth, Va.

Moon, John; 36, M.; dresser, North Adams; June 14, '61; dis. Aug. 2, '62, disa.; d. Jan., 1905, North Adams.

Williams, Samuel P.; 21, -; ——, Springfield; June 21, '61; in hosp. dep't. entire term of service; M. O. July 1, '64; in 1875, Springfield.

Wilsey, Buel G. (Willsey); 20, S.; weaver, Adams; June 14, '61; k. July 1, '62, Malvern Hill.

COMPANY C, NORTHAMPTON

NON-COMMISIONED OFFICERS AND PRIVATES CO. C

Braman, James H., (Sergt.), b. Northampton; 21, S.; Iron founder, Northampton; June 21, '61; k. May 31, '62, Fair Oaks; a member of Deluge Engine company, he was one of the first to enlist; bur. Northampton.

Brewster, Charles H., (First Sergt.), b. Northampton; 27, S.; clerk, Northampton; June 21, '61; prom. Second Lieut.; had been in the State Militia.

Clark, Frederick W., b. Northampton; 20, M.; paper-maker, Northampton; June 21, '61; wd. July 1, '62, Malvern Hill; dis. Oct 17, '62, disa.; do. 1908.

Clark, John C., b. Hadley; 23, S.; broom-maker, Hadley; June 21, '61; wd. May 12, '64, Spottsylvania; d. from wds., May 21, '64, White House Landing; bur. May 28, Hadley; one of the first to enlist from Hadley.

Coleman, Perry M., b. Southampton; 24, S.; carpenter, Southampton; June 21, '61; k. May 31, '62, Fair Oaks; he was the first to enlist from his town and the first to fall; his body, at first bur. on the field, was later brought home and was bur. in Southampton, June 18, '62.

Cooper, Henry W., b. North Adams; 22, S.; wool-sorter, Northampton; June 21, '61; M. O. June 1, '64. Also Coope and Coopee.

Goodrich, Frederick M., b. New York City; 20, S.; brass finisher, Williamsburg; June 21, '61; d. April 20, '62, Warwick Ct. House, Va.

Graves, Edward H., b. Townshend, Vt.; 21, S.; clerk, Brooklyn, N. Y.; June 21,' 61 Q. M. Sergt., Oct., '61; prom. Second Lieut.

Jewett, J. Howard, b. Hadley, 18, S.; clerk, Hadley; April 26,

'61; the first volunteer from the town; disa. Mar 10, '62, by reason of typhoid fever which sent him to hosp., where, during convalescence, he was detailed for duty as clerk at Mount Pleasant and Stone general hospitals until July 3, '63, when he was trans. to V. R. C.; prom. Second Lieut. in V. R. C., Oct. 28, '63; A. A. A. G. on staff of First Brigade, V. R. C. and A. A. Q. M. Second Brig., V. R. C. and four months was Post Adj., depot prisoners of war, Rock Island, Ill.; res. July 8, '64; since the war, in daily newspaper and magazine journalism and authorship, especially in juvenile literature as author of some twenty or more volumes of story-books for children; also some patriotic and army verse; residence, Dec., 1907, New York City; member, Authors' Club.

Kingsley, P. Wellington, b. Williamsburg; 35, M.; planemaker, Williamsburg; June 21, '61; M. O. July 1, '64; do. 1904.

Stanley, Edward H., b. Amherst; 23, M.; baggage master, Northampton; June 21, '61; d. July 27, '62, Harrison's Landing.

Wilsea (Willsey), Berea M., b. Troy, N. Y.; 22, M.; weaver, Adams, June 21, '61; M. O. July 1, '64.

COMPANY D, PITTSFIELD, POLLOCK GUARD

Captains

Clapp, Thomas W., b. Pittsfield; 31, S.; merchant, Pittsfield; June 14, '61; cashiered, Nov. 25, '62; S. W. No. 333, W. D.; in 1875, woolen manufacturer, Pittsfield; dead.

First Lieutenants

Wheeler, Charles, b. Sterling; 22, S.; paper maker, Dalton; June 14, '61; wd. July 1, '62, Malvern Hill, left arm amputated at shoulder; Com. Captain, July 21, '62 and declined; Regimental Quartermaster, Oct.. '62; res. Dec. 20, '62; in Fall of 1863, resided in Chicago and was agent for a paper warehouse; is said to have been killed two or three years since in a railroad accident.

Second Lieutenants

Hager, George E., b. Pittsfield; 20, S.; paper-maker, Pittsfield; June 14, '61; discharged Nov. 25, '62; Dec. 29, '63, enlisted, Sergt., Co. K, First Mass. Cav.; prisoner in Richmond, Andersonville, Florence and Charleston from May 10, '64 till Feb. 7, '65; M. O. June 26, '65; Aide-de-Camp, Dec. 29, 1890, staff of Commander-in-Chief W. G. Veazey, G. A. R.; Jan. 4, 1900, Aide-de-Camp, rank of Major, Staff of Gov. W. Murray Crane; in civil life, papermaker, Dalton; d. May 30, 1907.

Whittlesey, Elihu B., from Sergt. Maj. (F., S.), June 1, '62; M. O. July 1, '64; in 1875, wool manufacturer, Pittsfield.

Cassidy, James, b. Hinsdale; 24, S.; operative, Pittsfield; June 14, '64; k. May 5, '64, Wilderness.

Lane, Wm. T., b. Pittsfield; 43, M.; shoemaker, Pittsfield, June 28, '61; M. O. July 1, '64; d. before 1875.

Mason, Franklin B., g. Windsor; 20, M.; carpenter, Windsor; June 14, '61; wd. hand, Fair Oaks and foot, Gettysburg; M. O. July 1, '64; later in Co. I, Sixth U. s. Vet. Vols.; in 1873, clerk, North Adams.

COMPANY E

Timothy, Michael, b. Ireland; 30, S.; farmer, Northampton; June 14, '61; dis. Oct. 20, '62, disa.; d. N. S. H., Dayton, Ohio, Jan 24, 1895.

COMMISSIONED OFFICERS

First Lieutenants

Porter, Byron, b. Pottsville, Pa.; 31, M.; music teacher, Springfield; June 21, '61; prom. Captain, June 16, '62; res. and dis. Sept. 7, '62; captain, Asst. Adj. General; U. s. Vols., Aug. 7, '62; M. O. Sept. 1, '66.

COMPANY F

First Lieutenants

Eaton, Lemuel Oscar; Nov. 26, '62 from First Sergt.; wd. left knee at Malvern Hill and in left thigh, May 5, '64, Wilderness; M. O. July 1, '64; bvt. Captain, March 13, '65; until his retirement from business, Jan. 1, 1907, contractor and builder, springfield; member of E. K. Wilcox Post G. A. R.; member Builders' Exchange of which he was President two years; 1908, springfield.

NON-COMMISIONED OFFICERS AND PRIVATES CO. F

Gray, Henry W., (Wagoner), b. Wilbraham; 21, S.; hack driver, Wilbraham; May 31, '61; M. O. July 1, '64; in 1875, wilbraham.

Hendrick, Joel H., b. West Suffield, Conn.; 24, S.; mechanic, Chicopee; June 14, '61; wd. head by rifle ball, June 25, '62, Oak Grove; M. O. July 1, '64; in 1884 and 1885 member Common Council, 1886 Alderman, Springfield; 1897 to 1906 inclusive, County Commissioner, Hampden Co.; Commander Post 16, G. a. R. 1886; in 1908, Springfield; "James" on State House rolls.

COMPANY G

COMMISSIONED OFFICERS

Captains

Day, Edwin E., b. Gill; 35, M.; stone mason, Greenfield; June 21, '61; k. May 31, '62, Fair Oaks; his body was bur. on the field, but three and a half years afterwards, it was brought to Greenfield and reburied in Green River cemetery; his funeral was observed in the Unitarian church of Bernardston, June 15, '62, sermon by the Rev. H. B. Butler, singing, led by Wendell T. Davis of Greenfield, included an original poem composed for the occasion by a fellow member of the Captain in a local society; Capt. Day had belonged to the Greenfield Guards for several years, and from Aug. 5, '59, had been in command.

NON-COMMISIONED OFFICERS AND PRIVATES CO. G

Field, Albert A., b. Erving; 21, S.; mechanic, Erving; May 18, '61; Corp., June 20, '64; missed no battles, was not sick nor wounded in service; M. O. July 1, '64; later in Co. M, 3rd Mass. Cav.; M. O. Sept. 28, '65; in 1909, painter, Turners Falls.

Kellogg, Alvah S., b. New York City; 24, S.; tinner, Greenfield; May 18, '61; M. O. July 1, '64.

Parker, Alpheus B., b. Whitingham, Vt.; 21, S.; farmer, Colrain; June 13, '61; wd. face, Salem Heights, and by sharpshooter, June 10, '63, through both thighs, Fredericksburg; dis. Nov. 18, '63, disa.; in 1908, Erving; has held office of School Com., Assessor, Overseer of Poor, Selectman, etc.; P. O. Millers Falls.

Robbine, James E., b. Greenfield; 21, S.; farmer, Greensfield; Feb. 24, '62; d. Jan. 2, '63, Falmouth, Va.

Whitmore, George A., b. Spring Prairie, Wis.; 21, S.; miller, Sunderland, May 18, '61; M. O. July 1, '64; dead.

COMPANY H

COMMISSIONED OFFICERS

Second Lieutenants

Leland, Benjamin F., 38, S.; mechanic, Buckland; June 21, '61; wd. May 31, '62, Fair Oaks, d. from wds. the next day; his conduct in the fight was soldierly in the extreme, when wd. in the abdomen by a minie ball he tried to crawl off the field but could not, thus spending the night upon the ground; the next day he was brought in by his men and survived his wd. thirty-six hours; like a brave man he died saying, "I have done my duty and am ready to depart."

NON-COMMISIONED OFFICERS AND PRIVATES CO. H

Boswell, Dennis A., (R), b. Montague; 37, M.; laborer, Montague; Aug. 9, '62; d. Dec. 22, '62, Falmouth, Va.

COMPANY I

Cromwell, Luther F., b. Preston, Conn.; 30, M.; manufacturer, West Springfield; June 21, '61; dis. Jan 1, '63, disa.; in 1875, Fall River.

Falvey, John, b. Ireland; 18, s.; laborer, Holyoke; June 14, '61; on the visit of the allotment commission, he made over to the State Treasury in Boston, all of his wages except one dollar per month, the remaineder to remain on interest until his discharge, upon arrival of the Reg't. at Warwick court House, he fell ill of fever, d. May 1, '62, and was bur. near the center of the village, he left no relatives in this country.

Littlejohn, Otis H., (R); 19, S.; farmer, Montague; Aug. 9,'62; d. Feb. 3, '63, Falmouth, Va.

Otis, Abner D., Franklin, Conn.; 18, S.; machinist, Holyoke; May 31, '61; d. Armory Square Hosp., Washington, Sept. 17, '63.

COMPANY K

Kalfeur, Carl, b. Germany; 27, S.; cigar maker, Westfield; June 14, '61; d. Dec. 9, '62 and bur. in Smoky Hill Camp, Va.; name also given as Kalfear.

Mason, Wm. W., b. England; 34, M.; mechanic, Spencer; June 14, '61; M. O. July 1, '64; in 1875, mechanic, Spencer; d. June 7, 1883.

Toomy (Toomey), Edmund, b. Charlton; 22, S.; bootmaker, Spencer; June 14, '61; d. Aug. 11, '62; said to have d. of homesickness; body sent home to Spencer, date of death also given as July 19. (Unassigned Recruit.)

173

MR. & MRS. BEREA M. WILLSEY
FIFTIETH WEDDING ANNIVERSARY

**A LETTER APPEARING IN THE
NATIONAL TRIBUNE, WASHINGTON D. C.
A CLOSE CALL**

A Story of the Retreat From Malvern Hill, and How a Union and Confederate Soldier Met Afterwards.

Editor National Tribune: At the battle of Malvern Hill, July 1, 1862, the 10th Mass. (Maj. Ozro Miller) was in the Third Brigade, (Gen. Palmer), First Division, (Gen. Couch) Fourth Corps (Gen. Keyes); and I believe I was the last man that left the field on the morning of July 2.

I had been detailed, during the Winter before, as nurse in the regimental hospital and carried the hospital knapsack. Our hospital during the battle was located in the rear of our brigade on the left of the hill, where the 32-pounders were located and to the north of Gen. Porter's headquarters.

About 11 p.m., two of Co. B boys came to the hospital and told me my brother, Buck G. Willsey, was mortally wounded. They carried him off the field to a barn or shed. I told our Surgeon, Dr. Jewitt, and asked permission to go to him. He said that I never could find him, as it was extremely dark and raining very hard, but that I could take his horse in the morning and locate him.

About midnight, after attending to all the wounded inside and outside of the house, the Hospital Steward, C. C. Wells, and the Wardmaster, John Warner, said to me: "Come up stairs, we have found a room filled with feather beds." We camped there that night. Our Wardmaster got up about1 a.m., but soon returned with the cheering intelligence that the whole army had retreated to Harrison's Landing, and that the rear guard had passed about an hour before, and the Surgeon and nurse had been hunting us for over two hours.

The Steward and Wardmaster immediately retreated, while I remained, trying to induce the Surgeon to let me take the place of Nurse Sam Williams, and be taken prisoner. The Surgeon had a case of beautiful instruments and put it in my care, together with the old pill box, and told me to get out quick.

I went to the corner of the house to take a peep and saw a line of rebel cavalry coming very slowly. They passed the shanty where a lot of wounded were. I kept the house between us until I got to the bank where I could slide down to the road. Just as I got down a bullet went past my ear, and the next thing I knew I was rolling instead of sliding, and landed in the ditch filled with thin mud. I nearly suffocated before I could get the mud from my nostrils, mouth and eyes, and then I skedaddled across the road and thru another ditch into the woods, where I overtook Wells and Warner, and got to the landing about 11 a.m. There I found our hospital wagon and got a change of clothes.

In the Spring of 1869, I left Massachusetts, came to Nebraska and took up a homestead in Washington County. My wife and two children came in July, after getting my house built. My nearest neighbor (a German) lived near us. In November another German (Chas. Jordan) came with a bunch of three-year-old steers and stopped at my neighbor's until Spring to feed his cattle and get them ready for market. During the Winter evenings I met this man Jordan and learned that he had formerly been a Confederate soldier.

He had lived at Baltimore, and while in Richmond, Va., on business was pressed into the rebel cavalry. At the Second Bull Run he deserted and went to Washington and enlisted in the U. S. Army, and was sent West to fight Indians.

He said he had never deliberately shot at a Union soldier but once, and was very sorry he had done that, for he believed that he had killed him. He said that at Malvern Hill in the morning of July 2, he, with a squad of rebel cavalry, were feeling their way cautiously and came to a brick house with a lot of negro shanties in the rear, full of wounded of both armies - that it was raining very hard and very foggy, and when he got to the rear of the house he saw a soldier on the bank just going over. He fired and the soldier gave a spring and rolled over the bank. As soon as he could be followed on to see the result of his shot, but could see nothing, as it was so foggy.

I was thoroughly aroused when he told me that and made him give a description of the surroundings, the exact time, and who and how many were in the house. He told me that they had captured there a Surgeon, nurse, and two officers, also that one of the officers was mortally wounded. (The was Maj. Miller, who had command of our regiment, and the other was Lieut. Wheeler, of Co. D, who had his right arm amputated at the shoulder joint).

After all this talk I told him my story, and we were both convinced that I was the fellow he "helped" over the bank, and it appeared as if it took a load off his mind. In the Spring he loaded his cattle and shipped them to Baltimore.

Is it not very strange that such a meeting should occur after over seven years had passed and nearly 2,000 miles distant from the scene of operations?

B. M. Willsey, Co. C, 10th Mass, Scottsbluff, Neb.

A LETTER APPEARING IN
THE VALLEY NEWS AND TRANSCRIPT
NORTH ADAMS, MASSACHUSETTS
OCTOBER 15, 1863

10 Mass. Vols. Co C.,
Camp Stone House Mountain,
near Culpepper, Va., Sept. 26, 1863

    Mr. Coop — Dear Sir: — I take my pen to address to you a few lines at Henry's solicitation, he being rather unwell and just recovering from an attack of fever, a disease quite prevalent with us soldiers. This has been the first time I have seen Henry unwell since we left our home in the Beaver, some two years ago. We have both of us been very tough and hearty, not knowing hardly what sickness was. About two weeks ago I found Henry at his place of duty looking rather the worse for wear. At his request I write to inform you that he is better and will soon be as rugged as ever. Since his sickness, I have been to see him several times every day, and done all I could to make him comfortable. Henry and myself are friends, and when we came as soldiers, we both agreed to stick to each other through everything that might happen in our way. We are the only two persons from the Beaver village that are in the regiment, and I guess the only two now in the service. If the Lord is willing, we mean to go home together, and then live on something besides hard-tack and pork.

    I hardly know what to write in the way of news. We are all anxious to hear that Rosecrans has whipped the enemy, yet fear that he has got his hands rather more than full. The 11th and 12th corps of the army of the Potomac have gone to Washington, and some say they will join the army of the Cumberland. Our army are under marching orders with eight days rations in haversacks and seven days rations in the wagons. When we shall start or where we shall go of course is not known to the soldiers. We are having splendid weather, and everything requisite for a glorious campaign. The army are in good spirits, and all feel as if victory would be ours the next time we meet the foe. I am still nothing but a hospital nurse, and don't know that I shall be anything else during this campaign. I have but little to do now-a-days as we have but a very few sick. In fact the whole army was in better condition. Henry is on duty a a Provost Guard to the Sutlers of the 139th Penn. Vols. He is liked by every one—officers and men—that know him. He has always done his duty and always will do it, and let me say, Mr. Coop, that such a son as Henry is and has been since I became acquainted with him would cause any father's breast to be filled with pride, love and admiration. Hoping that these few lines will prove acceptable I sign myself,

Yours & c.,

Berea M. Willsey

OBITUARY

The following is Berea M. Willsey's obituary as it appeared in the Blair, Nebraska, *The Tribune* on January 31, 1918.

B. M. WILLSEY, PIONEER, BROUGHT HERE FOR BURIAL

News of the death of B. M. Willsey came to Blair last Thursday with the information that the remains would be shipped to this point for burial. Mr. Willsey died at the home of his daughter, Mrs. J. F. Kinney at college View, where he had made his home for the past two years. The remains were met by the Masonic lodge of this city and the burial services were held under their auspices.

Berea M. Willsey was born in Troy, N.Y, on June 26, 1839. His early life was spent in Massachusetts. At the outbreak of the Civil War he enlisted in Co. C, 10th Massachusetts Inf. where he served until the fall of 1864. In October of that year he was married to Lucy A. Goodrich, who survives him, together with three daughters, Mrs. J. F. Kinney of College View, Nebr., Mrs. G. G. Dennis, of Omaha, Nebr., and Mrs. J. B. Schrock of Scottsbluff, Nebr.

In 1869 he came to Washington county and settled on a homestead near what is now the town of Washington, Nebr. Eight years later he moved to the city of Blair where he engaged in the agricultural implement business. He moved to Omaha in 1897, where he entered the employ of the North Western road, retiring in 1909. A year later he moved to Scottsbluff, Nebr. where he remained for two years.

OBITUARY

The following is Berea M. Willsey's obituary as it appeared in the Blair, Nebraska, *The Pilot* on January 30, 1918.

Word was received last Thursday afternoon, Jan. 24th, of the death of B. M. Willsey, at noon at the home of his daughter, Mrs. J. F. Kinney, in College View near Lincoln, Neb., and that the body would be brought here Saturday afternoon for burial. The Masons met the funeral party at the depot and conducted the services at the grave, Mr. Willsey having always retained his membership here. All the near relatives came with the body from Lincoln, where the funeral service was held. Frank Willsey came up from Omaha, also Miss Frances Gross. Berea M. Willsey was born in Troy, N.Y., on June 26, 1839. His early life was spent in Massachusetts. At the outbreak of the Civil War he enlisted in company C, 10th Massachusetts Infantry, where he served until the fall of 1864. In October of that year he was married to Lucy A. Goodrich, who survives him, together with three daughters, Mrs. J. F. Kinney, of Collegeview, Nebr., Mrs. G. G. Dennis, of Omaha, Nebr., and Mrs. J. B. Schrock, of Scottsbluff, Neb. In 1869 he came to Washington county, Neb., and settled on a homestead near what is now the town of Washington. Eight years later he moved to the city of Blair where he engaged in the agricultural implement business. He moved to Omaha in 1897 where he entered the employ of Northwestern road, retiring in 1909. A year later he moved to Scottsbluff, Neb., where he remained until two years ago, since which time he has lived with his daughter, Mrs. Kinney. The many friends of the family here extend heartfelt sympathy, for we all have many pleasant recollections of Mr. Willsey's long residence among us.

OBITUARY

The following is Mrs. Berea M. Willsey's obituary as it appeared in the Blair, Nebraska, The Pilot on March 12, 1920.

The body of Mrs. B. M. Willsey was brought here last Sunday morning from College View and taken direct to the cemetery for burial by the side of her husband, whose death occurred two years last January. The funeral party was composed of Mr. and Mrs. Frank Kinney and son, Russell, of College View and Mrs. George Dennis and son, Waldo, of Omaha. Lucy A. Goodrich was born April 10, 1841, and was therefore nearly 70 years of age. Her death occurred Friday, March 5th. she was married to B. M. Willsey October 18th, 1864 and they came west in the spring of '69, locating first at Kennard, moving to this city in '77. They lived here until 1896, removing to Scottsbluff in 1910 and to College View in 1916. She is survived by three daughters, Mrs. George G. Dennis, of Omaha, Mrs. J. F. Kinney, of College View and Mrs. J. B. Schrock, of Scottsbluff, Neb.

OBITUARY

The following is Mrs. Berea M. Willsey's obituary as it appeared in the Blair, Nebraska, *The Enterprise* on March 12, 1920.

Former Blair Citizen Passes

The death of Mrs. B. M. Willsey former Blair woman, occurred on last Friday, March 5th at the home of her daughter, Mrs. Frank Kinney of Lincoln, Nebr., after an illness incident to old age as she was around seventynine years of age.

Funeral services were held Saturday afternoon at the Lincoln home and the body was brought to Blair Sunday for burial beside the body of her husband who died about two years ago.

She leaves three daughters, two of whom attended the burial on Sunday. They are Mrs. Kinney of Lincoln, and Mrs. Geo. Dennis of Omaha, the third daughter Mrs. Estella Schrock of Scotts Bluff, not being present. Rev. Wright of the Methodist church had charge of the services at the cemetery.

The Willseys lived in Blair over twentyfive years ago in the house now occupied by Dr. Murdoch which they built and the Kinney's lived next door. Both families were prominent in church and social circles for many years and were highly esteemed by Blair people.

Since the death of B. M. Willsey two years ago, the deceased has made her home at Lincoln.

INDEX

Abbott, Edith Public Library, vii.
Adamstown, 46.
Aldie & Snicker's Gap, 94, 96, 120.
Aldies Crossroads, 102.
Alexandria, 5, 42, 43, 64, 96, 107, 139, 158.
Althea, Cousin, 111.
Allen, Mr., 23.
Amidon, Lewis F., 25, 26, 167.
Andrew, Governor, 3.
Annapolis, 142.
Antietam, Battle of, v, viii, 42, 46, 47, 55, 69, 84.
Antioch Church, 30.
Aquia & Falmouth R.R., 62.
Aquia Creek, 43, 59, 62, 81, 146, 158.
Army of the Potomac, viii, ix, 1, 71, 84, 121, 143, 149, 159, 177.
Atkinson, Kate, 49.
Auger, Ken, 147.

Bakersfield, 55.
Baldwin, Capt., 131.
Baltimore & Ohio R.R., 46, 55.
Baltimore, 77, 158, 176.
Banks, 1.
Banks Ford, 89, 90.
Barbies Cross, 102, 103.
Barker, Charles, 91.
Barnesville, 45, 52, 98.
Bartlett, Lt. Edwin B., 81, 166.
Barton, Capt. Fred, 110, 154.
Barton, Rev. Frederick A., 4.
Baton Rouge, 81.
Bealeston Station, 134.
Bealton Station, 108, 109.
Beaver, 58, 110.
Belle Plain, 59, 62, 68.
Berdom's Sharpshooters, 95.
Berkeley Plantation (Landing), 31, 39.
Berkshire County, 62.
Berlin, Maryland, 55, 102, 112.
Bernard, Alfred, 64.
Bessy, 84.
Bidwell (Suttler), 17, 18, 71, 78, 79.
Bingham, Adoniram J., 49, 164.
Birkettsville, 46.
Birny, 84.
Bishop, Capt., 136.
Black, Levi, 63, 67, 68, 78, 79.

Blair, Mr. & Mrs., 4.
Blair, Nebraska, vi, viii, 179-182.
Blair Nebraska Public Library, vii.
Blaise, Napoleon P. A. "Biny", 37, 38, 167.
Bloody Angle, The, 147.
Blue Ridge, 56, 103.
Bollington, 55.
Boonsboro, 100, 101.
Boston Harbor, 111.
Boston, 6, 125, 156.
Boswell, Dennis A., 67, 172.
Bottom Bridge, 21, 69.
Botts, John Minor, 112.
Bowling Green, 150.
Braggs, 108.
Braman, James H., 27, 168.
Brandy Station, v, viii, 95, 108, 112, 114, 115, 143.
Brayton, Mr., 158.
Brewster, Charles H., 40, 168.
Briggs, Col. Henry S., ix, 24, 25, 50.
Brightwood, Camp, ix, 1, 2, 36, 37, 44.
Bristol Station, 109.
Broad Run, 98.
Brock Road, 144.
Brooklyn, 141.
Brooks Station, 62.
Bryan, I. H., 72.
Buddington, Rev. Mr., 141.
Buffords Cavalry, 114.
Bull Run, 2nd Battle, 42, 94, 120, 176.
Burkettsville, 46, 55.
Burnside, Gen. Ambrose E., 57, 65, 74, 90, 118, 132, 143, 147, 149.
Butler, Gen., 132, 133, 146, 148, 157.
Butterfield, Gen. (Daniel), 87, 119.

Cady, Henry, 123, 166.
Camden, 158.
Caseys Division, 23, 24, 27.
Cassidy, James, 122, 123, 170.
Catletts Station, 58, 109.
Cedar Mountain, 132.
Centreville, 97, 110.
Chain Bridge, 1, 2, 44.
Chamberlain, Dr. Cyrus N., 4, 13, 35, 47, 60-62, 91, 127, 135, 163.
Chancellorsville, Battle of and town, v, viii, 88, 146.
Chantilly, 110.
Charles City (Road), 22, 31, 40, 155, 156.
Charlestown, 102.
Cherry Run Ford, 53.
Chesapeake Bay, v, 72.

Chesterfield Station, 151.
Chickahominy River, v, 21, 22, 26, 30, 41, 156.
City Point, 157, 158.
Clapp, Mr., 27.
Clapp, Thomas W., 37, 169.
Clara, Cousin, 138.
Clark, Francis L., 165.
Clark, Frederick W., 168.
Clark, Dr. John C. (G. C.), 4, 5, 7, 10, 20, 52, 60, 83, 168.
Clear Springs, 53, 54.
Clegg, David, 111, 113.
Cold Harbor, Battle of, v, viii, 152, 153.
Coleman, Perry M., 27, 168.
Colista (Calista) (last name unknown), 35, 103, 105, 108, 110, 113,117.
College View, Nebraska, 179, 180, 181.
Columbia College, 3, 5.
Concord Church, 151.
Confederate Soldier, 176.
Coonradt, Willis E., 75, 80.
Cooper House, 158.
Cooper, Ferris A., 84, 167.
Cooper, Henry W. "Coop", vi, 11, 44, 81, 92, 104-107, 113, 129, 139-143, 157, 158, 168, 177.
Cornadt, Nellie, 111.
Corps, 1st, 99, 127, 131.
Corps, 2nd, 97, 114, 115, 128, 131, 138, 141, 142, 147, 149, 153, 155.
Corps, 3rd, 114, 126, 132.
Corps, 4th, 84, 175.
Corps, 5th, 112, 134, 143, 150-153, 155.
Corps, 6th, 82, 94, 98, 99, 111, 112, 114, 119, 144, 146, 147, 153.
Corps, 8th, 97, 134.
Corps, 9th, 143, 145, 155, 156.
Corps, 11th, 90, 108, 119, 138, 177.
Corps, 12th, 108, 138, 177.
Corps, 18th, 153.
Couch, General Darius, 1, 2, 20, 23, 30, 32, 45, 46, 50, 82, 84, 175.
Cousens, Lt. Wm. H., 77, 166.
Cousins, T., 106.
Cox, Ann Higgins, vii, xii, 71.
Cox, Michael, xii.
Crompton Gap, 55.
Cromwell, Luther F., 43, 58, 173.
Culpepper C. H., 107, 108, 112, 113, 129, 131, 137, 144, 177.
Culpepper Mine Ford, 115.
Cumberland, Army of, 111, 177.

Dalton, 146,
Davids Island, NY, 64.
Davidson, Gen., 14.
Day, Edwin E., 26, 171.

Deadwood, South Dakota, v.
Decker, Lt. Col. Jefford M., 22, 161.
DeMay, Jessica H., vii, xii.
DeMay, Richard F., vii, xii.
Dennis, Caroline "Carrie" Willsey, v, xii, 71.
Dennis, George G., v, xii.
Dennis, Mrs. George G., 179, 180, 181, 182.
Dennis, Lucile, xii.
Dennis, Waldo Willsey "Jack", v, xii, 181.
Denver Public Library, vii.
Devins, Gen., 25, 27, 45, 47, 84.
Dickinson, Aaron, 124.
Division, 1st, 152.
Division, 2nd, 137.
Dixon, Major, 139.

Doubleday Division,, 65.
Downsville, Maryland, 48, 52, 54.
Drainsville, 98.
Duffie, Ed. R., xii.
Dumfries, 94, 96, 120.

Eaton, Lemuel Oscar, 71, 136, 171.
Ecclestis, Mr., 129.
Edward Ferry, 98.
Edwards, Col., 144, 147, 157.
Ellsworth, Col., 6.
Enterprise, The, 182.
Eustis, Col. (later Gen.), Henry L., 43, 93, 110, 113, 123, 130, 138, 143, 144.

Fair Oaks Station, 23.
Fair Oaks, Battle of, v, viii, 24, 27, 29, 37, 69.
Fairfax Co. House (Station), 43, 94, 96-98, 110, 120.
Fairview, 53.
Falmouth, 61, 64, 74, 81, 89.
Falvey, John, 16, 173.
Fera, Charles, 71.
Field, Albert A., 124, 126, 172.
Fitz, 58.
Florence, Mass., 106, 124, 129.
Florida, 132.
Fogliardi, Gen., 87, 119.
Fort Collins, Colorado Public Library, vii.
Fort Darling, 28, 102, 155.
Fort Ethan Allen, 44.
Fort Magruder, 18.
Fort Marcy, Virginia, 1, 2.
Fort Pillow, Tenn., 141.
Fortress Monroe, 6, 11, 26, 42, 101, 158.
Franklin Crossing, 94, 119.

Franklin, Gen., 26, 50, 64.
Frederick, 98.
Fredericksburg, (Battle of or town), v, viii, 61, 64-66, 69, 89, 91, 119, 145, 146.
French, 84.
Funkstown, 101, 112.

Gainsville, 97.
Georgetown & Ohio Canal, 53.
Georgetown, 3, 96.
Georgia, 10.
Gerold, 133.
Germania Ford, 115, 114.
Germantown, 96.
Getty, Gen., 144.
Gettysburg, (Battle of or town), v, viii, 94, 99, 106, 126.
Gettysville, 99.
Gilman, John H., 93, 164.
Glendale National Cemetery, v.

Goodrich, Frederick M., 14, 16, 168.
Goodrich, H. P., 35, 49, 57, 104.
Goodrich, Lucy, See Lucy G. Willsey.
Goose Creek, 102.
Gordonsville, 88, 109, 119, 132.
Grand Island, Nebraska, vii.
Grange & Alexandria RR., 58.
Grange Co. House, 132.
Grant, Gen. U. S., 93, 115, 134, 136, 141, 148, 150, 153.
Graves, D. D., 134.
Graves, Edward H. (C.), 81, 106, 114, 124, 129, 151, 168.
Graves, H. R., 3, 84, 158.
Gray, Henry W., 116, 123, 127, 171.
Green, J. H., 122.
Greenbush, 108.
Greenland, 71.
Gross, Francis, 180.
Guiney Station, 150.
Gum Swamp, 98.

Hager, Lt. George E., 170.
Halifax, 54.
Halleck, 91, 136.
Hampton, 6.
Hams Creek, 98.
Hancock, 53.
Hancock, Gen., 147, 154.
Hanover C. H., 152.
Harpers Ferry, 44, 46, 121, 122, 137.
Harrison Landing, 32, 34, 42, 55, 84, 156, 175.
Hartack, Gen., 150.

Hartford, 158.
Haskins, Adelbert A., 40, 167.
Hatfield, Mass., 3, 24, 78, 103, 105, 111, 116.
Hayes, General, 3.
Hayward, 63, 92.
Heintzleman, 29.
Hendrick, Joel H., 64, 83, 84, 121-124, 127, 136, 138, 154, 171.
Hermon, 98.
Higgins, George M., xii.
Higgins, John R. Sr., xii.
Higgins, John R. Jr., vii, xii.
Higgins, Lucille Dennis, v, xii.
Higgins, Ray M., xii.
Higgins, Ray M. Jr., xii.
Hill's Troops, 144.
Hooker, Gen. Joseph (Division), 25, 27, 29, 30, 39, 64, 65, 83, 84, 87, 88, 90, 98, 114, 119.
Hooker's HDQRS., 79, 84.
Holyoke, Mass., 16.
Hooser Valley News, 124.
Howes Brigade, 48.
Howland, John W., 51, 163.
Hurd, I. F., 71, 72, 75, 79, 80, 87, 92, 93, 100-102, 104, 105, 113, 125, 128, 133, 134, 139.
Hyattsville, 98.

Indian Springs, 53, 54.
Ives, Ralph O., 106, 165.

Jackson, Stonewall, 30, 91, 152.
Jacobs Ferd, 114.
James River, 28, 31, 155, 156.
Jane, Cousin, 111, 123.
Jefferson, 46.
Jewett, George (Assistant Surgeon), 7, 16, 18, 35, 43, 46, 52, 164, 175.
Jewett, J. Howard, 168, 169.
Johnstons Army, 146.
Jones Church, 152.
Jones Ford, 156.
Jordan, Charles, 176.
Joy, Edward S., 37, 167.
Joy, Kate, 52, 94, 104, 105.

Kalfeur, Carl, 63, 173.
Keedeesville, 47.
Kellogg, Alvah S., 36, 45, 52, 72, 77, 106, 121, 123, 126, 137, 172.
Kellys Ford, 112.
Kennard, Nebraska, 181.
Kettle Run Encampment, 109.
Key West (Steamer), 43.

Keyes, Gen. Corps, 20, 35, 42, 175.
Kilpatrick, Gen., 133.
Kingsley, P. Wellington, 38, 169.
Kinney, Eloise May, xii.
Kinney, Mr. & Mrs. Frank, xii, 181.
Kinney, Harriet Jane, xii.
Kinney, Mrs. J. F., 179, 180, 182.
Kinney, Rothwell Jay, xii.
Kinney, Russell, xii, 181.
Kinney, Ruth Elaine, xii.

Ladd, Major, 38.
Lane, Wm. T., 33, 36, 40, 42, 43, 47, 48, 52, 55, 60, 66, 67, 93, 123, 129, 132, 135, 137, 170.
Lee, Gen. Robert E., 98, 101, 109, 150, 153.
Leland, Benjamin F., 26, 172.
Lewis, Mrs., 128.
Liberty, Virginia, 134.
Lincoln, Nebraska, viii, 180, 182.
Lincoln, President Abraham, vi, 34, 50, 84, 116.
Linoth, John, 71, 173.
Little River, 151.
Little Round Top, 94.
Littlejohn, Otis H., 75, 76.
Long Island Sound, 158.
Long Island, 117.
Longstreet, James, 99.
Loomis, Mr., 87.
Lovettsville, 55, 102.
Lucius, 102, 129.
Lute, 103.

Maders, Mr., 93.
Madison C. House, 133.
Malvern Hill, Battle of, v, viii, 31, 32, 39, 54, 69, 156, 175, 176.
Manassas R.R. (Junction), 56, 102, 103, 109.
Manassas, 1.
Manchester, 98.
Manchester, Henry, 103, 105.
Marsh, William R., 26, 162.
Marshall House, 6.
Martinson, Karen, xii.
Maryland, 4, 51, 54, 96.
Mason, Franklin B., 41, 51, 63, 84, 170.
Mason, Wm. W., 87, 106, 126, 127, 131, 142, 143, 173.
Mass. Inf. Regt., 1st, 29.
Mass. Inf. Regt., 7th, 1, 16, 21, 29, 30, 45, 48, 89, 90, 112, 119, 124, 126, 136, 138, 139, 140, 141, 143, 144, 147, 156.
Mass. Inf. Regt., 10th, v, ix, 1, 4, 16, 18, 21, 24, 25, 27, 31, 32, 44, 46, 64, 66, 71, 86, 89, 94, 99, 112, 114, 121, 136, 138, 143, 144, 147, 159, 176, 179, 180.

Mass. Inf. Regt., 12th, 65.
Mass. Inf. Regt., 15th, 45.
Mass. Inf. Regt., 16th, 41.
Mass. Inf. Regt., 19th, 125.
Mass. Inf. Regt., 27th, 154.
Mass. Inf. Regt., 29th, 125.
Mass. Inf. Regt., 32nd, 125, 134, 143.
Mass. Inf. Regt., 33rd, 43.
Mass. Inf. Regt., 34th, 43.
Mass. Inf. Regt., 37th, 50, 56, 61, 63, 83, 85, 103, 113, 119, 121, 138, 140, 141, 142, 144, 155, 158.
Mass. Inf. Regt., 57th, 90.
Massachusetts State Historical Society, vii.
McCall, Gen. George, 33.
McClellan Lancers, 1.
McClellan's Army of the Potomac, v.
McClellan, Gen. George B., vi, ix, 30, 32, 41, 43, 44, 46, 47, 57, 58, 84.
Meade, Gen. George C., 65, 84, 101, 141, 147, 150.
Medford, Mass., 37.
Methodist Church, 182.
Middle Town, 100.
Miles, Col., 46.
Miller, Major Ozro, 32, 162, 175, 176.
Millett, Samuel, 40, 82, 167.
Millimun, Mr., 44.
Moesby's Men, 111.
Mollie, 110.
Monitor, 6.
Monocacy Creek, 45.
Mon
Monrovia, 98.
Moon, John, 38, 167.
Mt. Pleasant, 98.
Mt. Vernon, 6.
Murdock, Dr., 182.
Murfreesboro, 71.
Mysick, Joe, 133.
Mystic (Steamer), 5.

National Archives of Washington, D.C., vii.
National Tribune, 175.
Nebraska, viii, 176.
New Baltimore, 57.
New Jersey, 18, 42, 43, 158.
New Kent C. House, 19.
New Market, 98.
New River, 73, 118.
New York City, 158.
New York Herald, 34, 71, 155.
New York Regt. 9th, 91.

New York Regt. 31st, 44.
New York Regt. 33rd, 11.
New York Regt. 35th, 86.
New York Regt. 36th, 38, 39, 45, 53, 55, 83, 86, 96.
New York Regt. 56th, 1.
New York Regt. 93rd, 14.
New York Regt. 126th, 98.
New York, 103.
Newburn, 101.
Newton, Gen., 56, 92.
Niel, Gen., 154.
Nine Mile Swamp, 31.
North Adams, Mass., vi, xii, 38, 50, 52, 72, 80, 84, 91, 105, 110, 111, 121, 126, 128, 129, 133, 135, 136, 158, 177.
North Adams Public Library, vii.
North Anna River, Battle of, v, viii, 150, 151.
North Carolina, 142.
Northampton, 27.
Northwestern Railroad, v, 179, 180.

O'Holleran, Molly Higgins, vii, xii.
O'Holleran, Timothy, xii.
O'Neal, Gen., 130, 135.
Occoquan Creek, 96.
Omaha, Nebraska, 179, 180.
Orange C. House, 144.
Orange, Mass., ix.
Orleans, 103.
Otis, Abner D., 107, 173.
Palmer, Gen., 27, 29, 32, 175.
Pamunkey River, 151.
Parcellville, 102.
Parker, Alpheus B., 95, 172.
Parker, Major Dexter F., 50, 162.
Parsons, Col. Joseph B., ix, x, 24, 45, 52, 89, 92, 94, 98, 99, 101, 112, 145, 161.
Peakes Station, 152.
Peninsular Campaign, v, viii.
Pennsylvania Ave., 5, 158.
Pennsylvania Regt. 23rd, 8, 11.
Pennsylvania Regt. 98th, 137.
Pennsylvania Regt. 139th, 60, 111, 142, 177.
Pennsylvania State, 51, 96, 99.
Pennsylvania Vol, Regt., 177.
Petersburg, 146, 153, 157, 158.
Phelmont, 56.
Philadelphia, 158.
Picketts Charge, 99.
Pilot, The, 180, 181.
Pittsfield, 24, 35, 36, 94.
Pleasant Valley, 55.

Pleasanton, Gen. (Alfred), 51, 52.
Plymouth, 142.
Polley, George F., 157, 158, 164.
Poolerville, 98.
Poolivar, 100.
Poolsville, 45.
Pope, Gen. John, 43, 59.
Port Hudson, 101, 104.
Porter, Byron, 12, 170.
Porter, Gen. (Fitzjohn), 27, 30, 57, 58.
Potomac Creek, 87, 93.
Potomac Crossroads, 44.
Potomac River, v, 1, 6, 158.
Prospect Hills, 1.
Purseville, 56.

Quaker Guns, 97.

Raccoon Ferd, 114.
Rand, H., 134, 141.
Rapidan, 108, 114, 115, 128, 132, 143, 144.
Rappahannock Station, 108, 109, 112.
Rappahannock, 64.
Rectorstown, 102.
Reedyville, 55.
Reynold, Gen., 87, 99, 119.
Rhode Island Regt., 2nd, 1, 16, 29, 56, 89, 119, 121, 133, 135, 141, 142, 144, 147, 154.
Richmond & West Point R. R., 156.
Richmond, Virginia, v, 2, 14, 17, 23, 27, 29, 35, 57, 64, 65, 132, 133, 139, 146, 148, 150, 152, 176.
Ritzville, 98.
Robbins, James E., 68, 69, 172.
Robertson, Mr., 127.
Robinson, Dr. A. B., 60, 91, 94, 117, 126, 127, 129, 164.
Roe, Alfred S., ix, xi, 161.
Rohersville, 55.
Ropers Church,
Ropers Church, 19.
Rosencrans, Gen., 74, 108, 177.
Rothwell, Hazel, xii.
Russell, Gen., 87, 119, 131.

Salbin, 102.
Salem Heights, 89.
Sandersky City, 122.
Savages Station, 25, 27.
Schrock, Mrs. J. B. (Estella), xii, 179-182.
Schrock, Joseph B., xii.
Schrock, Joseph Benson, xii.

Scottsbluff Historical Society, vii.
Scottsbluff, Nebraska, 176, 179-181.
Seashore, The (Steamer), v, 5.
Sedgwick, Gen. John, 88, 101, 105, 111, 116, 119, 130, 131, 141, 146.
Seneca Creek, 45.
Seven Day Campaigne, 29-31.
Seven Pines, 23, 24.
Shaler, Gen., 112.
Sharpesburgh, 47.
Shater, Gen., 94, 122.
Shellbourne Falls, 87.
Sickles, Lady, 84.
Sinkular, Lucy (Higgins), vii, xii.
Sinkular, Scott, xii.
Smart, Capt. Elisha, 26, 166.
Smith Division, 9.
Smith, Simion P. (of Co. I), 112.
Smith, Gen. W. F., 138.
Smoketown, 55.
Snickers Gap, 56, 96.
Snickersville, 56.
Soldiers Rest, 158.
South Adams, 11, 91, 125, 134.
South Aubrey, 158.
South Mountain Gap, 100.
South Mountain, 46, 55, 102.
Spauldings Point, 158.
Spotsylvania Court House, Battle of, v, viii, 145-150.
Sprague, Gov. (Rhode Island), 5.
Springfield Republican, 124, 132,
Springfield, Camp, ix.
St. James & Marys Colleges, 18.
St. James College, 48.
St. Marys Heights, 65.
St. Patricks Day, 81.
Staffords C. H., 59, 62, 94, 96, 120.
Staffords Store, 59.
Stamford, Vermont, viii.
Stanley, Edward H., 36, 37, 169.
Staunton, 107.
Stevensberg, 144.
Stewart, Burdick A., 130, 165.
Stewart, Henry C., 131, 133, 134, 165.
Stewarts Cavalry, 28.
Stocking Jessica, xii.
Stone House Mountain, 107.
Stone Mountain Camp, 177.
Stone Point, 53.
Stuart, Gen. J. E. B., 51, 52.
Sugar Loaf Mountain, 45.

Sulpher Springs, 107.
Sumner, Gen. Edwin V., 61, 64, 82.

Talbot, Gen., 130.
Taylors Ferd, 151.
Tennalytown, 1, 44.
Tenth Regiment Veterans Association, 161.
Terry, Brig. Gen., 104, 111.
Texas, 82.
Timothy, Michael, 33, 170.
Tom Powel, The, 158.
Toomy (Toomey), Edmund, 39, 173.
Tower, H., 72, 80.
Transcript, North Adams, vi, 72, 80, 82, 93.
Traver, Capt. Samuel C., 10, 38, 52, 166.
Trenton, New Jersey, 58.
Tribune, The, 179.
Troy, New York, viii, 179, 180.
Tunnel Hill, 146.
Turner, Eddie, 74.

Union, 56, 102.
Union Soldier, 176.
Upperville, 102.

VA-Central R. R., 152.
Valley News & Transcript, 177.
Vanderbilt (Steamer), 6.
Vedetto, Jake, 68.
Vermont Regt., 2nd, 116.
Vermont Regt., 3rd, 14, 133, 137, 142.
Vermont Regt., 4th, 127.
Vermont Regt., 8th, 116.
Vicksburg, 71, 82, 92.
Vining, John, 155.
Vining, Oliver S., 50.
Virginia Regt. 22nd, 99.
Virginia, 55, 102.

Warner, Jonathan D., 2, 4, 7, 33, 43, 51, 123, 129, 135, 165, 175, 176.
Warner, John A. (Steamer), 5.
Warren, Gen., 114, 115.
Warren, O., 133.
Warren, Rarid, 137.
Warrenton, 58, 103, 111, 112.
Warrenton Junction, 109.
Warwick C. House, 9, 14, 16.
Warwick, VA., 49.
Washington Chronicle, 91.

Washington City, v, ix, 3, 5, 6, 28, 37, 44, 48, 50, 57, 66, 81, 87, 96, 134, 135, 137, 140, 143, 146, 148, 158, 176, 177.
Washington County Genealogical Society, vii.
Washington County, viii, 176, 179, 180.
Washington, General George W., 6.
Waverly Magazine, 124.
Weaverton, 59.
Wells, Charles C., 2, 4, 10, 16, 18, 20, 73, 165, 175, 176.
Wells, E. E., 72.
Wells, Lt. David W., 10, 38, 62, 166.
Westbrook, 83, 124.
West Point, 17.
Westfield, Mass., 49.
Westminster, 98.
Whately, 138.
Wheatland, 102.
Wheaton, 56, 137.
Wheeler, Lt. Charles, 21, 32, 51, 169, 176.
White House (Landing), 25, 28, 30, 151, 152, 155.
White Oak Church, 64.
White Plains, 56.
White, Capt. J. J., 11.
Whitmore, George A., 95, 172.
Whittlesey, Elihu B., 11, 170.
Wilderness Tavern, 144.
Wilderness, Battle of, v, viii, 114, 144, 145.
Williams, Samuel P., 16, 18, 20, 54, 73, 77, 116, 139, 175.
Williamsburg, Battle of, 16, 18, 41, 69.
Williamsport, 47, 48, 52, 54, 69, 98, 101, 112.
Willsey, Caroline "Carrie", xii.
Willsey (Wilsea), Berea M., v, viii, ix, xii, 1, 71, 121, 161, 169, 176, 178-180.
Willsey (Wilsey), Buel G. "Buck", v, 2, 3, 7-13,19, 21-23, 25, 27, 29, 30-33, 52, 62, 83, 167, 175.
Willsey, Frank, 180.
Willsey, George, 132, 137, 141, 142.
Willsey, Hattie L., xii.
Willsey, Lois E., xii.
Willsey, Lucy Goodrich, vi, viii, xii, 2, 3, 8, 11, 24, 34, 35, 37, 42, 44, 51, 55, 58, 63, 66, 73, 75, 77, 80-82, 85, 86, 90-93, 96, 97, 100, 102, 103, 105, 108, 109, 113, 115-117, 123, 124, 128-131, 133, 135, 137, 139, 141, 142, 148, 150, 151, 154, 179-182.

Wilmington, 158.
Wright, Rev., 182.

Yankee Doodle, 26.
York River, 18, 43.
Yorktown, v, 8, 9, 17, 41-43.
Young, Capt., 113.
Youngs Mills, 9.

ADDENDUM

"The Tenth Regiment Massachusetts Volunteer Infantry 1861-1864" by Alfred S. Roe indicates that Berea M. Willsey is listed as a married soldier. Further research through the National Archives indicates at the time he applied for a pension on March 12, 1915, he wrote he had been married the first time on January 3, 1858, to Louanna Graves. He was divorced from her in September, 1864, at Northampton, Massachusetts - cause adultery!

In my first contact with the Massachusetts Historical Society in January, 1991, requesting information concerning the Mass. 10th Vol. Regiment they noted they had just received a diary written by a private in the Tenth Regiment by the name of George Arms Whitmore. After corresponding with Martha Whitmore Hickman (donor of the diary to the historical society) she arranged for me to receive a copy of the diary. It covers entries from October 1, 1862, to July 21, 1863. It was with great interest that I read it in its entirety and noticed many similarities between events in it and Berea's diary. I was very surprised by the entry on June 9, 1863. I quote in full: "Pleasant day. Lay still all day. Towards night the rebils shelled us. A little piece of a shell hit me on my breast boan (sic). Lucky for me it was a spent ball." On reading Berea's entry of the same day he mentions Whitmore being wounded! See page 95.